Power Steering

STUDIES IN GOVERNMENT AND PUBLIC POLICY

Power Steering

Global Automakers and the Transformation of Rural Communities

Michele M. Hoyman

 University Press of Kansas

Published by the University Press of Kansas (Lawrence, Kansas 66049),
which was organized by the Kansas Board of Regents and is operated and
funded by Emporia State University, Fort Hays State University, Kansas State
University, Pittsburg State University, the University of Kansas, and Wichita
State University

Library of Congress Cataloging-in-Publication Data

Hoyman, Michele.
    Power steering : global automakers and the transformation of rural
communities / Michele M. Hoyman.
        p.   cm. — (Studies in government and public policy)
    Includes bibliographical references.
    ISBN 0-7006-0818-4 (alk. paper). — ISBN 0-7006-0819-2 (alk.
paper)
        1. Automobile industry and trade—United States—Case studies.
    2. Rural development—United States.   3. Corporations, Japanese—
United States.   I. Title.   II. Series: Studies in government and public policy
(Lawrence, Kan.)
    HD9710.U52H69   1997
    307.3'3212'0976—dc20   96-45944

British Library Cataloguing in Publication Data is available.

Printed in the United States of America
10 9 8 7 6 5 4 3 2 1

To my family

Contents

Acknowledgments

I AM DEEPLY INDEBTED to many persons for their help with this book. I wish to thank the numerous public officials in the four communities without whose cooperation this study would have impossible, particularly the offices of Mr. Ralph Vaughn, Mayor Tom Kruse, and Mayor Tom Prather, who were particularly informative and gracious even with their busy schedules. Thanks to all the leaders, including the legendary Mayor Sam Ridley, who took two hours of their hectic schedules to be interviewed by yet another "outsider." I am indebted to Louis Ferman of Michigan, whose magical powers of grantsmanship secured the original Economic Development Administration grant (#99-07-13727) for the elite interviews portion of the research. His work as principal investigator, including the coauthorship of the project report, was tireless and inspirational. The interviewing acumen, research skills, stamina, and irrepressible wit of Lou Ferman (University of Michigan) and Al Tucker (Ph.D. program in political science at the University of Missouri Saint Louis) made the fieldwork a pleasure, even with sixteen-hour days. For the capable, even brilliant, research assistance, I am indebted to Ms. Christine Huang and Mr. Gong Chen. The following readers' comments were very valuable: Dennis Judd, Carol Kohfeld, Larry Malley, John Tryneski, Lana Stein; and also Bryan Jones and John Portz (the reviewers for the University Press of Kansas), whose care and labor helped transform the first version of the book into a much more finished argument. I owe an enormous intellectual debt to those scholars whose work on economic development and agenda-setting preceded and inspired me: Bryan Jones, John Kingdon, Peter Eisenger, Lynn Bachelor, Dennis Judd, Ann Bowman, Michael Pagano, Roger Cobb, and Sam Elder, to name a few. However, I remain responsible for any errors that remain after these careful readings. I am deeply grateful to the University Press of Kansas for its interest in germination of—and, indeed, loyalty to—the project. I thank the most patient and insightful of all editors, Michael Briggs. He was eternally encouraging and extraordinarily patient as the book took various twists and turns along the way, always able to keep his sights focused on the big picture. I also thank the University Press of Kansas for its fine copyediting, production, and marketing skills, especially those of the talented Susan Schott and Melinda Wirkus, as well as the fine work of Erica Fox, an astute freelance copy editor of Atlanta. Jan Frantzen, Lana Vierdag, Kristy Brooks, and John Kalinowski of the political science department provided enormous technical assistance in the preparation of the manuscript. The efforts of Sandy Crews in the last throes of the project were unparalleled in competence, drive, and efficiency; I am deeply grateful. I wish to thank also Elizabeth Sale, the head of the Survey Center at the Centers for Public Policy Research at the University of Missouri Saint Louis for her help in preparing the sample. Scott and Dotti Hoyman's helpfulness, support, and staying power sustained the project in the most discouraging phases of the manuscript's evolution. I greatly appreciate the generous efforts of the Department of Political Science of the University of Missouri Saint Louis and its Chairs, Dennis Judd and Lyman Sargent; the Dean of Arts and Sciences, Terry Jones; the Director of the Master's of Public Policy Administration Program, Carol Kohfeld, of the University of Missouri St. Louis; the Weldon Springs Fund of the University of Missouri; and the Centers for Public Policy Research and its Director, Lance Leloup, whose unit supported the collection of the public opinion data. Also, I wish to thank my friends, including Lana Stein, Carol Kohfeld, Tina Grossman, Robi Damyan, Ruth Przbeck, Karen Webster, Dianne Scaccia, Leslie Uljee, Carla Nolin, Lamont Stallworth, and Lou Ferman, whose friendship during rough times of this book's preparation sustained me. Finally, I wish to thank my immediate family, Michael and Courteney, and our trusty Airedale, Ginger, all of whom will celebrate if and when one morning soon as they ask the daily question at the breakfast table ("Is *the book* finished yet?") they receive an answer in the affirmative. They truly have earned the buttons I saw recently at a publication party which read "I survived the book."

1 | Introduction

A LINE OF PEOPLE winds down the walkway outside the Williamson County Chamber of Commerce in Franklin, Tennessee. It is 7:30 on a Monday morning, so the office is still empty. The job seekers waiting anxiously in line are excited because they may have a chance for jobs at the new Saturn automobile plant. Three days before, the company finally announced the site of the new plant—Spring Hill, Tennessee, in nearby Maury County. The people had come to apply for the 5,000 new jobs that had received so much publicity in the national news media. These jobs would be at an attractively high wage level, as is characteristic of the automobile industry. Some of the job seekers had driven all the way from California, starting the Friday before the announcement was made. They wanted to be the first in line. Even a young woman nursing her baby is standing there. Then comes the news: a chamber of commerce spokesperson announces that the plant will not be built for another five years; applications will not be taken for quite a while. Disappointed and confused, the crowd disperses.

Although this may sound like a scene from the Great Depression folklore or a Steinbeck novel about itinerant workers, the incident actually took place in 1985, the Monday after the Saturn Corporation, a division of General Motors, made its historic announcement that it would locate a plant in Maury County, Tennessee. The announcement generated enormous excitement. The scene just described followed a bizarre incident in which governors from more than twenty states paraded to Michigan in an attempt to convince Saturn to open the plant in their state. Then came the selection of the final few states and the announcement itself.

This study explores the impact of the Spring Hill plant and three other large automobile plants on the rural communities where they were built.[1] The changes in a community that occur after a plant opens—in its government, the structure of its elite, its level of optimism, and its sense of efficacy—are documented. The automobile plants discussed here ranged in size from 3,000 production workers to 8,800.[2] The four communities involved were Spring Hill, Tennessee, the site of the Saturn plant; Smyrna, Tennessee, the site of the Nissan plant; Georgetown, Kentucky, the site of the Toyota plant; and Marysville, Ohio, the site of the Honda plant.

Table 1.1 gives the size of each plant, the year the plant announcement was made, the year the plant was opened, the name of the automobile company, and the various political jurisdictions within the impact area of the company. Note that these plants opened on different dates. The Marysville site could be considered old, since the announcement that it was opening was made in 1977. By contrast, Spring Hill could be considered young. The Spring Hill plant did not open until 1990, although the plant announcement was made in 1985. The size of the plants varied, but all were large relative to the communities in which they were located. The demographics, such as the size of the communities where they were located, the educational level of the residents, the percentage of the community that was rural, and the level of infrastructure development, were similar with one exception: the level of unemployment differed at each site.

The plight of rural America is well known. The scope of its problems has reached new proportions, however, unparalleled since the Great

TABLE 1.1. Characteristics of the Four Sites

	Date Announced	Date Open	Workforce	Political Jurisdiction in Impact Area[a]
Spring Hill	1985	1990	3,000[b]	Columbia (city) Maury (county) Williamson (county)
Smyrna	1980	1983	3,500	Smyrna (city) Murfeesboro (city) Rutherford (county)
Georgetown	1985	1988	3,000[c]	Georgetown (city) Scott (county)
Marysville	1977[d]	1979	8,800	Marysville (city) Union (county) Logan (county)
			(7,700 Marysville) (1,100 Anna)	

a. Impact area is defined as those counties where 60 percent of workers in the plant live.
b. All of the 3,000 production workers were imported from outside the state, particularly from Michigan and Ohio. No bargaining unit jobs went to Tennesseans.
c. The Toyota workers reside in 108 of the 120 counties in Kentucky.
d. There were subsequent plants built on the same site in 1982, 1985, and 1987. See Table 2.1.

Depression. The failure of the agricultural economy, the exodus of young rural residents to the cities, the replacement of higher-paying light manufacturing jobs with service sector jobs at the minimum wage, and a myriad of environmental problems, such as tainted groundwater, overloaded landfills, and low-level radiation dumping sites, combine to imperil the rural community as we know it. This has led several authors, such as Fitchen, to describe rural America as endangered.[3] Each community faces policy choices: doing nothing, encouraging small business growth from within the community, or undertaking economic development through a large industrial siting. This study evaluates the third of these choices.

The findings from this study indicate that the economic development that occurs as a result of an event such as a plant opening can best be understood as a process rather than an outcome or series of outcomes. This means that the changes occur continually, not just when the plant opens. The effects of these changes are not solely economic but are political and cultural as well. Rather than a static process, economic development is dynamic and is affected by local forces, such as community leadership. The data from this study provide an opportunity to examine whether economic development is idiosyncratic by site or can be viewed as a generalizable process or set of stages.

FORCES LEADING TO GREENFIELD SITINGS

Recently, there has been a frenzy, even an obsession, over prizes such as the siting of a large industrial plant in one's state or town.[4] Competition for the Saturn plant, for example, was so fierce and public that a General Motors spokesperson said that the company had bids from "fifty-three of the fifty states."

Companies decide to move since capital is mobile and states are not. If a state is considered unattractive to business, because of, say, a workers' compensation law that is considered too protective of labor, then a company can relocate to another state or country.[5] This has led to the rise of what Peter Eisenger calls "the entrepreneurial state," as states vie to attract business.[6]

Capital flight is a complex notion that can take many forms: an industry can invest in more profitable enterprises or "cash cows," such as U.S. Steel's decision to invest in Marathon Oil of Ohio; it can relocate a plant to the Sunbelt; it can shut down an operation; it can slowly and invisibly phase out a plant; it can set up a "runaway shop" in a lower-wage area; and, finally, it can shift its entire operations from production to service.[7]

The increasing importance of globalization also has far-reaching implications for both cities and industries such as automobile manufacturing; it means a city must innovate over the long term and make cultural changes; it means restructuring the relationship between cities and nation-states, leading to the emergence of what Saskia Sassen calls the "global city," such as New York, London, and Tokyo, which have retained or enhanced their positions as leaders in the world economy based on their predominant status in global financial institutions rather than on the nation's economic growth. Sassen and others point out that globalization of the economy shifts the fortunes of one city to another.[8] One argument maintains that certain characteristics make a city global, that a community can position itself globally. For instance, it can "target" clusters, can control its land-use corridors, and can develop adequate access to transportation.[9] Thus, globalization can create several classes of cities, some of which are winners and some losers. The growth of global cities has implications for the distribution of income; in these cities there is a widening of the already growing income inequalities.

At the root of globalization is competition. Competition may not be a national phenomenon, but it is a community one. For example, communities can create a competitive urban political economy through the actions of their leaders.[10] The globalization of the economy has implications not just for the United States or the automobile industry, nor just for rural communities. Some authors have suggested that it has led to an increasing class polarization worldwide, that is, that the rich are growing richer and the poor poorer.[11]

Finally, globalization has implications for the individual employee, so that the type of labor a worker does can constrain his or her economic fate. Robert Reich in *The Work of Nations* argues that routine workers—blue-collar or production workers—are the least prepared to survive the rigors of world competition. They are in a "sinking ship" compared with workers doing more skilled, less portable work.[12]

In addition to the mobility of capital, deindustrialization has occurred in America over the last twenty-five years, resulting in plants closing in what were traditional manufacturing sectors. According to Barry Bluestone and Bennett Harrison, deindustrialization is defined as "the widespread systematic disinvestment in the nation's basic productive capacity," meaning there is no investment in basic industries. The effects of deindustrialization are universal, according to Janet Fitchen, affecting even the wage structure and prospects of rural communities.[13]

Has the automobile industry specifically been affected by globalization and deindustrialization? Automobile production has clearly changed dramatically; it can be shifted from one country to another based on labor costs, currency exchange rates, or changes in demand, much as textile production was moved from one community or region to another in the past, for example, from New England to the South. And, although U.S. automakers, particularly the Big Three (Ford, Chrysler, and General Motors), have been closing plants in the United States and "offshoring" production of their component parts, foreign automobile manufacturers have been hiring American workers. Between 1987 and 1990, the Big Three laid off 9,063 American workers and the Japanese hired 11,050.[14] Furthermore, no longer are exports from the United States purely American. A large percentage of U.S. exports is produced by foreign-owned companies, particularly Japanese firms, which alone accounted for 10 percent of America's total exports. In combination, the forces specific to the automobile industry work to create what Richard Hill has called the "global factory" in a company town.[15]

Because of globalization, products have become hard to identify as American, Japanese, or another individual country's. Exports from America, such as an American car, may look American but may have a far lower domestic content than Japanese cars sold in the United States. What would have been considered a "national product," like a Big Three car, may have an engine from Mexico, a body from Europe, wheels from Korea, brakes from South America, and small parts from all over the world.

All four of the plants discussed in this study are examples of greenfield sitings; therefore, to understand the discussion that follows it is critical to be familiar with their characteristics. A greenfield siting is a plant that is outside the jurisdiction of either a city or a town. It is in a greenfield, rather than in an urban, suburban, or exurban area. Siting a plant in a greenfield is an attractive way of doing business, as exemplified by recent sitings of a BMW plant in South Carolina and a Mercedes-Benz plant in Alabama. Besides the new mobility of capital and the desire to locate outside a political jurisdiction, other factors determine a corporation's decision to locate in a certain place.[16]

What do we know about siting decisions by corporations in general that can shed some light on this study? There is an acknowledgment by recent authors that siting is a multistage process.[17] Local and state tax systems, the educational level of the community, the industrial climate, and the labor skills of the residents must all be taken into account. According to Bryan Jones and Lynn Bachelor, the three most important variables are land costs, the available labor pool, and transportation costs. Their description succinctly explains the plant replacement strategy of General Motors and captures the incentives for a corporation to choose a greenfield siting: "Now city centers were filled up; little available land remained for building the linear one-story plants that were most efficient for modern productive process. Moreover, now labor was mobile; workers could come to the plant so the plants did not have to go to the workers. And both land and taxes were cheaper in the countryside."[18]

According to H. Brinton Milward and Heidi Hosbach Newman, one variable that has been identified as important in many studies is right-to-work legislation; however, it was not important in the four cases discussed in this book. Given the increasingly technological demands of modern sitings, some research indicates a preference for nontraditional criteria, such as education and quality of life, over the traditional variables of transportation and labor.[19] Specifically, Milward and Newman found in their study of six plants, including the Saturn site, that political and personal as well as economic variables were important. They point to other variables as well, including a state's commitment to have an ongoing relationship and to engage in follow-up, as well as its commitment to education and training. An examination of recent state incentive packages confirms this. Approximately one-third of the Nissan package was dedicated to training, whereas training constituted 39 percent of the Mazda package at Flat Rock, 38 percent at the Saturn plant, 48 percent at Chrysler-Mitsubishi Diamond Starr in Illinois, and 43 percent at Toyota.[20]

Infrastructure is also an important variable. In three out of four funds established for plant sitings, money was set aside for water improvement; in three cases, monies were allocated for site improvement and/or acquisition. According to some studies, incentive packages have been increasing in size in recent years.[21]

Tax incentives are another popular vehicle used to attract sitings to both urban and rural settings. Todd Swanstrom, in his book on Tom Kucinich, the populist mayor of Cleveland, describes the advantages of tax abatements: "Politicians supported tax abatement not because it was effective, but because it was a remarkably easy path to follow, one that allowed them to claim they were mounting a serious attack on the economic problems of the city." Swanstrom goes on to say that tax abatements have three key advantages for corporate siting recruitment as a community strategy: "(1) No requirement for up-front investment; (2) political virtue of finessing thorny distributive issues; and (3) very little staff and no delays and no bureaucracy."[22] There are some indications in the literature, however, that corporations do not consider abatements in making siting decisions.[23]

Of the four companies discussed in this study, Nissan, Honda, and Toyota were Japanese, and Saturn was American. Each company had a distinct organizational culture and long-range plan. The Japanese companies were motivated by the threat of more protectionism and the dollar-to-yen ratio. In addition, the Honda Corporation had a full-fledged plan to invest in America.

The location of the plant in a community that is in geopolitical limbo has several seeming advantages: the company is not subject to any planning or zoning regulations as it would be in a large city or town; the labor force is generally more docile than in an urban setting; transportation and other costs are lower; and a disproportionate number of the greenfield sitings are in southern "14.B." states, where there is little or no prospect of unionization.[24]

From the community's point of view, however, cynicism or wariness may be in order. Reich cautions about the viability of greenfield sitings over the long term. As he notes, smug politicians who congratulated themselves for landing the plants may be in for a surprise as robots replace humans:

> But as these ebullient politicians will soon discover, the foreign-owned factories are highly automated and will become far more so in years to come. Routine production jobs account for a small fraction of the cost of producing most items in the U.S. and other advanced nations and this fraction will continue to decline sharply as computer-integrated robots take over. In 1977, it took routine producers thirty-five hours to assemble an automobile in the U.S.; it is estimated that by the mid-1990s, Japanese-owned factories in America will be producing finished automobiles using only eight hours of a routine producer's time.[25]

In addition to the general trend in the automotive industry to establish greenfield sitings, even more compelling forces work in favor of Japanese plants doing so. These include the proximity to the U.S. market; the special free trade zone status awarded these sites; the hope that the American jobs from such "transplants" will help mitigate further U.S. protectionism; the shifting relationship between the yen and the dollar, resulting in savings for the Japanese of billions of yen in the 1980s and 1990s; and, finally, the motivation "to have a seat at the table" with the Big Three.[26]

ECONOMIC DEVELOPMENT AS A PROCESS OVER TIME

Economic development is a multistage, dynamic process that occurs over time. A community progresses through several stages, from the announcement that the plant will be opened to the point at which the plant is a regular and established feature of the community's terrain. Equally important to this process is the interaction of macroeconomic forces, such as globalization, capital mobility, and deindustrialization, with local forces, such as the community leadership. Much of the literature on deindustrialization and political economy suggests a different, more fatalistic process in which the corporation has so much power that the community is totally vulnerable. Three of the four communities examined here were essentially passive during the economic development process. By viewing economic development as a dynamic process, however, it is possible to see that the community leadership can make a difference, that is, that a dynamic relationship exists between the community and the corporation. Some recent literature, such as that by Pagano and Bowman and by Judd and Parkinson, suggests that leadership is terribly important in shaping the vision or image of the community.[27] From this perspective, the "new politics," including such matters as bargaining over the outlying costs associated with the economic development process, takes on increasing importance.

At the outset of this research project, it was expected that the economic development process would be totally idiosyncratic at each site. Rather, the results from the four sites support the idea that economic development occurs in a somewhat general way, in stages common to all sites. These stages are presented in detail in chapter 2. More than just economic changes occur from stage to stage; political and cultural transformations occur as well.

Why would one conceive of economic development as a process rather than an outcome? It stands to reason that the effects of a plant do not remain static over time; Anthony Downs, in his classic article on the issue-attention cycle, described the process by which an issue gets on an agenda.[28] This may give us some clue as to how the plant as an issue evolves and how the members of a community react to the plant over time (Figure 1.1). Downs describes the first stage of the issue-attention cycle as the preproblem stage. In this stage, all is quiet; the issue is invisible.

During the second stage, which could arguably be when the announcement is made that the plant will be opening, the problem, in this case the plant as an issue, is first discovered. Typically, there is one of two extreme responses: euphoria that something is being done about the economic problem or alarm and hysteria. The two extremes are intertwined and occur simultaneously. This certainly approximates the reaction of the four communities studied here. Many residents are "boosters" who view the plant as a savior, the answer to the community's economic problems. The boosters count on the plant to bring jobs and, like a magnet, to attract other industries and businesses. At the same time, a certain element of the community is aghast, horrified that the fabric of their small town might be ripped asunder. The preservationists and farmers fear the "sins" the plant will attract. According to Downs, eventually the issue dies down and reality sets in. The community begins to realize not just some of the

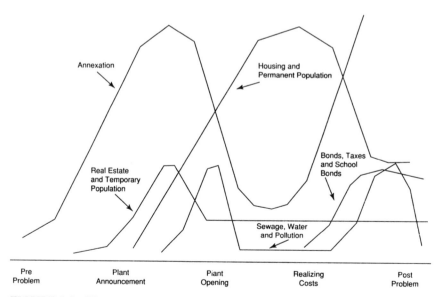

FIGURE 1.1. The rise and fall of plant-linked issues across time in the community.

costs of immediate problems relating to traffic and housing but also the costs of outlying problems of bonds, taxes, and particularly school bonds. The latter occur in a stage that Downs describes as "realizing the costs," as the community recognizes that it will be necessary to raise taxes and address such issues as annexation and development fees, and to float bonds for new schools and other public works.

Finally, there is a mature, or postproblem, stage when everything seems to be back to normal. At this stage no one can remember when the plant was not in their community—it is a nonissue.

PLANT AS A SERIES OF SUBISSUES OVER TIME

At first glance, the "plant" appears to be a single issue. In fact, over time, the issue of the plant disaggregates into a number of subissues, which rise or fall in importance as illustrated in Figure 1.1. The subissues are all related to the plant: real estate speculation, the temporary population explosion, construction, traffic, jobs, the greater demands on sewage, water quality and supply, schools, and annexation. How the town's leaders address these issues is important, as Jones and Bachelor remind us.[29]

The complexity of the meaning of the plant does not end there. The meaning of time measured in chronological age and the meaning of time measured in stages of development time are not the same. The chronological age of a plant and the stage to which the community has progressed in its process of economic development are not necessarily the same. A fully mature site is one that has gone through all of Downs's stages to the point that the plant is "no longer an issue." The town's leadership is completely transformed, and there is a new group of leaders. The community's public administrators are professionalized. There is a new way of doing the business of government that is more open and more formal, and there is a new emphasis on planning. As can be seen in Table 1.1, Smyrna is the only one of the four sites that has progressed through all stages of development; it took only six years, from 1980 to 1986, for it to do so.

There is one key way in which the plants do not follow Downs's issue-attention cycle. One interpretation of Downs is that the issue qua issue recedes, but no new policy has been made: some scholars have claimed that Downs was saying that, once life returns to normal and we are in the postproblem stage, there is nothing which has been done. The author feels that is too pessimistic. However, the fast succession of institutional changes described in chapter 2 is more typical of what Frank Baumgartner and Bryan Jones observe in the policy arena—there is a punctuated equilibrium, after which there are multiple institutional changes.[30] In other words, there may be no or few institutional changes and then numerous institutional changes. Baumgartner and Jones also suggest that any policy changes to the community's agenda differ depending on whether an issue enters the agenda when there is a mobilization of criticism or a mobilization of enthusiasm. As a result of the opening of the new plant, there will usually be a new or greatly expanded recreation department, a new emphasis on planning (with more staff and a new formalized procedure), a new group of community political leaders that is more pro–economic development and less like the good old boys, a new professionalization of police and fire chiefs, and major changes in sewage, water supply and quality, and other areas of public administration, as discussed in chapters 4 and 5 and in chapter 8 on political and cultural transformation.

There is also support in the agenda-setting literature for the notion that economic development is a process. How does the plant set the agenda? Roger Cobb and Charles Elder discuss different agents that can put an item on an agenda, such as interest groups, the parties to a dispute, a do-gooder, and the media.[31] Yet another possible agent, according to Cobb and Elder, is an unanticipated event, such as an earthquake, a war, or a natural disaster. The automobile plant functions as such an unanticipated event in that typically the community where it is sited is passive in recruiting it and its suddenness and magnitude are a shock to the community.[32] Yet one wonders why the impact is so sudden if, as shown in Table 1.1, there is a time lag between the announcement and the opening of the plant, in some cases as long as five years? The answer is that the community undergoes obvious changes as soon as the *announcement* of the plant is made. For instance, rampant real estate speculation begins immediately after the announcement. In fact, it has nearly stabilized by the time the plant opens. As will be discussed later, typically, there is approximately a 30 percent net increase in real estate prices as a direct result of the presence of a plant in the community; by the time the plant opens, however, prices have already leveled off. In sum, following the announcement that the plant will open, the community undergoes a sudden jolt, causing it to face many issues in rapid succession.

The economic, political, and cultural changes a community undergoes following the announcement that a plant will open occur not in a linear fashion but more in a series of waves. Increases in real estate prices and in the community's population occur first; next, wave after wave of public administration "problems" arise that need addressing, all washing over the passive and stunned community, which barely has time to come up for air before another wave crashes down (Figure 1.1).

There is a third way to visualize the plant: as a solution floating along next to the problem stream of the community. The plant is a single solution, but the community's problems are multiple. John Kingdon used the solution stream and problem stream metaphor to describe the way a policy is made: when the politics stream, problems stream, and solutions stream all have a window, a policy solution can couple onto a problem through a window of opportunity.[33] The problems in the problem stream of rural areas are multiple—the lack of economic growth, loss of small manufacturing, decline in agriculture, substitution of low-paying service sector jobs for manufacturing jobs, despair as young people flee to the big city, and the depression (psychic and economic) that is concomitant with being on the "outs" of the global economy. Janet Fitchen defines these problems as no different from many of the economic problems of cities.[34] Likewise, there are many possible solutions, such as preserving the agricultural character of the community, building small businesses from within the community, or recruiting a large plant from outside.

In only one of the four cases discussed in this book (Smyrna) did members of the community work to ensure that the plant opened in their community; however, in the other communities the plant was accepted once it was thrust upon them by the state. This study confirms much of the literature, such as work by Peter Eisenger, regarding the importance of the state as an agent in agenda setting. The element of randomness and timing that Kingdon so eloquently refers to in describing the way an idea for economic development emerges rings true for these sites also. The changes that occur as a result of the presence of the plant and plant-linked issues do not proceed in a linear, even, or predictable pattern. There are sudden surges forward. Call them progress; call them the bane of the community. There are also insurmountable obstacles and resistance. There are setbacks and stalls. A new political leadership emerges, including a second party and a new set of political leaders, usually within two to three elections, who have a new value system.

THE STUDY AS AN IMPACT STUDY
IN THE BROADEST SENSE

Putting this study in the broadest possible context, it asks whether, in terms of policy implications, economic development is a double-edged sword. This study not only addresses the economic impact, most significantly jobs, but also the governmental and cultural impacts of an automobile plant on a small, rural community. In the parlance of this literature, the automobile plant is the economic development "event."

There is a rich literature on the negative aspects of economic development, such as plant closings or the national trend toward deindustrialization.[35] However, there is an increasing amount of scholarship on the economic impact of large plant sitings and on the effects of tax abatements on the economic and fiscal health of communities, not to mention their politics.[36] The classic policy questions raised by impact studies are whether the economic development project was worth it and whether the community is better off overall. These questions raise some interesting methodological and policy issues regarding the wisdom of "smokestack chasing" as opposed to the value of nurturing small businesses from within.

Jobs mean votes. This was the hue and cry of the "old politics." Until recently, large industrial plants were an irresistible force, especially in inner and distressed cities.[37] Recently, communities, at least suburban or exurban ones and some rural ones, have started to balk at the idea of unfettered development; consequently, politicians have begun to pay political penalties for "giving away the store," and communities offer political incentives for curbing growth.[38] Even where a state sets a clear "no loss" criterion for approving abatement packages, such as Michigan did under Governor James Blanchard, the new objective criteria may give way to the "old politics" of wooing the plant with tax abatement packages.[39] There are, in fact, some challenging problems in assessing whether a package is "beneficial."

A favorite way that scholars have tended to measure whether packages are beneficial is to compare packages across communities using a dollars-per-job measure.[40] This has the advantage of enabling us to compare packages both across communities and across time. Another way is to calculate the cost to the government and the value to the firm in order to rank incentives, with those that minimize cost to the government and maximize value to the firm being the best.[41] It would appear that the more recent packages have been getting more generous, in other words, more costly to states.

It would also appear that estimates of multipliers vary radically even within the same industry. Clearly, some studies are commissioned more with political motivations than with candor or objectivity as the goal, such as the University of Kentucky study commissioned by Governor Martha Layne Collins, used to justify her expenditure of state funds for a Toyota plant in Georgetown after controversy arose. The study measured the impact of the plant on the state's economy broadly enough to ensure that there would be measurable positive results, starting from a conclusion and adducing the data to get to that conclusion.[42]

What do we know from these impact studies? What is clear is that the unit of analysis affects the results, that there are limits to the analysis, and that development is a value-based decision. The latter two points are inextricably bound to one another. Turning to the first concern, clearly the unit of analysis one chooses is critical in determining whether a particular abatement plan has net benefits or not. For instance, Bachelor points out that, with respect to the Flat Rock plant, when one moves from the measurement of net impact on Flat Rock to net impact on the state economy, the picture brightens considerably. At other sites, such as Diamond Starr (Bloomington-Normal), focusing on the smaller of two local government units yields more favorable results.[43] One study of the Toyota plant used a regional input-output modeling system and found that assessing the statewide benefits yielded $325.4 million in earnings for the state's investment. In the Toyota case, this approach helped justify the state's expenditure more than just looking at the county would have done. In this case, there was an estimated rate of return of 25 percent.[44] This may suggest that there is no objective truth to be found, search though we may.

Turning now to the second concern, the static nature of cost-benefit analysis, a methodological innovation was developed to address this deficiency: using a process approach, which allows the costs and benefits to be assessed over time rather than statically.

The third and fourth flaws involve the inherent subjectivity of cost-benefit analyses. Using cost-benefit analysis, Mary Marvel and William Shkurti were able to distinguish between direct costs and benefits and indirect costs and benefits. This is a very useful distinction. Looking at direct costs and benefits, they define the aggregate dollars collected in property taxes as benefits and the aggregate dollars of state investment as costs. They find that the Honda plant paid for itself within five years.[45] The indirect costs and benefits are more elusive. Some indirect effects are the attraction or retention of suppliers in the area, as well as growth for the entire region, a reduction in welfare expenditures, and the indirect payments demanded by the company locating in the community. For instance, Marvel and Shkurti count as indirect effects the loss of jobs in the domestic car industry and the additional incentive payments the state began to offer to domestic automakers after it had given Honda such an attractive package. According to Marvel and Shkurti, the tax abatement was $8.5 million, whereas the total package was $27 million, so that the tax abatement constituted a relatively small share of the total package. There are many intangible impacts of a plant that are difficult to measure.

There are limits to how much analysis, rather than underlying politics, drives decision making. In fact, we know little about how decision makers think.[46] This has led Fosler to label evaluation research on economic development as suffering from "the knowledge gap"; however, as Bachelor astutely points out, even if we get a negative calculus (the costs are greater than the benefits), there is a tendency for the old politics to prevail, that is, the community offers tax abatements no matter what the cost. One limit to analysis is how much the estimates of the costs and benefits vary. For example, the unit of analysis can determine whether one gets a positive or negative ratio. As Reich points out, communities foolishly make economic development decisions without looking at several long-term implications of their recruitment strategy:

> Subsidies and tax breaks obviously reduce the amount of public money available to support primary and secondary schools, local highways and bridges, recreation, waste treatment facilities, and local amenities. Ironically, as I have stressed, these are just the sorts of public investments that are necessary for building the good jobs of the future. Poorer states and cities, most of them desperate to obtain (or keep) routine production jobs, are thus placed in a bind: Either they provide such subsidies and tax breaks for routine jobs which may not even survive much longer than a decade or so, or they give up the contest and invest their shrinking bases in education and infrastructure, whose payoffs are decades away.[47]

Besides the limits to analysis, there is another factor that makes communities rush to recruit plants—the fact that, because of the mobility of capital, the company has the bargaining advantage over both the state and the community.[48] The community faces handicaps of analysis, as well as handicaps of power caused by capital mobility.

This study provides a solution to two of the problems that have plagued impact studies: the unit-of-analysis problem and such flaws of cost-benefit analysis as the static nature of the analysis. Obviously, neither this nor any other study can provide a solution to the limits of analysis or to the problem of how to assess the degree to which, case by case, economic development is a value decision. As noted earlier, choosing the correct unit of impact is a critical decision in any impact study. Many researchers make the erroneous assumption that the city or county nearest to the plant is the appropriate unit of analysis. Likewise, the state may not be the appropriate unit of impact. Although the state may have been the most important actor in initiating the incentive package, the plant may affect counties beyond state lines. For example, although it was located in Georgetown, Kentucky, a Toyota plant employed workers from 108 of the 120 counties in the state and had a three-state impact area. Conversely, sometimes only a small area within the state, rather than the entire state, may benefit from the plant. In this study, the unit-of-analysis problem was solved by focusing empirically on the areas from which workers were commuting. To do this, a line was first drawn around the plant and then extended to adjacent cities and municipalities until the majority of workers at the plant were included in the area of analysis.[49]

By viewing economic development as a process, this book attempts to address another flaw of many impact studies—that they create a static picture of the impact of economic development. The front-end figures—namely, the dollars-per-job calculus—tell only part of the story. Although the initial contours of the incentive package help shape the long-term fiscal health or stress of the community, this is just the beginning. The impact of the plant over time is also a function of how the leadership copes with such matters as sewage, water quality and supply, the increase in population, and so on. Thus, not only is there a uniform set of stages to economic development and a uniform sequence to this process, but the net benefits or net costs cannot be fully tabulated until the cycle of development has run its course.

Another flaw of impact studies is the subjective nature of cost-benefit analysis. One person's benefit can be another person's cost. Thus, even the decision to classify something as a cost or a benefit is subjective. For example, the increase in real estate prices that occurs after an announcement of a plant opening would be a cost to a future buyer but a benefit to the seller. Also, a cost can become a benefit over time and vice versa. One way to deal with this problem is to gather data from a variety of sources. One source of data for this study was the elite in each of the communities where the plants were located, a source most previous studies have used. These data were buttressed, however, by information gathered through public opinion surveys, as well as objective data from budgets and bureaucrats.

This study differs from previous impact studies in that it examines the impact of manufacturing plants on both economic and noneconomic aspects of communities. Some of the impacts were expected, such as the increase in jobs and traffic. Others were expected but were not corroborated by the data, for instance, the prediction that there would be growth in the retail and commercial sectors of the communities and in their housing markets. And some impacts were unanticipated, such as the passage of a law allowing liquor to be sold by the drink in the county, the pronounced increase in the number of business cards printed in Japanese, the internationalization of some communities, a referendum at one site to consolidate the city-county government, and, at another, the biggest educational reform in the state's history.

The influence of the plant extends way beyond jobs and over an extended period of time. Many of these effects are discussed at length in the literature: sprawl or uncontained growth, jobs, growth of commerce (retail), growth of secondary industry, changes in government (including change in the political culture or in government programs), changes in the way decisions are made, infusions of new capital and new knowledge into the community, increases in the cost of real estate, increases in traffic, increases in wages, and increase in the funds allocated to social services as a result of having to care for itinerants.[50]

All four communities discussed in this study had much in common. Consequently, one might assume that they were equally vulnerable. This was not the case, however. As we shall see, each community responded differently to its plant; community leaders at each site took a different stance in coping with the plant's impacts.

LOCAL LEADERSHIP

An important theme of this book is the idea that community leaders can change the vulnerable status of their community as it attempts to deal with the myriad changes that occur with globalization and, more specifically, the presence of a large multinational plant. Some of the academic literature suggests that a city's inherent characteristics determine whether it will become global or not.[51] This book takes a more sanguine approach; it shows that the community can affect its destiny. The process by which a community adjusts to being the site of an automobile plant involves a dynamic interaction between the forces of globalization and the effectiveness of the local leadership. This process dictates changes over time and differences across communities and companies. Some of the strategies adopted by community leaders are effective; others are not. This section discusses some of these strategies and the reasons community leaders play such an important role in the "new politics" of accommodation.

Bachelor and Jones, in their study of auto sitings, develop a particularly useful notion to describe the search-and-response strategy city leaders adopt with respect to economic development. They characterize it as a "solutions set" proposition.[52] Similarly, Michael Pagano and Ann Bowman speak of community leaders having a "vision" or image that guides their choice of economic development projects.[53] Wilbur Thompson argues that communities should encourage a strong sense of "civic loyalty" to fend off a hemorrhaging of talent in hard times.[54] Thompson sees five characteristics—entrepreneurship; central management; research, science, and engineering; engineering productivity; and routine operations—as critical if cities are to survive in a global economy. Pagano and Bowman view community leaders as engaged in a problemistic search that is motivated both by their overall vision of the community and by its political-economic needs. Finally, Dennis Judd notes that leadership may vary and may determine the future of communities in three important ways: the capacity of leadership, the choice of strategy, and the consequences of economic regeneration.[55] Thus, although there are cities that have become global because of their concentrations of financial institutions or their role in world trade, there are also cities that have created niches for themselves, such as centers for the development of research or centers for management activities.

In summary, there is a new feeling among urban scholars that how a city performs in the face of economic restructuring is important. Or, to put it another way, how does the city adjust to economic development events? In the words of Susan Fainstein:

> There are two ways of analyzing cities, neither incorrect. The first, or global, approach scrutinizes the international system of cities and its national or regional subsystems. While noting particularities the mode of explanation attributes them to the niche or specific node that a city occupies within

the overall network. Scholars using this perspective predict uneven development and consequent territorial difference; from their vantage point, which particular places win or lose matters less than that there inevitably will be winners and losers. In contrast, the second approach, which works from the inside out, examines the forces creating the particularities of a specific place—its economic base, its social divisions, its constellation of political interests and the actions of participants. Within the first framework differences among cities are manifestations of the varying components that comprise the whole. The second traces urban diversity to internal forces and the tactics used by local actors.[56]

What are the ways in which community leaders can make a difference? In the context of this study, what is the role of the political leaders of the city and county closest to the plant?[57] First, these leaders play a critical part in the second stage of negotiation of the incentive package, regarding the in-lieu-of-tax payments, after the state has negotiated the broad contours of the package (training, tax abatements), as discussed in chapter 4. Community leaders are often able to negotiate in-lieu-of-tax payments to offset the costs of running sewage and water lines out to the plant and the costs of expanding the schools as a result of plant-related growth. Occasionally, they are able to negotiate annexation of the site to the nearest town at this juncture, although of the four sites discussed in this study such an attempt was successful only at Smyrna. The precise deal that is cut determines whether the plant "pays for itself" or whether some of the jurisdictions will be in debt for years to come. At some of the sites examined in this study, the community leaders were more successful in their negotiating efforts than at others, although at all four sites the community leaders were encumbered by deficits of power, information, and time. Compounding these problems and further limiting the power of the local leadership, in many cases the state will not let the community "push too hard" for fear of losing the plant.

In most cases, the community leaders lose even more power after the second stage of bargaining and the emergence of the "new politics" in the community. Typically, within two elections, there is virtually a new set of leaders with a new set of characteristics. Usually a second political party gains in power, and the business of government gets done in new, more formal ways. Thus, in the time immediately after the plant opening, the community leadership begins what will be a continuous process of renegotiating resources as some of the costs associated with the plant are realized.

A variety of strategies are available to community leaders to offset the costs associated with having a large manufacturing plant in their town: annexation, development fees, community ownership of a utility, a requirement that the plant buy supplies locally, and increases in the amount paid by the company for in-lieu-of-tax payments. Chapter 9 contains an analysis of which strategies worked best and which strategies each of the communities adopted. In addition to their choice of strategies, community leaders can play a pivotal role in the economic development process, depending on their general stance toward economic development. The four sites differed in this regard, and leaders' attitudes changed over time as the leadership itself changed. Each community was so transformed that, generally speaking, by the mature point in the development process it had a different set of leaders with a different set of values. But even at the beginning, the leadership at each of the four sites took a different stance regarding the plant, and, because of an imbalance between taxes available and services demanded, the city's or community's stance was often not as rationally thought out as Pagano and Bowman might have anticipated. For instance, compare the stance of the leadership in Smyrna, as expressed by Mayor Sam Ridley's comment that "the plant must pay for itself," with the more passive or reactive stance of the leaders of the other three communities.[58]

METHODOLOGY

The first task of this study was to establish a baseline year. One finding the research team made during preliminary field trips to the sites was that in each case there were immediate impacts on the community as soon as the announcement was made that the plant was opening. We thus chose as the baseline year the year in which this announcement was made. The last year in the series was 1990.

One of the most challenging problems, as illustrated by Bachelor and others, is how to establish an accurate or correct unit of analysis or impact area. Unlike the community power studies of the 1950s, the impact areas in these cases were very diffuse. It seemed logical to follow the trail of the workers, so the general rule was to keep extending the area outward from the "bull's-eye" of the plant until the area encompassed 60 percent of the workforce.[59]

The data for this study came from three sources: interviews with the communities' elite, budget information from the year before the announcement of the plant to 1990, and public opinion data collected in 1992 based on a random sample of the residents of each of the four areas being analyzed, yielding approximately 600 interviews. The data on the elite were based on seventy-five interviews conducted in the spring of 1990. The budget data included total revenue and expenditure data, plant-related and non-plant-related revenue, as well as expenditure data broken into public administration categories: police, fire, planning, criminal justice, sewage, water, public works, recreation, and planning. At each site, the elite respondents or functionaries were the mayor, county commissioner, city manager, sewage or water director, recreation director, county unemployment officer, public health official, economic development officer, chief budget officer for the city and county, and superintendents of all city or county schools or other school districts within the impact area. Each of these respondents was given a partially open-ended and partially closed-ended two-hour questionnaire. The questionnaire given to the public was an abbreviated and simplified version of that given to the communities' elite; the shorter questionnaire was administered by phone and lasted twenty minutes (see appendix).

ORGANIZATION OF THE BOOK

Chapter 2 provides detailed accounts of how each of the four communities adjusted, or didn't adjust, to the news that an automobile plant would be opening and to the actual opening. To put the event in context, the chapter begins with a discussion of the demographics of each community before the announcement was made that the plant was opening.

Chapter 3 examines the attitudes toward the plant among the elite in each community. This chapter introduces a notion that is discussed in more depth in subsequent chapters: a plant can have multidimensional, noneconomic as well as economic impacts on a community.

Chapters 4 and 5 address the fiscal, budgetary, and public administration impacts. The contours of the incentive package determine the fiscal impacts, which are discussed in chapter 4. Then the patterns of revenue and expenditures are looked at across time and sites. In this chapter, there is the finding that the city or county adjacent to the plant often bears the brunt of the impact but has no "seat at the table" and therefore is unable to collect in-lieu-of-tax payments. Chapter 5 explores the specific impacts of the plant over time on such important public administration functions as police, fire, sewage, water, criminal justice, public works, recreation, and welfare. The discussion covers the percentage of change over time in each category and the absolute gains in the budget for that function over the entire period of economic development, but also the proportionate amount of the budget that went to each function before and after the plant was opened.

Chapter 6 focuses on changes in education, since it turned out that at each site the opening of the plant had a significant effect on this facet of the community. What was so remarkable was that more than just curriculum, enrollments, and staff were affected. The link between education and economic development was a revelation to these communities.

Chapter 7 covers the three policy choices communities face: they can do nothing (thus leaving the market in play), build small businesses from within, or recruit large industrial plants. Focusing on the third choice, the chapter sets forth a set of recommendations that communities can follow to maximize their bargaining positions with outside companies.

Chapter 8 looks at the changes each plant has wrought from the public's perspective. Chapter 9 elaborates on the long-term political and cultural transformations in the four communities. Finally, some tentative conclusions are drawn about the relative wisdom of embracing this form of economic development, which is the recruitment of a large "outside" industry rather than the percolation of jobs with small employers from within.

2 | Four Communities in Transition

THIS CHAPTER, which examines the context of each plant siting and its impact, will enable us to identify whether the economic development process is a generalizable one or not. The following topics will be discussed in detail: the nature of the community before the announcement of the plant was made; the company's, the community's, and the state's role in the siting, that is, how the siting fit into their respective economic plans; the incentive package, since its contours dictate the future of the community; the community's reactions to the siting; and the politics that evolved as a result of the siting.

This chapter addresses each site individually to provide a picture of the community before the opening of the plant, the context in which the siting decision occurred, and the contours of the incentive package, all of which influenced the community's reactions to the plant, the plant's impact, and the new politics, the change, and renegotiation executed within the community throughout the stages of the development process. The first case to be discussed is Smyrna, Tennessee, the success story of the four sites, which appears to have gone through all the stages of the development process. Next, Georgetown, Kentucky, and Marysville, Ohio, will be discussed, since the hypothesis is that they are the next most mature sites, followed by Spring Hill, Tennessee, the least mature both chronologically and in its stages of economic development. The data in this chapter will be adduced to test the categorization of the sites.

SMYRNA

Before the Plant

The Smyrna site is unique in this study in one respect. It is the only site where the local citizenry recruited the plant, as opposed to the state. As early as the initial site interviews when community leaders were asked to identify a single force responsible for bringing Nissan to Smyrna, they replied "Mayor Sam." The respondents went on to say that he was also the county's most decorated World War II hero. Along with local bankers and attorneys, he had acted aggressively to put together the industrial revenue bond package to finance the plant. Mayor Sam, with his considerable bargaining skills, was also terrifically successful in cutting an extraordinarily attractive deal for the community with Nissan.

The first question is, What impact did the plant have on the area around Smyrna? The distribution of the total workforce of 3,440 workers at the site by county was provided in an interview with Nissan officials. Of the 3,440 workers, 1,660, or 48 percent, were from Rutherford County. The rest were from seven other counties, most notably Davidson. Since Davidson is essentially made up of Nashville and has an abundance of industries, the impact area did not include Davidson County, only the city of Smyrna, the city of Murfreesboro, and Rutherford County. The importance of the 1,660 workers in Rutherford is very significant since there are not many large employers in the county. The other large employer is Middle Tennessee State University, located in Murfreesboro.

The fiscal impact of the plant on Smyrna was positive. The plant became a cash cow, and the city ran at a surplus for a decade after it opened. Revenue flowed into Smyrna because the city owned the gas utility, because the in-lieu-of-tax package had been large enough to make the improvements required by the advent of the plant, and because annexation had occurred.

Smyrna and surrounding Rutherford County were labeled "rural," but perhaps they should have been called "exurban." Rutherford County is in the growth line moving out from Nashville. The Smyrna site had experienced a steady growth rate for more than a decade before the plant was opened; it therefore did not experience traumatic levels of unemployment as it made the transition from an agrarian to an industrial economy. In fact, Rutherford's county seat, Murfreesboro, the site of Middle Tennessee State University, was a regional hub for cultural and commercial activity. As such, the impact on Murfreesboro and Rutherford County was not dramatic in creating new infrastructure and importing culture as in other sites. Rather, the rate of development accelerated, along with the concomitant growth in traffic. One other effect: the plant allowed Smyrna to experience the kind of prosperity long enjoyed by Murfreesboro.

The population was rising in Rutherford County even before the plant. This was because of Murfreesboro's music festival and its position as county seat and home of Middle Tennessee State University. The workforce at the Smyrna plant was 3,440 employees. The population for the city of Smyrna was 8,839 in 1980 and 13,647 in 1990—a 54 percent increase. The population for Rutherford County increased from 84,058 in 1980 to 118,570 in 1990. On the one hand, this countywide 41 percent rise was not entirely the result of the plant. However, Smyrna's economy was not bustling and vital before the plant, so one can safely assume that the difference between the county's population percentage increase and that of Smyrna could be attributed purely to the plant. That difference was 9 percent.

In terms of its political structure, Smyrna had had a small-town machine headed by Mayor Sam Ridley before the plant. It also had had a city manager prior to 1990. Combined with factors such as the reform of the town's charter, the plant helped unravel Mayor Ridley's forty-year-old machine. This was ironic given that Mayor Ridley was credited with getting Nissan to open a plant in Smyrna and with negotiating a very good deal for the community.

Siting Decision

Of the four sites, Smyrna was the only community that sought to get the company to invest in it. Why did Nissan choose Smyrna? Recall the discussion in chapter 1 of the incentives for Japanese companies to invest in America. There was another answer to "Why here?" given by both Nissan and the local leaders, and that was "the Tennessee work ethic," meaning Tennessee employees' reputed enthusiasm for hard work. The phrase is a vague reference to both Nissan's and the local leaders' anti-union attitude. Tennessee is a 14.B., or "right-to-work," state. There are some organized plants in the state, but in general the state is not organized. The details of the incentive package are laid out as follows:[1]

Company investment	State investment	Number of employees	Investment per employee
$743 million	$11 million (training)	3,000	$11,000 per job created
$843 million	$22 million (roads)		
$1.586 billion (total)	$33 million (total)		

Why was the local elite so eager to have an auto plant in their community? Two reasons: the industry was nonunion and it was stable. Unlike their American counterparts, Japanese auto companies did not tend to open a new plant and then close it during economic slumps. So a small group of local and state influentials approached the company with some sites around Smyrna. The final site selection story was apocryphal, almost serendipitous. Community and state officials were giving the Japanese a tour of the area when suddenly one visitor spotted a large, flat outcrop of rock, pointed to it, and said, "Now that would be a good spot for the plant." That spot, just outside Smyrna, became the precise site of the plant. The land was annexed to the town upon request from the Nissan negotiators.

How does this plant fit into Nissan's overall corporate strategy? The Nissan Corporation is the most guarded of the four companies studied. Therefore, the question cannot precisely be answered. The plant, opened in 1983, had been the object of an unsuccessful union organizing campaign, and local business leaders were happy about the result, proudly proclaiming that the union defeat "sent a message to the rest of the world." The company also employed the team concept typical of Japanese companies. A key part of the bonding process between employees and the company is an annual recognition awards ceremony. The company prides itself on good relations with the community.

Incentive Package

The 1980 Nissan package had certain basic contours. A goal of Mayor Ridley was that the plant pay for itself. This was achieved. As discussed in chapter 4, virtually no debt was encumbered by Smyrna, although there was substantial debt for outlying areas like Murfreesboro. The company initially invested $743 million and later an additional $843 million for the building of the plant. The state committed $22 million to roads and $11 million dollars to training. Nissan invested $64 million in training. (The original promise was for 6,000 employees but later was reduced to 4,400 employees and ultimately to 3,440 employees.) The cost per job was $11,000 when the expanded employment figure is used for the calculation; thus, the Smyrna package was the most reasonable of the incentive packages in this study, with "reasonable" meaning what is the most favorable to the community.

Nissan: "Annex Us!"

The story of how Smyrna was annexed is a testimony to Mayor Sam's bargaining skills. Nissan actually *requested* that Smyrna annex the plant site rather than the city pushing annexation. The company did this so it would be dealing only with Mayor Sam. This provided the same level of centralization on the community side of the table as on the corporate side.[2] For instance, on the community side of the table were representatives of both Smyrna and Rutherford County. Representatives of Murfreesboro, the city adjacent to Smyrna, were not invited to the table. Given the population influx and the debt ratio, it is unfortunate for Murfreesboro that it was not included in negotiations.

Mayor Sam Didn't Blink

At one point in the negotiations, it looked as though Nissan was going to renege on its agreement to fund a bypass. When the mayor pressed for it, the Japanese suggested opening the plant in Cartersville, Georgia, another community apparently wooing Nissan. Mayor Sam responded by saying that if the company was going to unravel all the previous agreements, it had better pack its bags for Georgia.

This anecdote illustrates several points. The company's reference to other sites was a way of reminding the community that capital is mobile.[3] Further, politicians can rarely afford to stand their ground when faced with the company's threat to go to another town. Why? Jobs mean votes, and politicians do not want to ruin their political futures by bargaining too hard and losing the deal.

New Politics

The last major impact was in the area of politics. A "new politics" emerges as a community's old guard is replaced by a new political elite, a second party develops, and the community renegotiates its deal with the auto manufacturer. When the data for this study were gathered in 1990, there was already a tight intermeshing of Smyrna personnel and local elite on a personal level, if not on official boards. For instance, one head of an area chamber of commerce had a spouse who held a high position in Nissan. Several area banks had had a high-level employee or two jump ship to Nissan. By 1990, the plant was a regular feature of the terrain. Virtually everyone in a community leadership position had someone in his or her family on the Nissan payroll.

One characteristic of the new political elite is that it scrutinizes and challenges the old machine. In Smyrna, this opposition took the form of a group that called itself the Watchdogs. Several issues sparked the Watchdogs' disenchantment with Mayor Sam—a local institution called the Town Club, the mayor's and his brother's low utility bills, and the town's purchase of a shredder.

Smyrna was described by many as a working-class town. Mayor Sam and other members of the elite from Smyrna, Murfreesboro, and surrounding Rutherford County saw the need for a club or gathering place to take business associates for lunch. The club was also available for family memberships and provided recreational activities. The city-built, members-only club would have been self-sustaining if it had recruited enough members, but although dues were set lower than at a country club, about $700 a year per family, not enough people joined. The club needed a city subsidy. That was when "all hell broke loose."

Then there was the matter of the utility bills. The mayor's opposition claimed that the mayor and his brother were paying a "minimum bill," which means they were being billed as if they had used no gas. This was discovered by an employee in the gas company's billing department who was a Watchdog and used this information in her own campaign for mayor.

The final incident involved a shredder. When Smyrna purchased a shredder, the citizens asked, "If there is nothing to hide, why buy a shredder?" In the midst of all this, there was an effort to change the town charter. The change centered on the tradition of appointing rather than electing a person for an unfilled remainder of a term. Through this form of successorship, the administration in power gave the appointee the advantage of incumbency.

The Nissan plant was not the sole cause of the downfall of the mayor of Smyrna. The outcry over the purchase of the shredder and the mayor's and his brother's minimum gas bills might have occurred regardless of whether the plant ever opened and still might have led to the mayor's demise; however, the events surrounding the Town Club definitely were associated with the plant and the mayor's desire to see Smyrna transformed from a working-class into a world-class town with all the associated amenities. In summary, it is unclear whether the opening of the plant directly caused or simply hastened the demise of the Ridley machine. What is clear is that the plant definitely led to some decentralization.

GEORGETOWN

Before the Plant

Georgetown was truly a sleepy, rural town with a failing agricultural economy before Toyota opened a plant there. The Toyota plant gave the community the economic and cultural jump start without which it would have continued to languish; however, even though the economic impact was dramatic, it was spread over a diffuse regional area.

Only 18.8 percent of the 3,182 Toyota workers live in Scott County, where the plant is located. The largest concentration of Toyota workers comes from Louisville, in Jefferson County. A sizable proportion also comes from Lexington, twelve miles away, and its surrounding county of Fayette.

The population of Scott County was 21,813 in 1980. The population of the county in 1985 was 22,073; it increased to 23,867 by 1990. These modest gains are consistent with the fact that of the four plants in this study the workforce at this site came from the most diffuse area. The city of Georgetown lost population between 1970, when it was 9,074, and 1975, when it was 8,892. The plant was announced in 1985, however, so it is useful to compare the population in the years closest to the announcement: in 1980, it was 10,792, and in 1990 it was 11,414.

Before the plant Georgetown had a council-mayor form of government and Scott County had a county commission. A progressive structure was already in place for the school district whereby there was a consolidated city-county arrangement.

Scott County government was dominated by rural and agrarian elements, but this was less true in the city of Georgetown. Mayor Tom Prather was appointed to fill the remainder of a term when the sitting mayor died in office. Prather attempted to institute many changes, including the annexation of the Toyota plant site, the professionalization of the public-sector employees in Georgetown, and an unsuccessful proposal to consolidate city and county governments, as detailed later in this chapter.

"From the Nineteenth to the Twenty-First Century"

"The plant took Georgetown from the nineteenth to the twenty-first century." This quote by one of the town's leaders epitomizes the Toyota plant's impact on Georgetown, Kentucky. The community was rural, dominated by horse breeding and tobacco farming. The economy had the agrarian characteristics of an earlier century; Georgetown was the small commercial center for a very rural surrounding area. Scott County is still described by one of the elite as 50 percent agricultural.

"Where Tradition and Progress Meet"

Scattered throughout the town and at its boundaries are signs proclaiming, "Welcome to Main Street Georgetown, Where Tradition and Progress Meet." Georgetown, the county seat, has two stoplights and an aging county courthouse. The downtown is two blocks square. The residential streets surrounding the downtown are speckled with Victorian houses. Georgetown College, a small school with a beautiful campus, abuts the residential houses and the downtown.

The city hall, which has had $300,000 worth of renovations, retains its traditional understated brick exterior. A proposed parking structure as well as the city hall were financed largely with revenue from the plant. At the time of the site visit in spring 1990, there were also several new fire and police stations scattered throughout town, and plans for a new $5-million justice building, which will hold a jail, a sheriff's office, and the district and circuit courts. Mainstreet Georgetown is a downtown renovation project whose goal is to preserve the historic character of the downtown and revitalize interest in downtown businesses. The program is affiliated with the Kentucky Main Street Program and the National Trust for Historic Preservation.

The downtown is so small it has only one restaurant, which serves country-style food. The mayor often eats there, along with numerous men in work clothes, seed caps, and overalls. The only women in the restaurant the day the research team was there were the city planner, with whom I and one member of our research team were having lunch, and the waitresses.

State's Role in Siting Decision

The story of Toyota's decision to locate a plant in Georgetown is one of aggressive pursuit. It was the dream of Governor Martha Layne Collins to get a Toyota Motor Manufacturing (TMM) plant in Kentucky. The local officials I interviewed said that the townspeople had nothing to do with pursuing the idea. The governor had made numerous trips to Japan, and after seventeen months of active recruiting, the deal was cinched.

Kentucky's success is also attributed to Jiro Hashimoto, the Far Eastern representative of Kentucky's state government and its trade representative. Hashimoto was the first person to present information on the state's labor and tax costs, its climate, and its location and to perform the role of liaison between Toyota and representatives in Kentucky.[4]

Community's Role in Siting Decision

The role of the local community in recruitment was minimal. The locals did not become involved until November 1985, about thirty days before the announcement about the plant was made. The immediate concerns at meetings in December 1985 and January 1986 revolved around the state's role in assisting in meeting the needs of the community. These were not direct negotiations between Toyota and local officials but meetings with the Office of Economic Development and commerce officials from the state, including the governor, who informed Toyota, the "county judge" or county commissioner for Scott County, and the mayor of Georgetown that the state would take care of the bypass construction needs of the community. "We will not forget you," said the governor.[5]

In some ways Georgetown was a natural choice, and in other ways it was an odd one. What made it a natural was its proximity to the University of Kentucky, in Lexington, only twelve miles away. Another attractive feature was its location in "auto alley," the tier of midsouthern states that had become popular because of their geographic centrality and convenience to several major interstates. Further, as a rural community, the Georgetown area had a vast supply of cheap land and energetic workers facing unemployment. Finally, because the particular site was outside the jurisdiction of the city of Georgetown, it had the advantages of a greenfield site.

In other ways, the choice was not a natural one. Kentucky is not a right-to-work state. The educational level is generally low and the dropout rate among high school students high, so that most people from Georgetown, Scott County, and other rural areas could not pass the literacy requirements necessary to get the good-paying jobs at the plant. Locals who had squeaked through high school were being rejected at the gates.

Incentive Package

The Toyota package negotiated by Governor Collins involved an investment by the state of $125 million to cover training, site purchases, and site preparation; Toyota's investment was valued at $1.1 billion, and the company made a commitment of 3,500 jobs, as displayed in the following:[6]

Company investment	State investment	Number of employees	Investment per employee
$823 million	$12.5 million (land)	3,000	$49,000 per job

This was reported to be the highest state package offered at the time.

When confronted with controversy over what some in the state considered the state's excessive outlay, the governor commissioned several studies by the University of Kentucky to estimate the multipliers, particularly the multiplier based on the growth of satellite industries throughout the region. The studies went a long way toward justifying the state's outlay in the package, although many said the multipliers were perhaps overly optimistic.

One study estimated that given the land speculation costs, the cost to the state might be as high as $325 million, roughly three times the $125 million that Governor Collins had negotiated with Toyota. The study estimated that these costs would be offset by additional plant-related industrial activity, by a multiplier effect to the economy, by the purchase of goods and services from local suppliers, and by added employment of more than 15,000 new workers in satellite industries. The study speculated that new jobs would be created that would increase demand for products and services, that wage and salary income would increase in the state, and that tax revenue would rise.[7]

Because of the town's negative reaction to the package, a study was commissioned to track public opinion. James G. Hoaglund Jr., of the University of Kentucky, examined what proportion of the population thought the incentive package was justifiable.[8] Data were gathered from the mid-1980s to 1990. For years, a minority of the population had reported that the package was justifiable, but its popularity steadily increased. Finally, in 1989, the majority of the population reported that the package could be justified.

Some literature has alleged that Toyota was a tough bargainer, at times pitting one state against another.[9] At one point during the site negotiations, for example, a late-night meeting was held in a hotel in the capital of Frankfort, at which state officials talked the locals into dropping the subject of annexation. The state officials were fearful that the plant would move "one state over," so they convinced the locals not to insist upon annexation. The threat that the company would open a plant elsewhere was taken extraordinarily seriously, since just months before Kentucky had lost the Saturn project to Tennessee. Although the deal with Toyota represented a huge outlay of resources by the state, it was finally accepted because of the fierce competition among states and the company's ability to play states off against each other.[10]

Soon after the deal was announced in the press, a lawsuit was filed against the state by angry citizens and other protest constituencies. At issue was whether the state had the power to raise and spend money for the benefit of a private business. The Kentucky Supreme Court dismissed the case and ruled that the incentive package was constitutional.

The siting process in Georgetown was marked by controversy, especially since two major plants in the area had been closed just before the announcement was made that Toyota was opening a plant in Georgetown. But even the promise of jobs did not mute the controversy, which centered on the feeling that the governor had taken "state dollars" and given them to a private company. Also, the size of the state's contribution to the package bothered some people. According to one study, the dollars abated per job created was enormous, estimated at $44,900, based on revised figures for the cost of land the state promised to buy.[11] The groundbreaking was picketed by labor groups that were upset over nonunion construction, by activists who thought the package was a giveaway, and by "conservatives" running the gamut from benign preservationists to raving xenophobes. In an interview with another leader, a local leader who exemplified the latter group was quoted as foaming: "The Japanese took Scott County without a single shot."

In addition, the governor commissioned both the University of Kentucky and the University of Louisville to conduct impact studies to justify the expenditure in terms of the broader state and regional economy. One study projected that, in addition to the direct and immediate effect of employing 3,000 persons and producing 200,000 cars annually, 1,500 persons would be employed by satellite businesses with a total investment of $250 million in plants and $450 million in machinery.[12] The researchers used a Regional Input-Output Modeling System[13] to estimate the multiplier effect. The initial construction and operation alone were projected to generate $1,908.70 million in output, $551.61 million in earnings, and 33,315 jobs. This projection was based on the conservative assumption that 60 percent of all construction and 30 percent of the machinery would be purchased in Kentucky.[14] The study projects an increase in the number of suppliers and in wage levels, a requirement of higher skill levels, and a more highly educated workforce. On a far-reaching note, the study ends by recommending long-term attention to the educational infrastructure of the state and long-term planning and cooperation among the auto alley states.

Community Impact

One of the most important effects of the Toyota plant on Georgetown was on its traffic. The prospect of waiting through two lights at the main intersection to turn left during rush hour is not a major problem compared with what many urban drivers face, but it was a huge change for Georgetown. The solution in the view of the city officials was to construct a bypass around Georgetown. The story of the bypass illustrates the challenges a community sometimes faces during the process of economic development.

Toyota's stance as a corporation is more open than that of other Japanese companies. It considers itself a good neighbor; it aims to fit into the community. The company did not want its higher personnel involved in politics, and it stood clear of the debate swirling around the city-county consolidation.

Toyota gave generously to the community in many ways: it gave a fleet of Camrys to the city for use by city services and an enormous grant to the University of Kentucky for a robotics center. The company also spent $1 million to purchase Cardome, a city facility housing a small conference center and some Georgetown city departments, and subsequently there was a substantial amount spent to remodel it. In 1986, there was $2.2 million dollars in general funds in the city of Georgetown, prior to annexation. In 1990, there was a budget of $4.6 million. Toyota contributed to many charitable causes. In a particularly powerful symbol of neighborliness, the head of TMM decided to live in Georgetown proper and, by definition, in Scott County, not in the more sophisticated city of Lexington.

When a community not accustomed to being part of a state or even an adjacent city is thrust onto the international scene, it may react with both euphoria and xenophobia. The elite in Georgetown was ecstatic that the Toyota plant enabled its frontiers to be opened. The person on the street was not as enthusiastic. There was some residual hatred over Japan's economic domination of the United States and a residue of xenophobia from World War II. More on this topic is presented in chapter 7.

One of the less concrete but long-term consequences of having a plant in one's community is the increased sense of efficacy it provides. For example, when the first car rolled off the line and it was higher in quality than those produced in Japan, the whole town celebrated. Finally the residents were confident that they could do something besides raise tobacco.

Members of the elite indicated that they had hoped more top executives would live in Georgetown instead of Lexington. In the words of one official, the city wanted "a full representation of all levels of employees to live in Georgetown." There were two other unfinished pieces of business. The first was in the area of housing. Three to four hundred Japanese live in Georgetown proper. Local officials indicated that they would have liked more executives to live in town. Mr. Cho, head of TMM in 1990, lived in a $500,000 house in Georgetown, but in general the housing built in anticipation of the plant did not match the income profile of the resident who decided to live in Georgetown. Housing in the expensive $100,000 to $200,000 range had been overbuilt, while more houses were needed in the $60,000 to $70,000 range.

Another area in which the goals remained unmet was the development of commerce. The Georgetown elite anticipated the growth of a healthy strip of service industries, including fast foods. This has happened but not as quickly as expected. People continue to travel to Lexington to purchase big-ticket items. The elite is excited about a new strip mall of small specialty shops that will be right off the interstate. This is expected to generate commercial activity. The goal expressed by local leaders was: We need to get people off the interstate.

Meeting of the Cultures

One of the broad effects of having not only a factory with outsiders flowing into a community but a foreign-owned firm is cross-cultural impact. Several top management persons at Toyota in Georgetown are American,[15] and, in fact, only about 3 percent of the in-migrant Japanese professionals were executives and trainers, the latter of whom moved out after the startup;[16] nonetheless, a fair amount of cross-cultural education occurred. For example, the state of Kentucky committed to fund Saturday school, the traditional conveyor of Japanese language and values. Similarly, members of the Georgetown political elite have visited Japan at Toyota's invitation, and Toyota has taken a whole party of local officials to the Kentucky Derby, paying for seats and hotel.

Enhanced Revenue

Besides Georgetown, Scott County comprises two small towns, Sadieville and Stamping Ground, both even smaller than Georgetown. Once the county and city annexed the plant, a substantial amount of revenue flowed into the city and the county from a payroll and profits tax. Thus, an important impact of the plant has been to enhance revenue to the area.

Moonshine and Mooning

Certain parts of the cultural blend did not translate well. For example, Scott County is a dry county, which means no liquor is served by the drink and no liquor can be purchased. The reason for the town being dry, according to one community leader, is the large number of churches; the town has thirty. In the words of one leader, Lexington is just down the road if "you want to party." It is lawful for citizens to keep liquor in their own homes, but when Japanese executives started living in Georgetown, they worried that the authorities would raid their private caches because they thought it was against the law to possess liquor. Georgetown officials explained that the law did not prohibit citizens from having their own supply of liquor and drinking it in the privacy of their homes.

Another incident indicates the stark differences in cultures. One afternoon, top Toyota officials were being given a tour of the downtown by Georgetown officials when an open truck filled with rowdy boys careened past the group. The truck stopped, and one boy pulled down his pants and proceeded to "moon" at the visitors. The Japanese were shocked and hurt. The Georgetown officials hastened to explain that this was a local custom that occurred when youths had imbibed too much local moonshine or Jack Daniels, or when one youth dared another to moon in public. The officials went on to say that it could have happened even if the Japanese had not been present. In fact, it happened regularly.

New Politics

The mayor of Georgetown, Tom Prather, seemed the model of a modern mayor, to paraphrase Gilbert and Sullivan. He represented the new breed of political leader that is the hallmark of the political transformation that accompanies the opening of a plant. Mayor Prather was, as others had described him, tall, suntanned, handsome, urbane, sophisticated, and professional. His office was sprinkled with Japanese mementos, such as origami, a beautiful geisha figurine, Japanese art, and copies of *The Road Less Traveled*, *Leadership* magazine, and *Toyota Today*. A groundbreaking spade stood in one corner, and on another wall hung a poster of A. P. Prather, a relative of Prather's who had run for mayor in 1933.

In the Georgetown site, the county commissioner represented the halfway mark between the good old boy type of leader who dominates many county governments in Kentucky and the new breed represented by Mayor Prather. The other county commissioners represented extremely traditional leadership: a farmer, a county resident who had moved to town and was a butcher at Kroger, and a retired extension officer who lived on a farm. The good old boys who had run the town neither recruited nor resisted the plant; however, the political changes started immediately after the plant opened.

Prather was appointed to replace the old mayor when a vacancy occurred midterm. Prather was progressive and favored economic development. He instituted a new professionalism to the public sector using merit-based national searches to fill the positions of a new planning director, police chief, and fire chief. The police chief was the head of the state of Kentucky chiefs association, a person who commanded the professional respect of his colleagues. In addition, much was done to upgrade service levels and hiring and promotion criteria.

After Prather was elected, he brought more changes to the community. He proposed that the city and county be consolidated, an idea too progressive for its time. In a second reelection bid after the Toyota plant opened, Mayor Prather was defeated by banker Warren Power, who some have described as a good old boy. The banker apparently had close ties to those in power before Toyota's arrival. It appears, therefore, that the road to a permanent change in Georgetown was uneven, marked by many bumps, detours, and switchbacks.

The head of the Georgetown Chamber of Commerce at the time of the study was very much in favor of preserving the rural character of the community. As he pointed out, 50 percent of the area was agricultural. One of his goals was to expand agricultural business opportunities. He ran on the platform of "preserving Georgetown as a peaceful college town."

Since the data for this study were first gathered in 1990, the community has reverted to its good old boys' culture. In addition to Mayor Prather losing his bid for reelection to the more conventional Power, the professional planner whom Prather hired has left. Some changes, however, such as the professionalization of public administration, have remained in place.

What role did the chamber of commerce play in Georgetown's economic development strategy? In many communities the chamber is dominated by small businesspeople who may be threatened by a large industry. In Georgetown, the head of the chamber had a keen interest in agriculture and agricultural products but also supported other forms of development. He took over in 1986, the year Toyota announced it would open a plant in Georgetown. In his words, "I know the Japanese culture." In fact, he had been a horse breeder and a vice president of a wholesale plumbing firm. He was a transitional figure between the old chamber of commerce small business type and the new guard.

The transformation of the elite in Georgetown has been dramatic but incomplete. First, there is a disjuncture between city and county governments in which, as in every other site, the county government has become more representative of rural districts. Currently, there are three elected county commissioners plus the county executive, George Lusby, referred to as "the judge." The county judge and the three commissioners are elected for four years and operate the Scott fiscal court, the governing body for the county. As of 1990, Lusby had served for thirty years in educational administration and twenty-six years on the city council. He had had Tom Prather as one of his students when he was a principal, and the two have a close working relationship. Lusby recounted that when he first became a city council member the job paid $5 a meeting and $10 a month. Now the job pays $6,000 a year. The county commissioners earn about $11,000 a year.

MARYSVILLE

Before the Plant

Marysville, Ohio, is a small community twenty miles off the interstate and twenty-five miles from Columbus, home of the Ohio State University. The Marysville site is considered quiet because the plant did not engender much controversy when it was opened and because there was no local input during the recruitment process. Many respondents simply said, "Honda happened."

Marysville is a quaint town, graced with a beautiful town square and an old brick courthouse. The town has been characterized by a sluggish commercial growth. Two small commercial strips have been built and are mildly successful, but the real commercial takeoff has not occurred. To understand Marysville's promise as well as its problems is to understand its proximity to Columbus. The good news is that the growth path is advancing in the direction of Marysville. The bad news is that Columbus is so close that area residents go there to purchase big-ticket consumer goods.

An anecdote about securing lodging for the research team serves as a good example of the problems of starting and keeping a commercial strip in Marysville. The first time we visited the site, in March or April 1990, there was only one motor lodge, and it did not belong to a national chain. Most of the businesses were Honda-related, and there was only one restaurant, considered upscale, although there were two fast-food restaurants on a strip across town. When we visited again, in June 1990, a new Day's Inn had opened; since then, the Day's Inn has closed, leaving only one motel on the strip. There was some concern articulated as early as 1977 that Marysville would suffer the plight of a bedroom community.[17]

The population of Marysville was 7,914 before the plant was announced in 1977 (and before it opened in 1979), and it increased to 9,656 in 1990. The plant had 8,800 employees, making it as large as the town of Marysville. In 1980, the population of Union County was 29,536; by 1990, it had increased to 31,969.

Regarding the economy when the plant came and in the early years, we see that Marysville and the two surrounding counties were very depressed, with unemployment in the 13 to 17 percent range. By 1990, thirteen years after the plant opened, unemployment had dropped to below the national average of approximately 7 percent. Clearly, the plant was a great economic stimulus to both Union and Logan Counties. By contrast, the counties just outside the hiring radius are still languishing at above-average unemployment.

Siting Decision

Why was the Honda plant opened in Marysville? Honda's decision can definitely be attributed to the efforts of Governor Jim Rhodes, to his commitment to economic development, and to his personal relationship with the Honda executives. Three other factors also influenced the selection of the site: the existence of an underutilized auto-testing facility (Transportation Research Center); the availability of farmland, which the governor offered to sell to Honda; and the governor's willingness to establish state-company partnerships. Given that there had been several plant shutdowns in the site area and the unemployment rate was 18 percent in Union County, Marysville was in no position to turn down the plant. Another reason the plant was sited here had to do with Honda's corporate strategy.

In 1988, Honda came up with a five-part strategy for future operations in the United States called "Honda's American Plan." The first part entailed the construction of a new plant and the expansion of the engine plant in nearby Anna, Ohio. An additional $380 million was committed to building an auto plant with a capacity to produce 150,000 cars per year and employing 1,800 associates. The plan cost $600 million and employed 1,500 associates by 1991. The second part of the plan was to export 70,000 cars per year to Japan. The third part was to increase the domestic content of cars from the 1988 level of 66 percent to 75 percent by 1991. The fourth part was the research and development strategy; this included increasing the number of employees in the research and development field from 180 in 1988 to 500 in 1991. Honda also had a plan to purchase the Transportation Research Center of Ohio for $31 million and to make it the site for its second automobile plant. The fifth and final part of the plan involved expanding Honda's engineering operations in the United States. The company perceived that the local workers had a strong work ethic. The hourly wages being paid to Honda workers today are comparable to those paid to union workers in the industry, although Honda workers do not receive negotiated benefits and do not have the job security rights concomitant with union jobs in the automobile industry.

As part of the work of the nonprofit part of the company, the Honda Foundation, Honda had already committed many long-term grants and resources to the engineering school at the Ohio State University. The goal of the foundation was to make the university the premier automotive engineering school in the country.

Incentive Package

From the point of view of the community, the Marysville package was the least generous but most prudent of the four discussed here (Table 2.1). No other state competed for the plant, driving up the price the community had to pay.

The Honda package was unique. There was a three-year tax abatement for existing buildings and a fifteen-year tax abatement for equipment and services. New buildings constructed after a three-year period of plant operation would be taxed at the going rate.

Community Impact

Marysville presents a very mixed picture. The plant has brought positive direct economic benefits and has had less impressive secondary and tertiary economic effects, but the transformation of the political elite from good old boys to professionals has not been complete. Further, Honda has not been completely absorbed into the community. The plant still exists outside the town; it is not integrated into its fabric.

To call the Marysville operation a plant is a misnomer; it is Honda city, a complex of several plants and buildings in Union County, seven miles outside the Marysville city limits. The focus here will be primarily on the impact of the large automobile plant. Also included in the complex is a motorcycle plant, which was the first part of the complex to be built. The announcement of its opening was made in 1977, it was built in 1978, and it opened in 1979. The auto plant was announced in 1980, constructed in 1981, and opened in 1982. Then, in 1984, an engine plant was built at Anna; the first engine was produced in 1985. Plans to build another plant in the town of East Liberty, located in Logan County just over the line from Union County, were announced in 1987.

Throughout this study when the "plant" is used, however, what is meant is the original motorcycle and auto plant in Marysville. Obviously, Logan County was affected by the original plant and is even more af-

TABLE 2.1. Marysville Incentive Package and Subsequent Packages

Date Announced	Date Open	State Investment	Number of Employees	Company Investment	Investment per Employee
1977	1979	$3.6 million expenditure for site improvements; $11 million for highways Limited property tax abatement	400	Motorcycle plant 400 workers	$9,474
1980	1982	$1.7 million expenditure for site improvements; $3.5 million for highways; $8 million for local sewage and water	Partial 2,000 tax abatement	$250 million auto plant	$307
1984	1985	Honda Resource and Development Center set up in Marysville		$240 million expansion	
	1987	$26 million direct economic assistance		Anna engine plant	$2,764
	1987	$65 million for highways		Second auto plant	$7,333
			Net employment 10,000		Net investment per employee $2,436

Source: Mary Marvel and William Shkurti, "Economic Impact of Development: Honda in Ohio," *Economic Development Quarterly* 7 (1993): 57. Copyright 1993 by Sage. Reprinted by permission of Sage Publications.

fected by the new plant in East Liberty. The decision to site the new plant in the adjacent county was a deliberate part of Honda's strategy of "sharing the wealth."

Honda of America Manufacturing was incorporated on February 15, 1978, in Ohio. The amount of investment Honda has made in Ohio since then has been substantial, starting with $35 million in 1979, rising to $285 million in 1982 when the first automobile was produced, to $720 million in 1987, to $1.2 billion in 1988, to $1.5 billion in 1989, and to $2.0 billion in 1990.

A major change in Marysville reported by both the elite and the nonelite is a noticeable growth in capital. One observer remarked that before Honda started its operations, the townsfolk attended parent-teacher meetings in jeans. Now they show up in nice clothes.

The employees in the impact area live in thirty-nine counties. The largest group (19 percent) comes from Logan County rather than Union County; however, this is only since Honda has expanded its operations. The second-largest group (or 14.5 percent of workers) comes from Union County, and the third-largest (13 percent) group comes from Franklin County. Champaign County claims 9 percent of the workforce, and Clark claims 8.5 percent.

The economy of Union County was very depressed before the plant, with unemployment in the double digits. Since the plant opened, the community has not only offset the impact of the closing of or layoffs in three industries in the area (Nestle's, O. M. Scott, and Rockwell); it has greatly reduced its unemployment, from an extreme of 18 percent in 1983 to a level considerably below the national average.[18] As of 1990, a total of 9,900 jobs had been created at Honda's Ohio operations: 8,800 at the Union County facility and 1,100 at the Anna engine plant. The investment by Honda in Ohio amounted to $1.8 billion in 1991. The weekly payroll in 1987 was $5.8 million.

Looking at secondary and tertiary effects, as of 1987 there was $936 million of activity generated among 515 suppliers, $540 million of which was within Ohio; $10 million was from Union County, and $64.4 million was from Logan County.[19] The budgetary impact on government units has been very positive. For example, property taxes alone went from $1.8 million in 1985 to $3.5 million in 1986 to $5.0 million in 1987[20] in Union and Logan Counties. There has also been a professionalization of civil servants' positions. As of 1990, plans were under way to establish a county courthouse by selling bonds to support the effort.

New Politics

The major changes in the politics of Marysville have centered on a partial transformation of the elite, a dispersion of power, and a new emphasis on economic development. Although support for this last goal is far from unanimous, the plant's entry into the community has meant the beginning of a commitment to economic development. One of the signs of innovation is the presence of a new full-time economic development officer, whose salary is paid jointly by the county, city, and private sources. Notably, she and her staff of two part-timers were placed in the Community Improvement Corporation; this entity is separate from the chamber of commerce, which could be characterized as still somewhat dominated by the old guard.

The economic development officer's first recruit was a controversial medical waste incinerator. When my colleagues and I visited Marysville in 1990, we saw signs everywhere saying "Stop DMI," the medical waste incinerator company. Ultimately, the city council convened an emergency meeting and passed an ordinance outlawing medical waste incineration inside Marysville city limits. Before that, no actual zoning code existed that would have prevented the siting. The economic development officer was under intense fire during our site visit. It looked as though the county commission might rescind its support of the position or of her personally.

The elite involved in the Honda deal was initially very small and acted like a tight clique. On the state level, there was an old guard of pro-development cronies, including Governor Rhodes and Jim Duerk, who was Jim Rhodes's economic development director and who is now associated with Rhodes and Associates in Columbus. Rhodes had been a real estate developer in the past. A couple of key banks were also involved in the initial recruitment of Honda.

The form of government in Marysville was changed in 1981, after the plant opened, from a council-manager form to a city-administrator form, but this apparently had nothing to do with the opening of the plant. Before the plant opened, a group of Republicans had controlled the county commission and the city of Marysville. After Ken Krause, now city manager, was thrown out of the mayor's office by the referendum concerning structural change, Knuckles took over as mayor. Subsequent to this and to Honda's arrival, one of the Democrats on the city council decided it was time for a change. This was Tom Kruse. Now Kruse is the mayor of Marysville, and former mayor Krause is city manager.

Mayor Tom Kruse, a Democrat, represents the new guard in this Republican county. He stands for "the winds of change" and professionalism in government. He is also more aggressive in addressing the challenges of economic development and has an openness not characteristic of the previous camp. The owner of a dry cleaning business, he wants to distribute some of the benefits of the plant "not just for himself" and his cronies but for a broader set of actors.

Although Mayor Kruse represents a new type of leader, it will be many more years before Marysville completes the process of political transformation. Both the old guard and the Young Turks are in evidence. The political culture has not been completely transformed to one of progrowth and professionalism. Interviews held at the site indicated that no single person calls the shots; rather, the government is more decentralized since the arrival of the plant. Why? Because the plant brings new actors into play and creates a different and rival power base.

SPRING HILL

Before the Plant

Spring Hill is located in Maury County, Tennessee. The impact area of the site is the city of Columbia and adjacent Williamson County. The town of Spring Hill proper has experienced virtually no benefits as a result of Saturn's opening a plant there except that there is a new fire station and a new city hall. Many Saturn workers live up the road in Columbia, the county seat of Maury County and the largest nearby town.

Columbia is more distinctly a town than Spring Hill. Columbia has an old rotunda-capped county courthouse in the center of the town square and a new county building across the street. The town abounds with quaint customs like free parking around the courthouse as long as one stays no longer than thirty minutes. There are no meters; a gentleman marks the cars with chalk, then returns to see if the time has expired. He is not a police officer but a traffic warden, an elected government official, and, parenthetically, his own boss; he also serves on the city council. He is a local character who seems to be familiar to all the locals and friendly to many outsiders.

Saturn prepared Spring Hill exceptionally well for the changes that would occur in the area in the years following the opening of the plant. Thus, when officials of Maury and Williamson Counties remarked that it would be useful to know the number of new persons coming to their counties each month and year, Saturn, which had been keeping track of these figures, kept the community closely informed. To minimize uncertainty, the company set up a transition team consisting of chamber of commerce and government officials of both counties and allowed information to flow freely. This was a slow plant startup and all of these efforts were attempts at coordination.

According to the Maury County Chamber of Commerce, the population increased from 51,095 in 1980 to 55,000 in 1985 to 59,200 in 1989. Without the Saturn plant, the population in 1990 would have been 59,200; with Saturn, it was 71,300; thus, a 20 percent increase was due to Saturn. The number of households was estimated to have risen from 18,203 in 1980 to 25,374 in 1990, which represents regular growth plus Saturn's impact. The school-age population increased from 10,798 in 1980 to 14,973 in 1990. The population would have been 12,432 in 1990 without the plant. This represents a 24 percent increase. The population in neighboring Williamson County, where one-third of the plant's workforce lives, went from 58,108 in 1980 to 81,021 in 1990, a 39 percent increase.[21]

The unemployment rate in 1985, before the plant opened, was 8.4 percent in Maury County; it was 4.7 percent in 1989 and 5.1 percent for the first months of 1990. Note that this improvement in employment occurred without the plant's actual opening, only with announcement effects. Furthermore, these positive employment effects occurred notwithstanding the fact that no locals were hired for bargaining unit positions. In Williamson County, the other impact area, the unemployment rate was constant at about 2.5 percent, practically full employment. The point is that the unemployment situation in Spring Hill before the plant was considerably better than in Marysville, for example, although not as robust as in Smyrna.

Mule Days and Yankees

Maury County is known for its rural atmosphere. One of the big social events of the year is Mule Days, "a remembrance and a testimony to the great animal, the mule," according to the promotional booklet from the chamber of commerce. There are contests for the best-dressed mule, not to mention pancake-eating contests. The contrast is dramatic between this and the urban lifestyle that typifies most of the in-migrants from large metropolitan areas in Michigan and Ohio.

Rural or Preindustrial?

Maury County certainly looks rural. One community leader, however, indignantly objected to the description, asserting, "We are not rural." He was making the point that, although the plant was surrounded by farmland, there were many diverse, scattered, and small plants in the fertilizer and petrochemical industries before Saturn arrived. In fact, there were eighty-four corporations that had a plant in the county, including Union Carbide, with 800 employees; Columbia Specialties, an air-conditioning company, employing 400; Spontex, a cellular space company, with 125 employees; Weather Tamer, with 200 employees; Gerber baby foods company, with 200 employees; Winning Moves, with 90 employees; Publix Shirt, with 500 employees; Rohn Polunc, a phosphorous enterprise with three facilities and 400 employees; and ICI Americas, an organic chemical firm with 300 employees. His definition of "rural" was preindustrial. Certainly he was correct in that the county did have industry. But rural can also connote population scarcity or a certain lifestyle, and, by this definition, Maury County is truly rural. Further, the industry that does exist in Maury County, being scattered and small, is nearly invisible.

By contrast, Williamson County, particularly an area called Brentwood, is a bedroom community for executives from Nashville. The town of Franklin, which is the county seat, boasts a rich history and a gracious charm. It has a beautifully preserved Main Street, and the requisite statue of a Confederate soldier keeps watch over the traditional square. The average income in Williamson County is much higher than the Tennessee state average. As in any county that is entirely suburban, there is a notable lack of industry in Williamson County. Community leaders have identified this as a problem. Since it takes many more residential than industrial buildings to garner the same amount of property taxes, the mainstay of school funding, the school districts in Williamson County are seeking to attract industry.

One of the pressing needs in the city of Franklin and throughout Williamson County is for moderately-priced housing, as embodied in the goal of the Franklin Planning Commission to provide multiunit housing; therefore, a need also exists to develop a commercial basis for the property tax. The community leaders are excited about plans for a new shopping mall off the interstate that should help alleviate their revenue problems.

Given the large number of executives who live there, it is no surprise that Williamson is solidly Republican on the local level, in striking contrast to the rest of the southern sites, which are strongly Democratic. Williamson is also wealthy compared with the surrounding counties. And, interestingly, many of the important decision makers in town are women. As of 1990, not only is the chamber of commerce president, Nancy Conway, a woman, but one of the largest banks is headed by a woman, and an influential woman heads a large temporary help agency. In fact, this agency landed the contract with Saturn for clerical workers. Along with one or two other important women, this group has formed what they call "the committee of last resort," which meets over dinner once every other week or so to discuss the important issues in the town.

Information regarding the residence of Saturn's employees was furnished by the public relations and personnel office of the Saturn Corporation. In 1990, the impact area included Maury County (the county in which the plant was located) and Williamson County (just north of Maury and adjacent to Davidson County, where Nashville is located). The plant is technically in Maury County, but it is near the border of Williamson.

Data from Saturn show that Williamson and Maury account for one-third each of the total workforce. Yet, after interviewing the two counties' leaders, it appears that the impact on Williamson was less significant than on Maury. In fact, representatives of Williamson were not invited to the table when the in-lieu-of tax payments were negotiated. The impact was also less clear-cut in Williamson because two additional events may have been responsible for recent growth there: the opening of an American Airlines office in Nashville and the opening of a new mall.

Siting Decision

The Saturn Corporation is a separate division of General Motors. It was meant to be a new organization with a completely new organizational structure that would create a new market for itself—a high-quality small car to compete with the Japanese cars already dominating that niche. Although a bold move for GM, the Saturn Corporation is not as separate as it was envisaged to be. What happened? GM formed Saturn in 1985 and appointed its first president, Joseph Sanchez, but he died three weeks later. A successor was then appointed. Although Saturn is a separate operating unit, it is accountable to GM. Because of record-level deficits and general corporate turbulence, the Saturn project has been reconceptualized to be a more modest endeavor. Although Saturn sales are strong, as this book goes to press, GM has been asking some hard questions of its affiliate.

The bidding war for the Saturn plant began the moment an announcement was made in January 1985 that the plant was going to be opened. One thousand sites from thirty-four states were in the running. GM announced that the plant would employ 6,000 workers, although this figure was revised to 3,000.

How, then, did Saturn make its selection? As reported to the advisory commission that wrote the report, GM gave this account. Selection activity began in December 1983, before the publicity began surrounding site selection. On January 8, 1985, GM announced that it was forming a new division called Saturn and that it was soliciting bids for a plant siting. Hundreds of bids, complete with incentives, immediately poured into the GM office.

A site selection task force was set up within GM. Chaired by the director of Argonaut Realty, it focused on many company functions, such as capital appropriations, personnel, marketing, industrial relations, and material management and purchasing.[22] A computerized model, developed and used to analyze cost data, took into account both initial and annually recurring costs over a long period of operation. Then the net current value and an average cost per unit were calculated. Different sets of assumptions obviously resulted in different cost projections.

To handle the volume of sites being considered, GM decided that each state needed its own screener to collect the proposals. A critical factor was that the plant had to be located where geographically related costs would be minimal. Some of the costs that were examined were construction, unemployment compensation, workers' compensation, health care benefits, electricity, natural gas, water, waste water treatment, inbound and outbound freight, local property taxes, state sales/use tax, state income tax, and franchise/inventory and other miscellaneous state taxes.[23]

An interview with a local chamber of commerce official from the Spring Hill site indicated that he thought Spring Hill was chosen for three reasons: in an effort to choose a nontraditional site, to ensure proximity to an interstate and a two-lane highway and access in less than one hour to an airport and a barge, and to take advantage of the quality of life, or livability, of Tennessee (Figure 2.1).[24]

The Spring Hill Package

The Spring Hill package was unusual because the production and maintenance jobs did not go to locals as was promised.[25]

Company investment	State investment	Number of employees	Investment per employee
$3.5–4.7 billion	$30 million (training) $50 million (roads) $80 million (total)	3,000	$26,666

Also, given the intensity of the bidding, not surprisingly, Tennessee Governor Lamar Alexander offered Saturn a substantial incentive package from public funds. The total investment from the company was $5 billion after an initial investment of $3.5 billion. The projected labor force at that time was projected to be 6,000, although it was scaled back later to 3,000.

There were many implications to the Spring Hill and other packages, the contours of which shaped the economic destiny of the communities. The Honda package was not as burdensome to the community since there were not many competitors and it was an inside deal. The Nissan package was the most successful because of the expert bargaining skill, astuteness, and sheer will of Mayor Sam Ridley in making the plant pay for itself. The Toyota package was very generous to the corporation and costly to the state. It would have been costly to the community had Mayor Tom Prather not had the patience and the bargaining skills to annex the plant to the town. Toyota gave up both its right to a hearing and its right to challenge the annexation. The implication of annexation was that the 1 percent profit tax and payroll tax that the county had in place

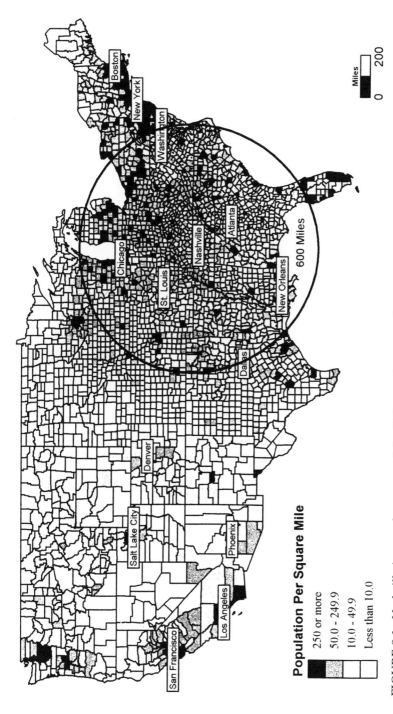

Population Per Square Mile

- 250 or more
- 50.0 – 249.9
- 10.0 – 49.9
- Less than 10.0

Miles

0   200

600 Miles

FIGURE 2.1. Nashville is near the center of the U.S. population; 50% of the U.S. population lives within 600 miles of Nashville. Population density of counties; 1980. (Urban Information Center, University of Missouri St. Louis; based on Bureau of Census data).

would be levied at 0.5 percent for the county and 0.5 percent for the city. A lasting legacy, however, is the rift between state and local officials caused by the bypass, which was promised but never built. The county officials in particular felt residual resentment toward the state. The Spring Hill package is the least favorable. After all, thirty-seven other states would have given up a lot for the plant. The chief and immediate benefit that a plant brings—jobs for locals—was missing in Spring Hill, a source of bitterness for the public and the elite.

Community Impact

To characterize the impact on Spring Hill, imagine the culture shock caused by an invasion of 3,000 "Yankee" strangers coupled with the population explosion on this essentially rural area.

Even though a community leader was adamant that the county "was doing all right before Saturn," he acknowledged that several suppliers had moved in as a result of the Saturn opening: Donnelly Corporation from Holland, Michigan, in a joint venture with Asihi, employing sixty, and Tentrec and Triangle Springs, producing windows and springs, respectively. Saturn's impact on the area was uneven. Columbia, Tennessee, is the county seat of Maury County and the nearest large town to the plant. As such, it was greatly affected. Many incoming employees chose to live in Columbia or on its outskirts rather than in Spring Hill.

The reaction of the locals to the large influx of persons who came to the area as a result of the plant is detailed in chapter 7 and is merely summarized here. Their reaction was truly ambivalent. Although the townspeople recognized that the town was more vital and bustling than it used to be, they also were aware that the jobs did not go to Tennesseans. They were heartened that businesses were popping up all over, but they did not like waiting in the long lines at the new stores.

Some of the effects on the Spring Hill area were typical of the effects that occur immediately after an announcement is made that a plant will be opening in what could be called time 2 of the stages of development, such as real estate speculation and increases in population. Later this chapter will address whether this time period and its characteristics are typical or not. Property adjacent to the plant rose sharply in value, and one restaurant reputedly changed hands six times, in each instance for a higher and more outrageous price. Even mediocre farmland changed hands rapidly, and its price skyrocketed.

Anticipating some of the potential problems, the community asked for several projections to be done detailing the effects of the plant on the community. The projections, which were paid for by Saturn as a result of the negotiations over the in-lieu-of tax payments, were detailed in a report by the Tennessee Advisory Commission on Intergovernmental Relations (TACIR) and were not very sanguine. There were three scenarios, which varied depending on the amount of in-migration the community experienced.[26] The multiplier and the net fiscal loss to the community were both estimated. The first scenario, based on 25 percent migration with a multiplier of 1.1, would result in a net fiscal loss of $1,356.5 (thousands) in 1985 dollars. The second, or most likely, scenario, that of 50 percent migration with a multiplier of 1.1, would result in a net fiscal loss of $2,290.9 (thousands) in 1985 dollars. The third, or high migration, scenario assumed 75 percent migration with a multiplier of 1.2, and yielded a net fiscal loss of $2,407.6 (thousands) in 1985 dollars.[27]

One immediate impact was that there was controversy over jobs. The locals felt they were promised jobs that were not delivered. The dramatic influx of job seekers prompted the Spring Hill government to buy them one-way tickets out of town if they were unsuccesssful in finding employment.

The view of the person on the street was harsher than that of the elite. With the exception of Spring Hill's mayor and one or two people in the chamber of commerce, the elite was enthusiastic. Members of this group generally thought the plant put the community on the map, and they anticipated many secondary and tertiary effects, if not many direct jobs. Although absolute increases were made in the budgets of the police and fire departments, no proportionate increases were made in the area of public administration. The fire department underwent notable changes, including the addition of staff and three new pumpers and a 14 percent increase in electrical inspections in Columbia. In addition, a new chief was brought in. The police department also got a new chief, an increase in staff, and significant increases in training and money for that training. There was also an increase in crime and an upgrade in 911 services.

New Politics

Unlike Smyrna, where politics has been significantly transformed, Spring Hill, which is still a very immature site, has not advanced beyond the early stages in its emergence of a new politics, and this process has been marked by controversy. George Jones, the mayor of Spring Hill, not only continued to attempt to annex the plant to his community but, as is typical when a site is in the early stages of the development cycle, he campaigned against the plant when he was up for reelection. The process whereby the good old boys in government are replaced by more professional, urbane, and pro–economic development leaders, which typically occurs at a mature site, has not happened in Spring Hill.

Changes in values and lifestyle have occurred in Spring Hill, however. The newcomers expect to be able to purchase liquor by the drink, to participate in certain city and town recreational programs, and to expose their children to a varied curriculum in the schools. There was an influx of Catholics and Republicans to Maury County. By contrast, Williamson, which had been solidly Republican, experienced an influx of Democrats. It is too early to say whether the newcomers' culture will be absorbed or will exist parallel to that of the locals, or ultimately whether the situation will explode into conflict. Just after the opening, housing and the problems of the permanent population dominate the elite's and the public's mind. This is the beginning of what was called earlier the "realizing the costs stage." At this stage, issues may be put on the agenda as the result of mobilization of criticism, which may lead to amicable changes in policy or to open conflict. This stage also includes an upsurge in tax and school bond issues. This stage of realizing the costs is followed by the "postproblem stage," in which the plant becomes an ordinary feature of the community's terrain. This set of stages of the development process will be applied to all sites and summarized in the next section.

RESULTS

Now that each site and the characteristics of each stage of economic development have been described, it is possible to address the empirical question of whether this process follows a universal or an idiosyncratic pattern. Based on the data from these four sites, there is strong evidence that each site undergoes similar stages of impact. This does not mean that all the sites have completed the entire process and are fully mature, that is, have progressed to time 8. As shown in the classification scheme in Figure 2.2, each site is at a different stage and is pro-

FIGURE 2.2. Stages of economic development process: time 1 through 8 in four sites.

Pre-Problem	Alarmed discovery & Euphoria		Realizing Costs			Post Problem		Downs (Top Row)
Time 1 Site Announcement	Time 2 Real Estate Speculation	Time 3 Population Increase	Time 4 Immediate Effects	Time 5 Medium Long-Term Effects	Time 6 Long-Term Effects	Time 7 City or Town Responses	Time 8 Plant Becomes Normal Feature to Town	Total Time to Complete Stages
A 1) 1985 Spring Hill*	---1985-89*---	O >1990*[2]					---> Not Complete	
A 2) 1980 Smyrna#[1]		O >1983#	>1984-1986#		>1986#	>1986#	>1986-1990#---> 6 Years	
A 3) 1985 Georgetown⊗		O >1988⊗[2]	>1985-1986⊗		>1986⊗	>1986-1990⊗[3]	---> Not Complete	
A 4) 1977 Marysville♦		O >1979♦	>1979-1986♦	>1987♦	>1987♦	>1990♦	---> Not Complete	

Legend
* Spring Hill
# Smyrna
⊗ Georgetown
♦ Marysville

A = Announcement
O = Opening

[1] Annexation was part of package in Smyrna (Time 1)
[2] Georgetown and Spring Hill are not yet at Time 8
[3] December 1986 - Negotiations began--annexation was 1987

gressing at a different rate. These results illustrate the advantage of using a comparative as opposed to a single case-study approach.

Classification of Sites by Stages of Development

It is now appropriate to develop the concept of stages of development and to examine the impacts associated with each period. Below is a detailed description of Downs's stages and time periods, which indicates the stages each site must pass through in the developmental process (see also Figure 2.2). Each site was classified using these criteria.

1. Preproblem and site announcement. This period is characterized by the two extremes—euphoria and doomsday predictions.
2. Recognition of problem and post–site announcement. This period has impacted real estate speculation, the influx of a temporary population of construction workers and consultants. Again, alternate euphoria and alarm.
3. Recognition of population increase. This is the stage in which the permanent population increase occurs.
4. Recognition of problem and immediate effects. The immediate effect is jobs. There are other immediate effects, not all of which are positive, such as traffic.
5. Realizing costs and medium long-term effects. At this point, certain costs such as upgrading of water and sewage systems and a concern over revenue (taxes). During this period there is also a transition in government to a new set of political leaders, a group of leaders who are more committed to economic development. In this stage what begins is the process of continuous negotiation between the community leaders and the company to cover some of the costs the community is trying to recover.
6. Realizing costs and long-term impact. The effects in this time period are the professionalization of public-sector jobs, the building of additional roads (not negotiated in the package), and recreational programs.
7. Realizing costs and town or city's response strategies. The town attempts to make its adjustment to the new situation—by annexing, by passing a payroll tax, by raising new revenue through other devices, or by coordinating with other governmental entities. The focus and locus of activity shift from the plant to the governmental units of the city and county.

8. Postproblem plant no longer an issue. Once a community has been through all stages, the plant is considered a normal feature of the terrain.

Translating the "preproblem and site announcement stage" into particular events in the community, we see that townspeople's responses take the form of one of two extremes: euphoria over the good or hysteria over the sins that will occur once the plant is opened. The boosters count on the opening of the plant to result in jobs and, like a magnet, in the creation of related industries and businesses in the community.

This euphoric reaction resembles what Baumgartner and Jones describe as a wave of positive mobilization, which results in a set of powerful policy and institutional changes, a sort of policy activism. As Baumgartner and Jones point out, the mobilization of enthusiasm and the mobilization of criticism usher in different policy implications or different results, and the latter does not necessarily yield policy activism.[28] The subissues during this stage of development and the beginning of the next are whether to annex the plant to the city and how to deal with the transient population, construction, and the sudden rise in property values and business and residential turnover. Attention may also be focused on how best to spend the increased revenue being collected in sales taxes as the transients spend money. These effects hit a peak after the announcement that the plant will open. When the plant opens the important issues become sewage, water, and pollution.

Just after the opening, housing and the problems of the permanent population dominate the elite's and the public's mind. This is the beginning of the "realizing the costs stage." At this stage, issues may be put on the agenda as the result of a mobilization of criticism, which may lead to amicable changes in policy or to conflict.[29] This stage also includes an upsurge in tax and school bond issues. Finally, in the "postproblem stage," the plant becomes an ordinary feature of the community's terrain.

One major change in all of the towns studied is that planning has taken on increasing importance. This is in part because the early stages of development are ipso facto destabilizing because of the sudden rise in real estate prices and the influx of itinerant job seekers. Also, controversy inevitably arises around issues of planning and zoning decisions. Even a community like Spring Hill suddenly needed planners. Furthermore, each planning and zoning decision becomes a lightning rod, an occasion to revisit the decision to site the plant in their town.

In addition to economic changes, political changes take place over the stages of development. A new set of leaders takes over who are more committed to economic development. A new political agenda emerges. What the agenda items are and whether or not they are universal across sites is the subject of chapter 3.

The differences between the old and the new leaders at a site are pronounced. The former have a limited vision for the community, value the community primarily as it was, want to recruit industry from the outside only if it "does not rock the boat," and do not want to change the political leadership currently in power, the wage structure, or the way of doing business.

By time period 5, a process of continuous negotiation between community leaders and the company is in full swing (Figure 2.2); this includes annexation and other efforts. Time period 6 involves long-term impacts, including costs and such issues as the need for increased professionalization of the public sector, which strictly speaking is not a cost. (Professionalization may lead to new expenditures, however, thereby representing a cost; it is also a real benefit to the community.) Other long-term needs of the community that have been put off usually surface in this period, such as a highway or bypass the community needs that it did not negotiate in the beginning. The need for recreational programs may also become important.

Time period 7 is the final phase in which town or city leaders can realize the costs involved in having the plant in their community. During this period, the leadership may make an aggressive bid for annexation. Other revenue-garnering devices also increase in importance, such as bonds and taxes. All of these developments are addressed more thoroughly in chapter 8.

Spring Hill

Spring Hill provides the best example of the first stage of development. One usual short-term benefit of the plant siting is that there is a sudden increase in jobs. Since virtually all the blue-collar workers were imported from laid-off UAW members largely from Michigan and Ohio, the Spring Hill site is not benefiting in this classic way in terms of jobs; thus, adjusting to the new incoming population may be more of a rub. Nor has Spring Hill yet experienced the longer-term costs. As of 1990, Spring Hill appeared to be in time period 3, the stage characterized by a temporary population explosion. Since the plant opened later in 1990 than when the data were gathered, Spring Hill was only in the postannouncement and barely in the postopening stages when the data were collected. Time period 3 is only the third of eight time stages that constitute full maturity. Thus, Spring Hill is our least mature site.

Georgetown

Georgetown is classified as in time period 7, the period in which the city or town must deal with the costs associated with the new plant. The Prather regime sings the praises of Toyota, classifying most of the impact as positive. Further, the new guard leadership in the form of Mayor Tom Prather, began trying to get the land where Toyota is located annexed to the town in 1986 and was successful in 1987. The process of transformation to new-guard leaders is not complete, however, nor is the change to a new political culture. Thus, the site cannot be classified as completely mature.

Nowhere is this message clearer than in the public opinion of the masses. Of the four sites, Georgetown had the highest percentage of people, 39 percent, who said that the package the state and town offered Toyota was unjustified or only partially justified. The validity of the classification of Georgetown as not completely mature was confirmed during the last election, when the progressive Mayor Prather was replaced by a traditional representative of the old guard.

Marysville

Marysville was also classified as in time period 7 because economic development was not yet a well-established value. Another hallmark of a mature site is that the elite is generally uniformly enthusiastic about economic development.

Chronologically, Marysville is the oldest site of the four. Plans to open the plant were announced in 1977, thirteen years before the measurement date. Nonetheless, it is classified not as mature but as in time period 7, the phase in which the city or town responds to the plant through such means as renewed efforts to annex the site to the community. In the case of Marysville, the town's main goals are to annex the plant after annexing some land between the plant and the town, to distribute debt load in a manageable way, and to institute an impact fee. Thus, data about Marysville suggest that there appears to be no relationship between chronological time and a site's stage of development. Further, progression through the stages of development does not appear to occur at a steady rate. Although it is the oldest site chronologically, neither the political leadership nor the political culture of Marysville has been completely transformed and thus it is classified in time period 7, just short of complete maturity.

Smyrna

The hallmark of a mature site is that the plant has become such a normal feature of the terrain that no one can remember when it was not there. Of the four sites we studied, Smyrna was classified as the most mature, not because it was the oldest chronologically but because it had progressed through all stages to time period 8 of the cycle of development.

SUMMARY

That a universal process of development can be identified is noteworthy and enables us to develop a knowledge base from which to make generalizations that are not possible with case studies. What we now know is that as long as a community is rural or exurban and has a limited infrastructure and very few signs of progressive urbanization such as professionalization of its police and fire departments, the site should follow a predictable progression of stages.

These findings support the notion that, at least theoretically, growth is generic. On a practical level, these findings provide a primer for public administrators in other communities facing a plant siting. The problems that public administrators will face in rural areas such as Wentzville, Missouri, where there is a GM plant, in South Carolina, where there is a new BMW plant, in Alabama, where there is a Mercedes Benz plant, in upstate rural New York, or in tiny farming communities in California will be similar to those faced in the four communities examined here. The solutions to these problems will vary, however, depending on each community's leadership as it engages in the process of continuous renegotiation that is called the "new politics."

To guide the reader through the rest of the book, I shall briefly characterize each site. Smyrna is the success story and the most mature site.

Georgetown was the site that jolted from agrarian sleepiness and a languishing economy into the future virtually overnight in a swirl of controversy over the incentive package. Marysville was the quiet site with impressive employment gains. Finally, Spring Hill did not get the front-end jobs it expected, but it did transform itself, both economically and culturally. It experienced controversy because outsiders "invaded" from the north.

3 | The View from the Top: The Plant as Agenda Setter

THIS CHAPTER begins to address the important question of how the members of the elite in each of the four towns under study assess the impact of the plant on their community and explores in depth their assessment of the economic impact. In this book I treat economic development as a process, not an outcome; rather than a single, simple event, development entails several transforming stages. Each community exhibits similarly sequenced stages in this process, up to the most mature stage (time period 8), when the plant is a normal feature of the terrain. As illustrated in Figure 1.1, Figure 2.2, and Table 3.1, the impact of a plant on a community is more pronounced in some time periods than in others.

Further, the impact of a plant is felt in several distinct areas of the community: the economic life, the governmental or political arena, the quality of life, and the culture. As a result of the changes in these areas, there often emerges what is called the new politics.

Based on these notions, the hypothesis is that the opening of a plant establishes an agenda for the community for years, even decades, to come. Why is this so? Because the plant sets in motion a series of problems the community either would never have had to tackle or would not have had to confront as quickly. These problems are identified as issues on the community's agenda if the public identifies them as issues that need to be addressed by the leaders of government. This idea that the plant sets in motion the items on the community's agenda is tested empirically later in the chapter. A related question is whether these issues that become so important are unique or are common to each site. The data for this chapter come primarily from sixty-seven interviews conducted with members of the elites in the four communities in which the plants were located. The budgetary data and other objective data are from the eleven jurisdictions, city or county, that form the impact areas of the four sites.

* * *

TABLE 3.1. Categories of Impacts and Time Range
of Influence on the Community

Impact	Time period
Economic	
Jobs	2
Commercial activity	3–8
Industry	3–8
Capital	3–8
Higher wages	3–8
Cost of real estate	1
Cost of taxes	6–8
Government	
Infrastructure	1–8
Government	4–8
Government programs	4–8
Decision making	7–8
Professionalization	7–8
Quality of life	
Population	1–3
Charity	5–8
Traffic	1–8
Pollution	1, 8
Knowledge	6–8

LEADERS' PERCEPTIONS OF PLANT'S IMPACT

As can be seen in Table 3.2, in general, the members of the elite of these
communities have a very positive view of the impact of the plant: depending on the impact, 78 to 85 percent of the leaders in the total sample
have such a view. Further, 80 to 83 percent of the leaders cited the classic economic benefits of plants, namely, that jobs, commercial activity,
and industry were positively affected.

Concerning the costs of the plant, 52 percent of the leaders mentioned that wages increased. Only a minority cited the increased cost
for social services, the higher taxes, and the increase in pollution. Nearly
all the leaders acknowledged the impact of the plant on human services,
such as education and fire and police protection, but not on health care.
Finally, the elite was less likely to observe changes in the government,
such as professionalization, the way decisions are made, and the introduction of new programs, than to observe economic changes. Probably
bureaucrats would be more likely than elected politicians to notice governmental changes.[1]

TABLE 3.2. Survey of Community Leaders'
Perceptions of Plant's Impact on the Community

Impact (N = 67)	Percentage
Economic and governmental	
Jobs	83%
Commercial activity	84
Industry	80
Professionalization of public-sector jobs	52
Decision making	52
Creation of new programs	52
Human services	
Human services	94
Education	88
Social services	93
Fire	75
Police	82
Health	40
Benefits	
New capital	85
Commerce	84
Industry	80
New knowledge	78
Costs	
Wages	52
Social services	46
Taxes	38
Pollution	23

ECONOMIC IMPACT

Community leaders were very enthusiastic about the stimulation the plant provided for their local economies; therefore, as Table 3.2 demonstrates, a high proportion of the leaders reported that their community displayed classic economic benefits.

Jobs

The primary and most immediate effect the leaders and the public alike anticipated was that the plant would provide jobs for local residents, the quid pro quo for the tax abatement. These included jobs at the plant as well as those generated through a multiplier effect in satellite industries, in other large industries, or in the retail or commercial sector.

The job picture varied across the sites. The leaders of Marysville and Smyrna were satisfied with the new jobs created. In Georgetown, the reaction was more mixed. In both cases, however, the larger the unit of analysis the leaders used, such as the state or the region, the more satisfied they were with the job situation.[2] Only at Spring Hill were the leaders disappointed with the job situation. Here the leaders had been promised that the first 6,000 jobs at the plant would go to locals; then, in 1986, they were told that the first 3,000 production jobs would go to laid-off union workers largely from Michigan and Ohio. The clerical jobs went to locals but were subcontracted through a temporary firm, so the employees did not earn the good wages and benefits or have the job security characteristic of other workers in the auto industry.

Despite the leaders' disappointment, the employment figures for Spring Hill were positive. Unemployment in Maury County, which had been 8.4 percent in 1985, was only 4.7 percent in 1989 and 5.1 percent for the first months of 1990. For Williamson County, the unemployment rate was constant at about 2.5 percent—practically full employment.[3] This is notable since itinerants usually converge on a town in the early days after an announcement that a plant is opening. This site is still in the early stage of development.

The value of the new jobs generated after the opening of the plant varied in each community since each started from a different economic baseline. Marysville, with unemployment in the 18 percent range, according to the leaders, was very depressed, so the plant represented a miraculous recovery to the national average. At the Smyrna site, the plant meant more jobs, revenue, and national publicity for this community, as opposed to Murfreesboro, which historically had had the advantage because of its status as the county seat and home to a university. For Georgetown, the plant meant the town could reverse the bad fortunes that had resulted from a burley tobacco crop, an outflow of small manufacturing jobs, and the exit of the young generation of county residents.

Industry

Besides jobs, one argument for recruiting a large plant is that it attracts other large industries. Not only did satellite suppliers, such as glass window plants, parts plants, trim plants, and seat belt plants, move into all four communities, but, more subtly, supplier plants were saved from closing. For example, a network of suppliers across three states in the Golden Triangle region around Georgetown had begun closing in response to Big Three automobile plant closings but were able to stay open after Toyota announced it was opening a plant in the area.

Commissioned University of Kentucky researchers estimated that the additional employment from satellites in the Georgetown area would be 1,500 with an investment of $250 million in the Toyota plant and $450 million in machinery.[4] The studies projected that 3,000 workers would be employed directly and immediately and 200,000 cars produced annually. H. Brinton Milward projected that a total of 35,520 jobs could be created in secondary or satellite industries by the time the plant began operation. He estimated that these workers would generate an additional $3,792 million in output and $768 million in earnings annually in direct and indirect effects. According to Milward, 63 percent of the total economic effect would occur in the automotive sector and 37 percent would be dispersed among the other sectors of the economy. Jobs would be distributed unevenly across several sectors. Interestingly, only 26 percent of all the jobs generated would be in the auto industry.[5]

One study calculated the internal rate of return to be 25 percent.[6] The study concluded that Toyota was a sound financial investment for the state of Kentucky. The net effect at peak production was calculated to be $3,792 million in additional economic output, $768 million in additional wages, and 35,000 additional jobs. The economic effect of start-up alone, meaning construction and initial operation, was estimated to be $1,908.7 million in output, $551.61 million in earnings, and 33,315 jobs. This projection was based on what the study called the "conservative assumption" that 60 percent of the machinery would be purchased in Kentucky.[7] These estimates, however, could be described as too optimistic, according to some experts.

In Smyrna and Marysville, there was no groundswell of controversy to warrant the commissioning of such reports. The towns were satisfied with the direct jobs created and with the incentive package and siting. According to estimates, as of 1987, $936 million of activity was generated among 515 suppliers, $540 million of which was within Ohio. Ten million dollars was generated for Union County, and $64.4 million was generated in Logan County.[8] Satellite industries prospered at all four sites.

Build It and They Will Come

One assumption behind recruiting a plant is the idea of "build it and they will come," to quote a line from the movie *Field of Dreams*. The communities built the plant, but "they" (retailers and small commercial businesses) did not come. When leaders were asked in the closed-ended portion of the interviews whether commercial activity increased, 84 percent answered "yes"; during the open-ended portion of their remarks, however, a fair number expressed disappointment over the sluggishness of the retail sector. It grew, but not by as much as expected.

Several reasons may account for this. First, workers reside not in a tight group but across many counties. Second, the interstate highway system makes it easy to travel great distances to purchase large consumer items. Third, the proximity to larger cities, Nashville in two cases and Lexington and Columbus in the other two, stymied commercial growth. Two laments from community leaders illustrate this point: "People still drive to Columbus for their big-ticket purchases," and "We have to get the people off the interstate." Marysville aspires to be the site of a Wal-Mart, but so far it has landed only a few shopping strips that have mostly fast-food establishments. Given that small, longtime downtown merchants are often threatened by Wal-Mart, the community may experience ambivalence toward this goal.

Capital

The promise of capital was fulfilled. All four sites had large payrolls and attracted a new bank after the plant opened. For example, Honda's weekly payroll in 1990 was $5.38 million. One leader commented that notwithstanding the sudden soaring of wealth of the townspeople, there was a potential for anomie. He noted that twenty-year-old farm boys who suddenly make $15 an hour may have "more money than they know what to do with" and may "turn to drugs." In general, however, the leaders thought the influx of capital was a definite benefit.

Higher Wages as a Cost

Higher wages can be a cost or a benefit, depending on one's perspective; 52 percent of the leaders said it was a cost. Obviously, higher wages would be a cost to the employer and a benefit to the employee. But consider the surprising perspective of a maintenance worker in the city public works department (who was mistakenly included in the sample with the elite). He had less than a high school education and worked as a mechanic on city vehicles. He loathed the very idea of the plant. He had to battle more traffic each day and pay about 30 percent more in rent, and he still worked for the city at the minimum wage, not for Toyota. Thus, he experienced higher wages as a cost, not a benefit. This example supports two notions: economic development is uneven in its impacts, and one person's benefit may be someone else's cost.

Real Estate

The higher cost of real estate is commonly perceived to be an impact of the plant. Recall that, in terms of the stages of economic development, real estate prices rise dramatically immediately following the announcement that the plant will be opening (Figure 1.1). Locals try to sell previously undesirable farmland at ten times its former value. Outside speculators and developers buy the land at a frenzied pace, apply for development permits, then drop the idea and sell again.

Real estate frenzy occurred at the restaurant in Spring Hill adjacent to the plant's property (mentioned in chapter 2), and in Georgetown, where the state's commitment to buy the land where the plant was sited combined with rampant real estate speculation to raise the cost of the package from $125 million to $250 million. Prices drop by the time of the permanent population influx; however, they never go back to normal. In the last stages of development, a permanent increase of 30 percent in the price of real estate often occurs as a result of the plant's presence.

In addition to the boom, Georgetown's housing supply and demand were substantially mismatched. Developers overbuilt in the $80,000 to $200,000 range and ignored moderate-income housing. Developers were too eager to move in and were working from the wrong set of assumptions. This did not occur in Marysville, Spring Hill, or Smyrna.

An important benefit of the plant is that there is an influx of executives into the surrounding community. They are savvy citizens and a particularly valuable resource to local nonprofit organizations. At Georgetown, the executives largely settled in Lexington because of its big-city amenities; the exception was Toyota's chief executive officer. At Marysville, the executives lived in a few suburbs of Columbus with superior schools. At the Spring Hill site, they lived in Columbia, the county seat, in one of the well-to-do suburbs in neighboring Williamson County, or in the other suburbs of Nashville. At Smyrna, they tended to live in Murfreesboro or in the suburbs of Nashville. In these communities, the goal of attracting executives to live near the plant was an unfulfilled dream.

In Marysville, the "real estate strategy" included attracting more people to live in Marysville proper. In a moment of frustration, the economic development officer told some of the local elite that the town was not attractive because it did not have a first-class restaurant. One of the leaders said enthusiastically: "Good news! A Bob Evans restaurant has decided to open here!"[9] Furthermore, despite its articulated real estate strategy, Marysville has no moderately priced new housing.

Cost of Taxes

Typically, taxes go up after a plant opens; however, only 38 percent of the leaders thought that higher taxes were a cost of the plant. The feeling among the public is much stronger that higher taxes are a cost.[10]

The leaders interviewed described the process whereby taxes are raised by floating bonds for large capital improvements, such as school buildings. This would occur late in the cycle of development, in the period called "realizing the costs." Jobs, sales taxes, and other front-loading benefits provided some relief in the earlier stages. But later, overflowing schools and crowded roads give way to the need for new school buildings, public works, and other large capital-investment projects. Although the state is usually responsible for roads, it often makes vague promises or abandons them, as in Georgetown. The city of Georgetown had to bear the entire cost of a bypass. This burden is uneven across political jurisdictions, as discussed in chapter 4.

POLITICAL AND GOVERNMENTAL IMPACT

Questions concerning the impact of the plant on the local government were stated broadly. For example, respondents were asked: "Was there an impact on government?" The answers covered a myriad of changes. The respondents in Marysville, Smyrna, and Georgetown all said that their towns underwent structural changes in the system of government. In Georgetown, there was a radical proposal on the ballot to consolidate the city and county government. Another impact is that the cast of characters in political leadership positions often changes. In other cases, new government programs may be introduced. For instance, an International Friendship Center was created in Marysville, an enhanced 911 system was created where a basic one had existed in Georgetown, and volleyball and soccer programs were created through the recreation department in Georgetown.

Other governmental impacts are budget and debt increases, and budget and substantive changes in such areas of public administration as fire, police, sewage, water, planning, public works, recreation, welfare, and criminal justice. Changes in sewage and water service, called the "two guns" of economic development by one leader, are usually potent enough to give the community substantial leverage with the corporation. There were significant water supply challenges in all four of the communities. Georgetown had to close its historic water supply, the spring that flows through the center of town, because of benzene tainting.

Increases in the number of substations, personnel, and equipment were among the plants' impacts in the area of police and fire service. A more important and permanent change was that public-sector jobs were professionalized, meaning that public servants were selected based on merit after a national search. Two other dramatic changes occurred: one in the area of town planning, which went from being marginal before the plant to being centralized, and one in the area of education.

QUALITY-OF-LIFE AND SOCIOCULTURAL CHANGES

The quality-of-life and sociocultural changes that occur in a community after a new plant starts operating are profound and varied. Sometimes they are palpable and visible; other times they are nearly invisible. These include physical changes, changes in traffic patterns, cultural changes, increases in pollution, changes in charitable giving, and a variety of changes in the popular culture.

Physical Changes

Before visiting the sites, physical changes were visualized as taking the form of the sprawl Joe Feagin described in Houston.[11] I also thought the patterns of growth might have resembled a bull's-eye, surrounded by concentric circles in which degrees of growth have occurred. In fact, the plant sites are so removed from the hustle and bustle that the landscape around them appears deserted, almost lunar. The surrounding lands are almost untouched, and the plants rise surrealistically from them, looking like extraterrestrial crafts. The best examples of this are the Spring Hill and Georgetown sites.

The physical landscape around the Saturn plant in Spring Hill, Tennessee, looks untouched. Spring Hill, located about an hour's drive south of Nashville, was virtually unheard of before Saturn began its great bidding war in early 1985. Spring Hill is the site of an old mansion, called Haynes Haven, which is still preserved and is part of the Saturn site. There is also a working farm adjacent to the plant on the plant property, a fact in which the Saturn Corporation takes pride. Maury County, where the plant is located, is a county rich in churches and Civil War memorabilia.

The Saturn plant is so unobtrusive, it can barely be seen. It is a long, flat building peeking over the top of the lowest hills. At dawn and dusk the building seems to evaporate into the shadows as its blue color blends with the surrounding hills. Indeed, only when the plant spews exhaust from its stack or when the parking lot bustles with traffic is one convinced that there is an automobile plant in the area.

The parkway that leads off the interstate is called Saturn Highway, and the other driveway leading off it is named after Don Ephelin.[12] Saturn's theme is down-home country, bucolic, back-to-the-farm values. Standing in the plant, one can look out the windows and see a working farm and a field of cows. The picture is of a caring company, and virtually every advertisement has a farm with a cow ruminating nearby or a concerned worker who has just traveled to the farthest corner of the country to help a Saturn customer.

Spring Hill itself has no center and is almost invisible. Although this description is hackneyed, Spring Hill is the kind of place one can miss completely by blinking while driving through town. A road sign shows the population, but there is little other evidence of a town. A cluster of mailboxes stands by the side of the road, but the houses are set far back and there are large spaces between them in a typically rural pattern. Scattered across the landscape are a few decrepit structures among the billboards, a couple of abandoned gas stations, a feed store, and a fire station. (Since the opening of the plant, there is a new fire station.)

The Toyota plant in Georgetown is located on a spanking-new dual parkway lined with trees and a median called Cherryblossom Way. The local schoolchildren had a contest to choose the name. The plant itself, located in a beautifully landscaped industrial park, is such a flat, low island and so surrounded by grass that one could almost miss seeing it.

What is absent at both these sites is the telltale, endless strip mall, hallmark of plants in suburban and urban locations. All four communities studied did have large population increases after the plants were opened, but these increases were over a more diffuse area than expected.

Traffic

At the time of the site visits, traffic had increased in all four towns since the plants opened, and in Georgetown and Marysville traffic was considered a problem. One Georgetown leader complained of "megatraffic"; at one of the town's two stoplights, he had to wait through two complete cycles before making a left turn. The traffic problem will be alleviated by the bypass, which the city had to pay for on its own. Recall that the governor had promised, "We won't forget you," but the next gubernatorial administration forgot the commitment. After the county commission balked at the prospect of splitting the cost of the bypass with the city, the city of Georgetown paid for it in full.

Another town where the traffic became horrific, with very real costs, was Marysville. The chief of police has a chart on which areas with high numbers of accidents are marked with red dots. The entrance to the Honda plant was marked with hundreds of them. One respondent attributed this explosion in accidents to Honda's strict policy regarding tardiness, which sends employees speeding into the entrance at starting time. Many more accidents occur as people hurry to get home. In Allen Township, the closest township to the plant, the number of traffic accidents has risen fourfold, from 36 in 1982 to 129 in 1989. This has led to an increase in the number of new police officers and to a huge increase in the town budget.

An increase in the amount of traffic should be anticipated; therefore, as a planning exercise, a community should predict where the increase will occur. In Georgetown, the leaders and public knew that motorists coming from one direction would have to cross town, causing a jam unless a bypass was built. Similarly, the community leaders in Marysville knew that the two state roads leading to the plant needed to be widened. Since traffic problems can be predicted, can they be avoided? Yes and no. Although a community can predict what it needs, it often cannot get the state to allocate resources. Essentially, the police function is local. The company does not usually want to fund roads and bypasses that are for the convenience of the community, not the business. In fact, the company is reluctant to fund even the highway projects it needs to get its product to the interstate.

Culture

With the advent of the plant, the culture of the small town, where everyone knows each other and where merchants let customers "run tabs," gives way to more sophistication and more economic optimism but also to an influx of more "strangers," an increase in crime, and other urban ills. The locals regard many of these changes as positive, many as negative, and many as mixed. Public opinion surrounding these changes is discussed in chapter 7.

Pollution

Pollution is clearly a problem after a plant opens, and it is almost never an invisible one. The leaders of the four communities studied, however, appeared to be in a state of denial; only 23 percent said that pollution was a cost of having an auto plant in their town. Pollution is one issue, however, around which evidence can be adduced to see if the leaders' thinking is accurate. The objective fact is that the rural counties surrounding Nashville and two of these plants, the Nissan and the Saturn plant, have levels of air pollution that are among the highest in the country for rural counties.

In Maury County, for example, the Industrial Development Board announced pollution control revenue refunding bonds in the amount of $65 million in October 1986. This is reminiscent of Matthew Crenson's analysis in which he argues that pollution is viewed as a nonissue by elite structures where one industry dominates the town and is the source of pollution.[13] There was even a move by federal and state Environmental Protection Agency officials to include the rural counties outside Nashville in Nashville's nonattainment zone during the time when the study was conducted.

During one site visit, I observed the political leaders testifying on televised hearings against including the counties surrounding Nashville in the nonattainment zone, and yet they responded on the questionnaire that pollution "has not been a cost" of having the plant in their town. The leaders testified that to include Maury and Williamson Counties in the nonattainment zone would have made them "no-growth" areas; thus, the leaders were saying that pollution was not a cost because they felt business interests would be compromised if businesses needed to meet environmental standards, not because they thought there were no effects from the pollution.

Charity and Knowledge

The role of the new auto executives in increasing both the knowledge base and the financial resources of the charitable and nonprofit sector was viewed as important by the leaders of the four communities. The auto companies made substantial contributions to the United Way and to local universities. Toyota contributed to the robotics institute at the University of Kentucky, and Saturn donated the land for a new high school in the Spring Hill area. Toyota also donated twelve Camrys to the city of Georgetown and $1 million to convert the Cardome Center into a conference center and city office building. Nissan was active in mentoring programs involving local high schools and in advancing technology. It also made a large commitment to business-educational partnerships in the community. The Honda foundation has invested huge sums in the engineering school at the Ohio State University. The activities that all four corporations sponsor are uncontroversial and largely educational, or, as one mayor described them, "warm and fuzzy."

Cost of Social Services

It was predicted that during the early stages of development, many transients would be attracted to the areas where the plants were being built and then would linger, remain jobless, and strain social service resources. In fact, as can be seen in Table 3.2, only 46 percent of the leaders thought the plant put a strain on social services. Because this issue did not become a concern, state and county unemployment office experts were not interviewed. One of the reasons social services did not register as a cost, however, is that providing unemployment and welfare-related services is a federal and state, not a local, function, although the services are administered through counties.

AGENDA SETTING

The plant was a seemingly simple and single "solution," floating in a stream of solutions, to use John Kingdon's parlance,[14] adjacent to a stream of rural problems—economic distress, the failure of the agrarian economy, the loss of population to large cities, and threats to a traditional lifestyle.[15] In actuality, rural problems may look like urban problems. In Jones and Bachelor's terms, the plant fits the "solution set" of the community leaders nicely;[16] however, as Baumgartner and Jones point out, "Issue definition, then, is the driving force in both stability and instability."[17] Thus, issue definition propels the agenda-setting process forward.

Since "the plant" is not a single issue, it disaggregates into multiple issues, and these issues ebb and flow throughout the development cycle, as described earlier. The changes that occur after the plant opens are not incremental or small; rather, there may be a massive number of institutional changes, what Baumgartner and Jones call "punctuated equilibrium."[18]

An "issue" or "problem" in agenda-setting theory is an item everyone acknowledges is a problem that needs to be addressed. It is on the systemic agenda. Once an issue is on the formal agenda, as opposed to the systemic agenda, it is under consideration for action by the government. Most issues must get on the systemic agenda before being placed on the formal one; however, that is not always the case, especially when insiders catapult items onto the formal agenda without public recognition of the issue via the systemic agenda.[19]

Agenda-setting theory applied to economic development would hypothesize that a common set of problems or issues exists across each site. Thus, if an issue is named as important by the elite at one site and then is named as important by the leaders at another site, this would support the notion of a common agenda. Chapter 7 contains a fuller comparison of how the public versus the elite views the issues. Table 3.3 lists the sites and the problems in rank order.

Looking at Table 3.3, we see that three issues—real estate, traffic, and housing—were common across all four sites.[20] Further, they were given approximately the same ranking relative to other issues at the sites.[21] Thus, they can be viewed as universal issues. Looking at the character of these issues, we see that they have to do with creature comforts and are very tangible problems. Insofar as problems related to growth in rural areas look like problems related to growth in urban, exurban, and suburban areas, this might suggest that growth is a generic process.

What about the issues that were nearly universally viewed as issues? The leaders at three sites, everywhere but Georgetown, mentioned that school bonds were a problem.[22] Some issues, including wages, water, sewage, and taxes, were perceived as problems at two sites. The increase in overall wages was considered a problem only at Smyrna, where it

TABLE 3.3. Most Important Problems, by Site

Problems for each site by rank

Spring Hill			Smyrna	
Real estate	1		Traffic	1
Traffic	2.5		Wages	2
Taxes	2.5		Real estate	3
Housing	4.5		School bond	4
School bond	4.5		Bonds	5
Water	6		Housing	6

Georgetown			Marysville	
Traffic	1		Real estate	1.2
Housing	2		Traffic	1.2
Real estate	3		Roads	1.2
Water	4		School bond	1.2
Annexation	6		Housing	5
Sewage	7		Wages	6
			Sewage	7.25
			Bonds	7.25
			Taxes	7.25
			Pollution	7.25

Problems common to all sites. The criterion for inclusion was if 50 percent or more of the elite named it as a problem.

All sites	Real estate, traffic, and housing
Three sites	School bond
Two sites	Wages, water, sewage, and taxes
One site	Roads, pollution, and annexation

Number of problems across sites (maximum score = 12). The number of problems each leader named was averaged within a site.

	Raw mean	S.E. of mean
Spring Hill	8.5	2.5
Marysville	9.0	.89
Georgetown	9.6	.66
Smyrna	9.2	.89

ranked second, and at Marysville, where it ranked sixth. This is interesting since Smyrna is the most mature site and Marysville is fairly mature. Thus, community leaders might not notice the plant's effect on the community's overall wage structure until the plant has been operating for a while. In the case of Spring Hill, the plant was reasonably new when the interviews were conducted and all the workers had been imported; therefore, no hometown employers had lost employees to the higher-paying auto plant. In Georgetown, the increase in wages has not been an issue, probably because only a small number of employees from Georgetown proper and Scott County proper work at the plant.

The quality of the water supply was not viewed as a problem in Smyrna or Marysville. By contrast, Georgetown had tainted water and Spring Hill had to float a bond for water pollution cleanup. The two towns whose leaders mentioned that sewage was a problem were Georgetown and Marysville. What made sewage a problem in the latter community was that the rates had to be raised to meet the community's portion of the funding to receive matching federal funds. Surprisingly, only 50 percent or more of the elite at two sites—Marysville and Spring Hill—listed taxes as a problem. Recall that at Spring Hill a controversy swirled around the issue of the amount of revenue that should go to the town as opposed to the county. Similarly, the leaders in Smyrna did not list taxes as a problem since the town had a very favorable revenue profile.

What issues had little universality and were named at only one site? Roads were named only at Marysville (where it was ranked first, tied with traffic, school bonds, and real estate); pollution was mentioned only at Marysville; and annexation was mentioned only at Georgetown in spite of the fact that the plant had already been annexed to the town.[23]

Number of Issues

What about the number of issues that were viewed as problems? Table 3.3 lists the twelve issues that were mentioned across the sites.[24] The leaders at Spring Hill named seven, and the leaders at the other sites listed ten. Probably the reason Spring Hill listed fewer problems was that it was the least mature. Of the twelve issues named at the other sites, nine were named at all three. Further, three issues were identified universally across the sites as of the most concern to the community. These were creature comforts: traffic, real estate, and housing. Thus, economic development imposes a common agenda of problems on a community.

Front-End Benefits and Back-End Costs

One would expect that increases in the number of jobs and other benefits would occur early in the economic development cycle and that costs would be recognized later on. A crude but straightforward way to test this is by comparing the average number of benefits cited per leader at the least mature site, Spring Hill, to the most mature site, Smyrna. The benefits should be greatest in Spring Hill. In fact, it is just the opposite.

Spring Hill should have experienced an increase in jobs, but there was no such increase. One would expect the most mature site to have the highest average number of costs. Smyrna did have the highest number, which is consistent with the idea that costs are recognized later in the economic development process; however, Georgetown and Marysville, which should have had the next highest number, actually had the lowest number.

There were not many leaders per site, so these averages must be interpreted gingerly; however, as shown in Table 3.4 and in Figure 3.1, there appears to be a curvilinear relationship between the number of impacts mentioned and the age of the plant. If we arrange the sites by stage of development ranging from youngest to most mature, we see that the increase in the number of impacts over time is neither linear nor monotonic. Costs do load later to the extent that the Smyrna site has the highest number. Benefits should front-load, so Smyrna should have the lowest average number of benefits. Spring Hill should have the highest average number of benefits; however, it did not have jobs, the most important single benefit that should load near the front of the process of development. Thus, Spring Hill is not typical of an immature site.

If economic development is an agenda setter, the plant should have much more than just economic effects. It is appropriate, therefore, to test whether the elite thinks the plant's impact is one-dimensional or multidimensional. This can be done by performing a factor analysis in which the empirical question we are addressing is, Do the leaders conceive of economic development as a multidimensional concept and the plant as having political and cultural as well as economic impacts?

The factor analysis is reported in Table 3.5.[25] Notwithstanding the limitations of factor analysis, the results suggest that the leaders conceive of economic development as three-dimensional. The promax version of the factor analysis program was used. This means that there was no assumption that the factors were uncorrelated or independent. The

TABLE 3.4. Variation Across Sites of Average Number of Impacts, Costs, and Benefits

	Spring Hill	Marysville	Georgetown	Smyrna
Broad impacts (maximum score = 7)	2.8	3.8	5.6[a]	4.5
	(.34)	(.39)	(.37)	(.27)
Brimjobs Jobs				
Brimbus New businesses				
Brimtrff Increased traffic				
Brimgovt Government				
Brimprof Professionalization of public-sector jobs				
Brimdecn The way decisions in government are made				
Brimprog New government programs				
Benefits (maximum score = 5)	2.5	3.9	4.7	4.7
	(.36)	(.12)	(.15)	(.12)
Benjobs Jobs				
Benindus Industry				
Bencomm Commerce				
Benknow Knowledge				
Bencap Capital				
Costs (maximum score = 5)	2.3	2.0	1.5	3.1
	(.35)	(.42)	(.50)	(.37)
Costtax Higher taxes				
Costpoll More pollution				
Costsserv Higher demand for social services				
Costwages Higher wages				
Costrst Higher real estate prices				

Note: Sites are in progressive order from left to right, least to most developed in stages completed. Numbers in parentheses indicate standard error of mean.

a. Statistically significant.

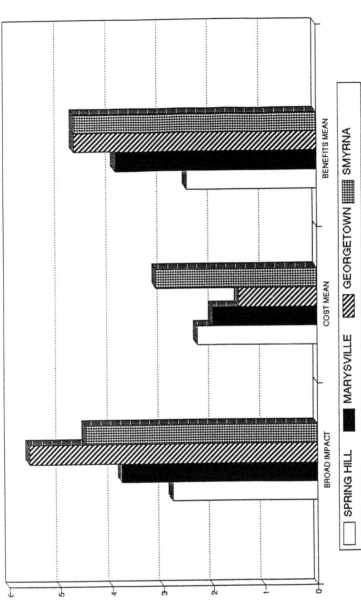

FIGURE 3.1. Cross-site variation in average number of impacts, costs, and benefits. M. Hoyman, "The Impact of Economic Development on Small Communities: The Case of the Automobile Industry" (paper presented at the annual meetings of the American Political Science Association, Washington, D.C., August 29–September 1, 1991).

TABLE 3.5. Factor Analysis of Broad Impact, Cost, and Benefit Variables

| | Political and Economic Growth | | |
	Primary (factor 1)	Secondary (factor 2)	Sociocultural Long-Term (factor 3)
Benjobs[a]	.84[b]	.15	.17
Brimjobs	.76[b]	.14	.07
Bencap	.70[b]	−.21	.18
Costrst	−.17	.05	.08
Costsserv	−.51[b]	.19	.28
Brimbus	−.11	.85[b]	.01
Benindus	.25	.75[b]	−.09
Bencomm	.20	.63[b]	0
Brimgovt	.38[b]	.63[b]	0
Costwages	.27[b]	.40[b]	.27
Brimdecn	.03	.36	−.29
Costpoll	.14	−.06	.64[b]
Costtax	−.51[b]	−.14	.64[b]
Brimprof	0	.21	.48[b]
Brimprog	.29	.19	.48[b]
Benknow	−.12	0	.47[b]
Brimtrff	−.06	.19	−.36
Variance explained	.14	.27	.11

Note: Interfactor correlations are factor 1 + factor 2 = .41; factor 2 + factor 3 = .27; and factor 1 + factor 3 = .12.
a. Abbreviations for these variables are explained in Table 3.4.
b. Statistically significant.

three factors that emerge do not parallel the convenient economic, political, and cultural categories used at the beginning of the chapter, making the results all the more interesting. The first factor is called political and economic primary growth. The variables that load high on this factor are as follows:

Jobs are a benefit	.84
Jobs are a broad impact	.76
Capital is a benefit	.70
Social services are a cost	−.51
Broad impact on government	.38
Cost wages are a cost	−.27
Cost taxes are a cost	−.51

One can make several noteworthy comments about factor 1. First, some of the variables that load on this factor are economic; some are political. Second, the variables are both costs and benefits. Third, these variables tend to be most salient in the early stages of the process of development. For instance, jobs are most on people's minds when the plant is announced. This is the point at which politicians present the political justification for why the plant is a boon to their community: the plant may bring jobs. On the cost side, the cost of social services soars in the early stages, as the temporary workforce of job seekers, construction workers, and hangers-on lingers after the announcement of the plant is made.

The second factor is labeled political and economic secondary growth and includes the following variables:

New business is a broad impact	.85
Business is a benefit	.85
Industry is a benefit	.75
Commerce is a benefit	.63
Broad impact on government	.63
Wages are a cost	.40

Factor 2 is also a mix of economic and government variables; however, all the economic variables loading on factor 2 are associated with the secondary stages of growth. For example, jobs do not load on factor 2, but business, industry, and commerce load quite high. These are classic secondary economic effects. A political variable (broad impact on government) also loads very high on this factor. Also, one of the cost variables (the higher cost of wages) loads high. It stands to reason that higher wages would be a secondary impact: the plant has already been announced, and new workers have been hired. Finally, enough time has passed for the original employers to have raised their wages to retain their employees or to have lost employees to the higher-paying plant.

The third factor is labeled the sociocultural, long-term factor. It includes these items and these loadings:

Cost of pollution	.64
Cost of taxes	.64
Professionalization of public sector	.48
New government programs	.48
Benefit of new knowledge	.47

Factor 3 effects occur during the final stages of the economic development process (see Table 3.1). These changes are immutable and permanent, not just narrow economic impacts. For example, the "benefit of new knowledge" is felt as plant executives and other plant personnel become a presence in the community, sitting on community boards and participating as volunteers on the boards of nonprofit organizations. This is a longer-term impact for the community than the increase in jobs, for example.

Two other changes are long-term: the professionalization of public-sector jobs and the creation of new programs. These changes occur as part of a process of what Baumgartner and Jones describe as punctuated equilibrium, in which there are no institutional changes for quite a while and then suddenly a raft of new policies. The plant acts as a catalyst, enabling many institutional changes to occur.

Economic development may thus be conceived of as three different kinds of growth: short-term primary, secondary political-economic, and long-term sociocultural. Those who conceive of it as a short-term primary growth phenomenon do not think of it as a secondary political-economic phenomenon. And neither of these groups views it as a long-term political cultural phenomenon. Furthermore, not only does economic development appear to involve several dimensions, but it appears that the dimensions embody a time component. The agenda-setting results are consistent with the notion that development is a uniform set of progressive stages.

What about alternative explanations for the leaders' conception that economic development is multidimensional? If there is variation by site, what explains these differences? There is some variation by site, but it does not undercut support for the agenda-setting hypothesis.

Can the variations be explained by the leaders' role? If one is in business, for example, is one's conception of the economic development process different than the view of a person who is not in business?[26] The results are constrained by the fact that there are too few leaders to divide the sample in this way and get a statistically robust answer, but they are suggestive. The results suggest that businesspeople, economic development persons, and elected leaders are very concerned about the primary growth factors associated with the opening of a plant in their community and less concerned about the other costs and benefits. Elected officials view economic development as valuable because it results in an increase in jobs. This fits strongly with the idea that jobs represent great political capital. The opposite is true of nonelected officials or bureaucrats. As can be seen in Table A-1 in the appendix, the factor scores are both highest and negative for factor 1, second highest for factor 2, and positive for factor 3.

SUMMARY

This chapter has presented an overview of community leaders' perspectives on the diverse costs and benefits of a plant to the surrounding community. We have discovered that economic development affects more than the economy of a community; it affects the politics, the government, and the sociocultural life as well. The elite perceives economic development not entirely in economic terms but in three dimensions and as embodying a time component: short-term political and economic impacts, medium-term economic impacts, and longer-term sociocultural impacts. There is some indication, though no statistically robust evidence, that elected leaders define economic development primarily as the first dimension.

The elite interviewed perceived a common agenda of problems experienced by all towns with a new plant. About nine problems are universal, and three are always named as the "most important" issues: real estate, traffic, and housing.

4 | Impact of the Package on the Town's Budget, Revenue, and Debt

ANY COMMUNITY in which a plant opens hopes it will bring revenue into the public coffers. Because of incentive packages, however, some revenue is often lost in the form of tax abatements. The assumption is that the flow of revenue will increase enough to government units in the impact area to offset the loss of taxes. This chapter examines whether and when this is a valid assumption.

Because economic development is a process, it is important to examine the flow of public-sector revenue throughout all stages, not just at one point in time; therefore, the sequence of annual percentage increases over the development cycle will be examined to see if there is a discernible pattern. One point of view among scholars and policy makers is that, since the government is subsidizing the industry that is opening the plant, the net benefit to the community may be decreased. Thus, recruiting the plant may not be worth the costs involved. This view is based on a process of determining the calculus of dollars outlaid per job created. When using this calculation, one gets enormous dollars-per-job figures.[1]

Although this is sound analysis insofar as it is calculated from the time the package is announced, it reveals only part of the picture. The benefit-cost ratio obtained from taking the cost of the total package and dividing it by the number of jobs and getting a dollars-per-job ratio gives the front-end calculus only. Furthermore, it assumes that jobs are the only benefit; in fact, the plant has fundamental governmental, political, and public administration impacts. These could be considered benefits or costs depending on one's value system. Also, the ratio of benefits to costs varies over time, and the plant's impact is diffused across multiple jurisdictions.

This chapter provides an over-time, cross–government unit and cross-site analysis of the impact of economic development on city and county budgets, including overall revenue.[2] For each site several counties and sometimes several small cities form the impact area. The units for the Smyrna site are the city of Smyrna (the plant site location), Rutherford County (the surrounding county), and Murfreesboro (the town adjacent to the plant). The units for Georgetown are Georgetown (the plant site location) and Scott County. The units for the Marysville site are the city of Marysville (the plant site location) and Union County (the plant site location). The units for Spring Hill are the city of Columbia (the nearest town to the plant), Maury County, and Williamson County.

HOW BARGAINING FOR THE PACKAGE AFFECTS THE COMMUNITY'S DEAL

Because there may be some confusion about the term "original package," a brief discussion of its meaning is in order. The original package usually refers to the state's abatement of taxes and any in-lieu-of-tax payments the plant made to the community. The package may contain a guarantee of a certain number of jobs or a clause requiring the company to buy all new materials within the county. Sometimes packages include provisions concerning water and sewage lines and the construction of a bypass or road from the plant to the interstate. In recent packages, the state has also funded job training. The community usually pays for sewage, water, and power, and it attempts to estimate the cost of providing these services. Since taxes usually have been abated, the community negotiates in-lieu-of-tax payments from the company.

Unlike the conventional wisdom, communities are far from weak or powerless relative to corporations.[3] Specifically, it is at the critical stage when communities are bargaining the in-lieu-of-tax payments that they can make a difference. The original package is imposed upon the community by the state and the corporation, but in-lieu-of-tax payments enable the community to garner substantial resources. If the community bargains effectively, it will be well situated for years. The press, scholars, and policy makers have traditionally overlooked the importance of this stage of negotiation.

Who Does the Bargaining

The state, not the community, is the most important component in attracting automobile plants, and it does the initial bargaining. The state has more power than the community, and the corporation has more power than either one because capital is mobile; the state and community are not. The state's interest is in "getting the plant," not in its long-term implications for public administration in the community. The city and county bureaucrats may have a different perspective than that of elected officials.[4] The community is vulnerable, particularly a small one.[5] The parties usually present during the second stage of bargaining are representatives of the city where the plant is located, or the nearest city to the plant if it is on nonannexed land, and the county where it is located.

Characteristics of the Bargaining Process

Bargaining does not end with the initial package but continues to the agreement of the in-lieu-of-taxes package:

1. States bid for plant site.
2. Bid is awarded to a state. (State informs community of abatement which it has offered.)
3. Negotiation between community and company begins. Very little advance notice is given to community. Power imbalance between company and community. As a bargaining ploy, the company often raises other communities as possible sites.
4. Final package signed. Element of controversy regarding the terms.
5. Community will attempt annexation and payroll or profit tax as a strategy for gaining revenue once costs start to be realized.

All through the process, company representatives remind the community that other states and towns are standing in the wings. Even after the announcement is made public and the plant's opening appears definite, a company representative may say, "If we can't reach an acceptable agreement, we will go somewhere else." Under this pressure and that engendered by the publicity surrounding the package, politicians may find it difficult to stand firm. Irate citizens would blame them if they failed at the negotiation and all the jobs went elsewhere.

Other factors decreasing the power of the community are time and information. The corporation has months, even years, to research the costs of a site. One respondent reported that his company had eight file cabinets filled with information on one site alone. In addition, the employer has one of the most critical pieces of information since it knows how many new workers it will hire. In contrast, the community receives confirmation of the siting just before the public does. The head of one community chamber of commerce said he received word less than twenty-four hours before negotiations started. Another official said he heard the announcement on the evening news.

These instances confirm what other studies have said about corporation-community inequalities.[6] Information is a critical problem for a community that has no way of arriving at accurate estimates of the costs it will incur once a plant opens. Many small communities do not have an economic development officer or a full-time planner. Several community leaders we spoke to went scrambling to local universities to find economists who could estimate the costs of accommodating the plant.

Given that many communities lack information about the costs involved in becoming the site of a plant, perhaps one should not be surprised that three of the four packages examined in this study generated significant amounts of controversy.[7] This is particularly interesting given what has been written in the urban and policy literature on regime theory and preemptive power.[8] This literature suggests that politicians and even the public resort to "chasing smokestacks." In the cases of Georgetown and Spring Hill, community leaders were angry at the state about their agreements. As one Georgetown respondent described the situation, referring to Martha Layne Collins, the governor of Kentucky who recruited Toyota to Georgetown, "She could not have been elected dogcatcher" after she announced the package.

Following are some variables related to whether a small community is successful in obtaining a positive result. These are important in negotiating the original package and are under the community's control. (The strategies a community can adopt to further its own aims are covered in chapter 9.)

Bargaining Skills of the Chief Negotiator

Marked differences existed across the four communities in their degree of success in "cutting good deals."[9] These differences were attributable largely to the bargaining skills of the chief negotiators, usually the mayor. Smyrna and Georgetown cut the most favorable deals for themselves if one defines favorable as success at annexation and the development of other strategies that bring in revenue and offset losses from abatement. Annexation is important because once the plant is annexed, sales taxes and occupational or payroll taxes begin to flow into city coffers. Smyrna was successful in obtaining annexation as part of its package. This was and still is virtually unheard of. After all, there are reasons companies choose sites that are in "geopolitical limbo."[10] Georgetown annexed its plant within a couple of years of its opening.

Bargaining skills are not usually a criterion for electing a mayor or county executive, although both Mayor Sam Ridley and Mayor Tom Prather had exemplary skills in this area.[11] Communities could consider hiring professional negotiators rather than risk losing resources at the table because of the ineptitude of local officials at bargaining.

Centralization of Power on the Community Side

According to Jones and Bachelor, centralization of power is important on the community side in automobile plant siting decisions: the more centralized the decision making, the more favorable the deal for the community.[12] This is because the corporation nearly always speaks with one voice, while the power of a community is nearly always divided among multiple city and county units. Mayor Tom Prather of Georgetown attempted to solve this problem by offering to consolidate city and county governments, but when this proposal appeared on the ballot it was defeated. At the time of the research, fragmentation was still evident in Georgetown in the form of tension between the city and the county over the bypass.

One difference between city and county leaders was in their expectations concerning the plant. In general, county leaders felt that their counties did not gain as much revenue from the plant as the cities did. This feeling was prevalent across the four sites. In the case of Spring Hill, members of the community felt, overall, that it had been given short shrift. In 1985, the community ended up getting a favorable reallocation decision out of Michael Cody, the attorney general of Tennessee, which gave Maury County and the city of Spring Hill a reallocation of the in-lieu-of-tax payments in the form of a greater portion to Spring Hill.[13]

Availability of Information

The corporation has much more information than the community. In recent abatement packages, however, the company has recognized the need for it to help communities make up for their information deficits.

For example, the Saturn package included resources for Maury County and the city of Columbia, Tennessee, to commission consultants and for university researchers to collect data on which to base growth and need projections and to develop a master plan for the community and the area. In the case of Spring Hill, in preparation for the opening of the plant, some county and city of Columbia planners visited other greenfield sites and attended conferences with persons from other sites. This "lateral learning" across sites proved to be valuable.

Communities preparing for the opening of a plant are in need of resource people with experience at other sites of similar magnitude. One effective community strategy is to have the cost of doing impact studies included in the package; the company would then pay for consulting studies to help the community prepare.

Time

Time is the scarcest commodity in communities preparing for a plant to open. The community needs time to bargain with the corporation and to prepare for the population influx. Some plants studied were "fast-track"; they opened within two years of the announcement. Others, such as Spring Hill, were "slow-track"; these opened in five years.

EFFECT OF THE PLANT ON GOVERNMENT BUDGETS

As was mentioned in the policy section, one of the desired benefits of a plant is that it enables a community to have an even flow of capital. One important question is, Is there an incremental increase in expenditures and revenues, or are there extreme ups and downs?

As can be seen in Table 4.1, none of the ten government units followed an incremental pattern of increases across the years. The most stable was Rutherford County, the first unit listed and the county in which the Smyrna plant is located. All the other units experienced dramatic ups and downs in their percentage increase in revenues over the years. Marysville is a good example; it had a 447 percent increase in revenue from 1980 to 1981, a 5 percent increase from 1987 to 1988, and a decrease of 95 percent in 1982.

Table 4.2 shows the average and cumulative percentage increases, averaged by site. Independently from this the sites were coded from most skillful to least skillful in bargaining. Smyrna was ranked most skillful, Georgetown second most skillful, Marysville third most skillful, and Spring Hill least skillful. Tables 4.1 and 4.2 show that the sites with the highest average revenue and cumulative percentage increases were the most skillful at bargaining. Smyrna, with a cumulative site percentage increase of 308 percent, was the most skillful. Georgetown was also skillful, having the second-highest cumulative increase in county revenue— 220 percent and a site average of 131.5 percent. One may conclude, therefore, that success in using bargaining strategies, as opposed to such factors as serendipity or the features of the original package, leads to high percentage increases in revenue. The jurisdiction adjacent to the one where the site is located may present a different picture, however.

Budget for the Site as a Whole

How good was the budget for each site as a whole? Figure 4.1 and Table 4.3 enable us to look at the very large absolute increases and average annual percentage increases for all four sites from the baseline year to the year the study was done. The A in Table 4.3 indicates when the plant announcement was made, and the O represents the opening. To determine more precisely when shifts occurred and to see if they happened systematically at or after the opening, we can divide the series of years into three time blocks: baseline to announcement, announcement to opening, and postopening.

Table 4.3 shows that the pattern of preannouncement and post-announcement and preopening and postopening averages varies by site, although one general statement can be made: there is a larger increase in revenue between the preannouncement and the postannouncement period than between the preopening and the postopening period. The announcement itself, rather than the opening, seems to trigger the increase in revenue. Bear in mind that each site is at a different stage in its development. Spring Hill is the least mature. Georgetown is the next most mature, having opened in 1988. Smyrna, the next to the oldest, opened in 1983. Marysville is the oldest, having opened in 1979.

The question remains whether some or all of this increase would have occurred even if the plant had not opened. At some sites, such as Smyrna, there was a steady pattern of growth in the larger region before the siting; thus, the opening of the plant enhanced an already steady period of growth. In Marysville, however, which had a 14 to 18 percent unem-

TABLE 4.1. Revenue Increase (and percentage change) by Government Unit, Except Adjacent Units

	Smyrna: per site (+/-%)[b] cumulative 308; average 38			Georgetown: per site (+/-%) cumulative 131.5; average 18.2	
	Rutherford County	Smyrna (City)	Murfreesboro[c]	Georgetown (City)	Scott County
1977	12,407,277				
1978	23,101,171 (86)				
1979	25,011,651 (8)				
1980	28,904,095 (15)	2,395,045			
1981	33,075,312 (14)				
1982	33,560,129 (1)				
1983	34,660,579 (3)				1,454,415
1984	37,289,116 (8)	8,502,909 (255)			1,611,401 (7.2)
1985	47,795,595 (28)	8,812,130 (4)			2,027,948 (26)
1986	52,533,527 (7.2)	10,221,894 (16)			3,138,670 (55)
1987	55,299,503 (5)	11,639,338 (14)		3,801,504 (58)	3,940,728 (26)
1988	61,065,346 (10.4)			4,075,564 (7)	4,381,924 (11)
1989	72,665,847 (19)	12,407,277 (6)		3,177,278 (−22)	4,658,808 (6.3)
1990	74,661,478 (3)				
Entire site: cumulative (+/-%)	501	518		43	220
average (+/-% per year)	15.9	59		14.3	22

Note: Sites are arranged left to right from most skillful (Smyrna) to least skillful (Spring Hill) at bargaining. Figures in parentheses indicate percent change.

TABLE 4.1. *Continued*

Marysville: per site (+/-%) cumulative 139; average 17.3		Spring Hill: per site (+/-%) cumulative 83; average 14.4		
Marysville (City)	Union County[c]	Columbia	Maury	Williamson County[c]
2,276,184				
2,362,480 (3.6)				
2,498,425 (5.7)				
3,091,052 (24)				
16,918,902 (447)		7,160,044		
796,864 (−95)		6,866,826 (4.1)		
		7,015,205 (2)		
5,768,463		7,756,928 (10.5)	28,441,504	
364,238 (−93)		8,666,809 (11.2)	30,382,556 (6.8)	
1,595,845 (338)		9,328,289 (7)	42,035,238 (38)	
4,819,211 (201)		10,871,369 (17)	45,435,766 (8)	
5,187,609 (7)		15,964,715 (47)	48,267,958 (6)	
128		123	70	
93		14.1	14.7	

a. Per site.

b. The per site cumulative average and the per site average +/-% include the adjacent unit figures in Table 4.2. Therefore, the two numbers under "cumulative" do not average to the per site figure.

c. See Table 4.2.

TABLE 4.2. Revenue of Government Units (and percentage change) Adjacent to Plants: Union County, Murfreesboro, and Williamson County Compared to Average for other Units in Site

| | Spring Hill | | Smyrna | | Georgetown[a] | Marysville | |
	Williamson County	Average for Other Units in Spring Hill Site	Murfreesboro	Average for Other Units in Smyrna Site	(includes city of and Scott County)	Union County	Average for Other Units in Marysville Site
1977			139,536,299			2,201,286	
1978			149,615,945 (7.7)	86		3,750,557 (70)	2.6
1979			157,207,379 (1.5)	8		3,985,567 (6.3)	7
1980			354,361,802 (125)	15		4,379,268 (10)	24
1981			380,914,058 (7)	14		4,286,485 (−2.2)	447
1982			424,462,962 (11)	1		4,674,126 (8.3)	−95
1983	34,148,976		457,094,363 (7.7)	3		4,447,500 (−5)	
1984	42,008,356 (23)	4.1	463,942,144 (1.5)	132		4,837,075 (8.8)	
1985	46,865,875 (12)	2.0	492,396,125 (6)	16		5,236,478 (8.5)	−93

TABLE 4.2. *Continued*

	Spring Hill		Smyrna		Georgetown[a]	Marysville	
	Williamson County	Average for Other Units in Spring Hill Site	Murfreesboro	Average for Other Units in Smyrna Site	(includes city of and Scott County)	Union County	Average for Other Units in Marysville Site
1986	69,605,884 (12)	10.5	10,221,894 (−98)	11.6		5,359,197 (4)	26
1987	70,931,803 (48)	10.7				5,556,295 (3.6)	5
1988	53,245,837 (2)	26.5					8
1989	(25)						
1990							
Entire site: cumulative (+/−%)	56	83	−93	509	131.5	150	128
average (+/−%) per year)	17.5	14.4	8.6	48	17	11	93

Note: Figures in parentheses indicate percent change.
a. Both Georgetown [city] and Scott County were present at table. In Georgetown, no single adjacent area had significant impact due to diffuse impact.

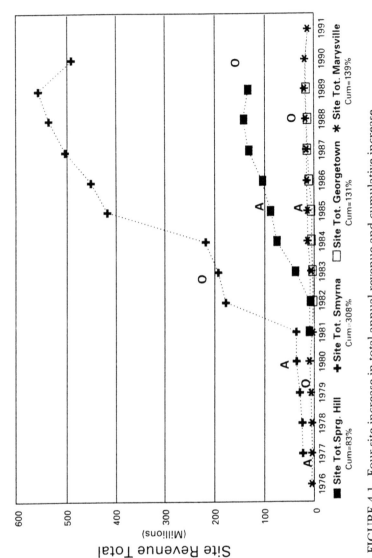

FIGURE 4.1. Four-site increase in total annual revenue and cumulative increase. A = announcement; O = opening. Cum = cumulative site average percent increase averaged for each site.

TABLE 4.3. Average Revenue Percentage Change by Site Before and After the Plant Announcement and Opening

	Smyrna	Georgetown	Marysville	Spring Hill
1977			12.4 A	
1978	8.3		22.3	
1979	15.6		38.6 O_1	
1980	14.4 A		15.0	
1981	1.5		228.6 O_2	
1982	3.3		−41.8	4.1
1983	7.4 O	7.2	9.0	2.2
1984	16.6	10.8	−4.9	15.2
1985	43.8	25.9 A	−14.0	8.9 A
1986	13.3	54.8	17.1	18.2
1987	11.9	42.1	3.6	29.8
1988	13.3	9.2 O	5.6	9.6
1989	2.1	−7.9	9.7	13.5
1990	6.1		−2.5	O
1991			7.8	
Preannouncement	12.7	14.6	12.4	7.6
Preopening	11.9	25.0	24.4	11.6
Postannouncement	11.9	24.6	21.5	17.7
Postopening	15.3	0.6[a]	20.9	missing data

Note: Sites are listed in order of skillfullness, from most skillful (Smyrna) to least skillful (Spring Hill). A = announcement; O = opening; O_1 = opening of motorcycle plant; and O_2 = opening of automobile plant. These percentages are an average across the whole site, so do not necessarily correspond to those reported in earlier tables.

a. 1988 and 1989 used in calculation of postopening; otherwise, it would have been only one year, which was 1989.

ployment rate before the plant siting,[14] the rate decreased to about the national average after the siting. Much of the improvement in this community's fortunes could be attributed to the plant. In Spring Hill, the results cover only the period from the announcement to the opening of the plant; nonetheless, the revenue effects look hefty. In Georgetown, the plant's revenue flow clearly offsets the negative effects of the plant and has placed the community in a positive cash-flow position.

In Table 4.3 the revenues in the announcement era appear to have had important impacts. This can be seen by comparing the differences between the preannouncement and postannouncement averages and between the preopening and postopening averages. The fact that revenue begins to increase immediately after the announcement has interesting implications. On the one hand, this is good for the community since revenue may be needed to offset the costs of the population influx and the rise in real estate costs that occur immediately after the announcement. On the other hand, since information about the impact of the plant on the community is incomplete, revenue is starting to flow before adequate planning has taken place.

What about the effect of the plant opening on revenues? As Table 4.3 shows, the preopening and postopening averages do not follow a discernible pattern and do not move in the predicted direction.[15] In Smyrna, the opening had a positive impact on revenues, while in Georgetown and Marysville the opening had no positive impact on revenues per se.

One way to assess how the overall budget of a site is affected by the plant opening is to examine the cumulative percentage increase in all revenue.[16] Smyrna experienced the largest such increase, followed by Spring Hill, Georgetown, and Marysville, respectively. Looking at the average annual percentage increases, we see that all four sites are roughly comparable, particularly if we take into account the possibility that Marysville's high average may be a function of an extreme scorer.

All the sites experienced substantial increases in revenue after the opening of the plant, although the increase was only modest in Marysville and Smyrna fared significantly better. In addition, there was variation across years. In general, the impact of the plant was generally positive; however, the question remains whether all units within a site were affected equally.

BUDGET FOR EACH UNIT WITHIN THE SITE

The preliminary findings from the interviews with community leaders suggest that the town or county adjacent to the one where the plant is located may get much of the pain but not much of the gain when a plant opens. It experiences increases in traffic, tightness in the housing market, and increased demands on its police and fire departments and schools, and a possible need to build new roads; however, it receives no taxes, even after the abatement period is over.

Representatives of the adjacent town or government unit are not invited to the table to negotiate in-lieu-of-tax payments because the impact area is assumed to be more concentrated than it really is. Thus, the county or city adjacent to the plant, not the political unit that recruits the corporation, often experiences major, if not the most important, effects of the plant. The policy implication is that the parties represented at the table when the package is negotiated are not the only parties that are affected. The adjacent units in this study are Murfreesboro in the Smyrna site, an adjacent city to Smyrna; and Williamson County in the Spring Hill site, an adjacent county to Maury County where the plant is located.

In Georgetown, there is no good way to test this proposition since the plant's impact was diffuse and the adjacent county contained Lexington, which had a variety of employers. Any revenue increases in the county where Lexington is located could have occurred because other employers came into the area. Looking at Spring Hill, we see that the cumulative percentage increase for Williamson County is lower than the average increase for the other two units. Likewise, at Smyrna, the percentage increase for Murfreesboro is lower than the average for the other two units.

The summary measures used were the cumulative percentage and the average percentage increase. The cumulative percentage is the percentage difference between the first year for the community, usually the baseline or the figure for the year before the plant announcement, and the last year in the series (1990). The cumulative percentage is more meaningful since it tells us what has been the net gain. Within the limits of the analysis, it looks as though the data support the notion that the adjacent community loses.

The results are shown in Table 4.2. The percentage increases for Murfreesboro, adjacent to the Smyrna site, Williamson County, adjacent to the Spring Hill site, and Union County, adjacent to the Marysville site, show the following pattern: Williamson County had a cumulative percentage increase of 56 percent versus 61 percent for Spring Hill as a whole; Murfreesboro was most dramatic, with a cumulative percentage decrease of 93 percent versus a 434 percent average for the Smyrna site overall; Union County has a substantially lower cumulative figure of 150 percent, compared with 423 percent for the site overall.

Revenues and expenditures do not always match, however.[17] For example, the cumulative percentage gain in revenue discussed earlier is not always the same as the cumulative percentage gain in expenditures. Thus, the cumulative percentage gain for the units of the city of Murfreesboro, an adjacent unit to Smyrna, is different than the average percentage gains for the Smyrna site as a whole, and the figures for

Williamson are different than the average in Spring Hill for both expenditures and revenues.

Does Murfreesboro have a revenue disadvantage compared with other government units at the site, as we would predict? At first, we see that Murfreesboro's percentage increase in revenue both after the announcement and after the opening of the plant is *more* than the site's average percentage increase in revenue as a whole. When the extreme scorer in this series of data is removed, however, we see that the revenue increased almost twofold after the announcement and more than twofold after the opening.[18]

Williamson, the county adjacent to the Spring Hill site, is a good site with which to test the "one county over" argument on revenue. Before the announcement that the plant was opening, the county had higher average annual increases in revenue than the other units at the site, but after the announcement the percentage increases in revenue for Williamson County were roughly comparable with those for the rest of the site. Thus, the Williamson data confirm the "one county over" hypothesis, although the data are not as strong as the data for expenditures.[19]

REVENUE GENERATED BY THE PLANT

Direct Revenue

Besides the general revenue patterns, it is useful to look at how much direct revenue can be attributed to the plant. Direct revenue may include funds negotiated in lieu of tax payments or any other direct payments so labeled in the public budget. Direct revenue does not include sales tax that could be attributable to the plant or extra revenue from property taxes due to the escalation in real estate prices.

The absolute amount of auto plant–related revenue varied from site to site. Smyrna reported a twentyfold increase, from $300,000 to $8 million, between 1985 and 1989. It dipped to zero in 1990. In Georgetown, the beginning figure was unknown, but it was probably zero; it reached $2,281,472 in 1990. In Marysville, it was nil,[20] and it did not go up from 1977 to 1990. In Spring Hill, there was a huge increase—from zero to $7 million. The conclusion is that the sites did not do equally well: Marysville was the least endowed, followed by Georgetown and Spring Hill. Smyrna did the best in terms of direct revenue.

Looking now at the percentage increase from one year to the next, Spring Hill increased 8.9 percent in 1987, –5.9 percent in 1988, and –32.3 percent in 1989. Smyrna started with a –23 percent increase in 1978, went to 86 percent in 1979, –19 percent in 1980, 23 percent in 1981, 27 percent in 1982, 76 percent in 1983, 157 percent in 1984, 0 percent in 1985, 1.6 percent in 1986, 2.2 percent in 1987, –1.7 percent in 1988, and –2.2 percent in 1989. The pattern is filled with ups and downs, with peaks of 86 percent in 1979 and 76 percent in 1983.

In Georgetown, revenue data are missing for the period 1983 to 1987. The figure was probably zero and then increased 33 percent in 1987, decreased by 3 percent in 1988, and reached 103 percent in 1989. This revenue coincided with the opening of the plant (1988), then lagged by a certain amount due to the payroll tax being implemented after the plant opening. In Marysville, data are missing for all the years; there was thus zero identifiable revenue associated with the plant.

Indirect Revenue

Sales. Interviews with the elite did not shed any light on the precise amount of the revenue from sales taxes that was due to the opening of the plant. In Spring Hill, Smyrna, and Georgetown, the revenue from sales taxes increased astronomically; however, in Marysville, the revenue from sales taxes actually went down, from $63,000 to $14,950, in 1991.[21] One can conclude, therefore, that sales taxes were a major source of revenue everywhere except Marysville.

Property. Property taxes would be expected to be an important source of revenue even if the tax rates remained the same after the plants opened. This is because real estate prices escalated by about 30 percent from the baseline to 1990. In Spring Hill, revenues from property taxes went from $1 million in 1981 to $10 million in 1989. In Smyrna, the revenue was $5 million in 1977 and $460 million in 1990, a ninety-fold increase. In Georgetown, the revenue was $445,000 in 1983; it had doubled to $986,938 by 1989. In Marysville, it increased from $1,200,000 to $1,572,000, a 20 percent change. The amount of revenue due to property tax increased dramatically for all sites, although the increase was comparatively less dramatic in Marysville.

Total Revenue. Total revenue—the sum of auto plant–related revenue and total official revenue—gives us a good idea of the resources available to a community.[22] In all but one site (Marysville), there has been a strong and dramatic gain in total revenue since the announcement of the plant.

Debts

Does the plant go into debt? To answer this question, we must examine the debt pattern as well as the revenue pattern. There are two measures of debt: the absolute amount of debt and the debt-to-revenue ratio (or expenditures). In looking at the second measure, we find no substantial differences between expenditures and revenues. The absolute amount of debt increased after the plant opened at each site except Marysville. The debt in Marysville was finally reduced from $357,338 in 1990 to $340 in 1991. It seems that Marysville, the oldest site chronologically, has almost eliminated its debt. Speaking more generally, though, it looks as if debt load and the plant go hand in hand.

Ratio of Debt to Revenue

In these four communities, the expenditures tended to equal the revenues, perhaps because of state laws mandating that communities balance their budgets. Examining the debt-to-expenditure ratio, we see some interesting variations across government units. At Spring Hill, for instance, Williamson County had the highest debt-to-expenditure ratio of any government unit studied—almost 18 percent in 1983 and again in 1989. This was several percentage points higher than Maury County. Most important, the debt-to-expenditure ratio for Columbia, another government unit within a site, was much different. In 1985, it was 0 percent, and it ended up at only 2 percent in 1989. Thus, there is much greater variation in the debt-to-expenditure ratio across a site than over time. These findings support the notion that the impact of economic development is uneven across units at a site. They also support the point that the way the initial package is negotiated determines how much of a burden will be borne by the community.

Looking at the debt-to-expenditure ratios, we see that Smyrna's ratio remained zero, while Murfreesboro and Rutherford County had double-digit increases. Looking at the city of Georgetown, we see that Scott County's ratio decreased from 16 percent to 8 percent in 1989. Finally,

Logan County's debt-to-expenditure ratio was zero, and the ratio at Marysville was only 2 to 5 percent.

SUMMARY

It appears that the initial package negotiated between a town, county, or state and a corporation defines the broad contours of the financial arrangement for the community. The variables identified so far as important in getting a "good deal" are whether the city or county retains ownership of utilities, the bargaining skills of the chief negotiator, whether power is centralized on the community side, how much information is available to the community, and how much time the community has to prepare for the opening of the plant. Whether a community is able to work out deals such as annexation of the plant site to the town or city seriously affects the community's financial future.

Regarding the plant's overall budgetary effect on government units, we find, in general, that revenue is enhanced significantly throughout. Percentage increases vary by unit within an impact area, and adjacent cities or counties fare the worst. At all sites except Smyrna, the pivotal moment when the increase in revenue occurred was the announcement, not the opening, of the plant. This is interesting and unexpected; it means the plant's impact is immediate.

A similar picture emerges regarding expenditures. Thus, not only was there variation over time, but there was variation across sites. The most striking finding was that at Spring Hill expenditures increased enormously, probably because revenues started at such a paltry base.

How is the budget for the site as a whole affected by the plant? Clearly, significantly. With the exception of Spring Hill, the four sites had impressively large increases in revenue. Smyrna had the largest cumulative percentage increases in revenue (308 percent for Smyrna and 131 percent for Georgetown) because they successfully annexed the sites to their towns and had chief negotiators who were highly skilled at bargaining.

As to whether the plant affects each government unit equally, the results indicate that counties or cities adjacent to plants get the pain but not the gain. To a certain extent these differences are a function of the packages that were negotiated. Representatives of these adjacent units were not invited to the table.

What about revenue? Looking at specifically plant-related revenue first, we see that the sites varied: Spring Hill went from zero to $7 million, and this was before the plant even opened. In Smyrna, plant-related revenue was also impressive; it went from $300,000 to $8 million between 1985 and 1989, a twentyfold increase. In Georgetown, the beginning level is not known, although presumably it was zero and increased to $2,281,472 in 1990. Marysville remained flat, from zero to zero; therefore, Spring Hill and Smyrna increased their direct revenue most dramatically. In terms of indirect revenue, three out of four sites, all but Marysville, saw their sales revenues skyrocket, and property tax revenues were even more impressive.

What about total revenue? The total revenue in effect includes plant-related revenue twice if, in fact, that revenue is embedded in the regular budget. Dramatic increases occurred at all sites except Marysville, where there has been a loss of revenue since the plant was announced.

As to whether the site goes into debt, we find that at Spring Hill the debt increases have been enormous; however, Marysville, the oldest site chronologically, has almost eliminated its debt. We also find that the debt increases from the time of the plant announcement to when it opens. There are very interesting variations across government units within sites. In Spring Hill, for instance, Williamson County had the highest debt-to-expenditure ratio—almost 18 percent in 1983 and again in 1989. The percentage for the city of Columbia was radically different, hovering between 0 percent and 5 percent. Thus, in terms of the burden of indebtedness, it appears that different units within one plant's impact area have radically different fates. This variation seems to be more important than the variation across time.

5 | Impact of the Plants on Aspects of Public Administration of the Communities

ONCE A PLANT is opened in a community, the town's priorities and long-term agenda are changed significantly. One indication of this change is in the community's budget. This chapter focuses on the effects of the plant on the following public administration functions: fire, police, water and sewage, recreation, planning, public works, and criminal justice. Education is covered in a separate chapter because the changes in this area are so numerous, far-reaching, and subtle.

Four measures in the communities' budgets were used over time to evaluate changes: absolute increases in the amounts budgeted for each category; percentage increases each year; proportionate amount of the total budget allocated to each category; and substantive changes, including qualitative changes, for instance, in the professionalization of public employees, upgradings in ISO ratings,[1] and changes in selection criteria for police or fire chiefs. The percentage increase per year in the amount budgeted for each category is a good indicator of major shifts in commitment.

The absolute number of dollars allocated to each category is a good indication of the local government's commitment to ensuring that the community has a certain service, for example, police protection. The problem is that the overall budget could have increased enormously as well. Thus, the absolute amount may not tell us whether the community has reallocated resources in a particular direction. To evaluate this, the proportionate amount of the budget allocated for a particular service provides more useful information, as well as the proportion before and after the opening of the plant. Finally, the percentage increase indicates whether a particular public "problem" was seen as more important in one year than in other years.

FIRE PROTECTION

Dramatic increases were evident in all four communities in the absolute amounts budgeted for fire protection.[2] Although the prediction was that the proportionate amounts would also increase, no patterns or shifts were found. Much variation occurred across time, but there was no consistent pattern in the percentage increase in the budget for fire protection; for example, there were no huge increases immediately after the plant opened. If any pattern exists, it is that the budgets for fire protection increased about one year after the announcement was made that the plant would be opening. The largest increases tended to occur between the announcement of the plant and the opening.[3]

Information on the substantive changes that occurred in fire protection came from the interviews with the elite.[4] These included changes in demand, such as the number of inspections, the number of square miles covered, and the administration of special programs; in the development of new stations; in the amount of new equipment purchased; in staff, including new staff and increases in professionalization; in status, from volunteer to paid; and other changes.

Changes in Demand

Improvements in the physical facilities and the addition of new staff are evidence of increases in the quality of fire protection. In Murfreesboro, the fire department was upgraded to a class 4 ISO rating and, as of 1990, was considering going for a class 3. Georgetown's department went from a rating of 6 to 5[5] and was considering further improvement. Clearly, such changes benefited these communities. Not only did these changes indicate that the communities' citizens had better fire protection; they also meant homeowners' fire insurance premiums were lower by 10 to 12 percent, according to Chief Adkins, fire chief of the city of Georgetown, as conveyed in an interview on June 7, 1990.

Most of the fire departments indicated that their communities' burgeoning populations were the main reason for the increase in demand. The city of Columbia, for example, reported a 14 percent increase in electrical fires; by contrast, the arson rate remained the same. In Georgetown, there were 300 responses by the fire department in 1984, 310 in 1988, 540 in 1989, and 600 in 1990. Thus, there was almost two times the number of responses in the year after the plant opened (1989).

In some sites, the impact was felt in terms of increased inspections rather than actual fires. For example, in Scott County, the number of inspections went from 8,500 in 1984 to 13,500 in 1990. In Marysville, there were a greater number of apartments to inspect; there was also a shift from residential to a commercial-industrial mix in building inspections.

New Stations and Equipment

Three of the four communities needed new fire stations after the plants opened. Marysville, the exception, had just built a station in 1973. Murfreesboro added two new stations, an enormous increase.

In terms of equipment, the city of Columbia, Rutherford County, Murfreesboro, and the city of Georgetown purchased or refurbished pumpers after the plants opened. When Georgetown purchased a new pumper and refitted its old one, the cost came to $350,000. Georgetown also had to spend $1 million for a new training center; this joint venture was funded by the city, county, and Toyota, starting in 1990 and extending over the next five years.

Professionalization and Staff Additions

Overall, the fire chiefs in place after the plants were opened were no longer "good old boys" but professionally trained chiefs selected for their merits. This change was typical of what occurred among the political elite. In three out of the four communities, either the city or the county chief changed because of the advent of the plant. The new chiefs represented different outlooks and exhibited an enthusiasm for professionalization rather than cronyism. Columbia has probably gone the furthest in making changes in this direction; it has proposed creating a new training facility, underscoring its seriousness about training and upgrading its fire and police personnel. In only one government unit, Scott County, has no upgrading occurred. Another trend is toward the addition of new staff; for instance, Marysville had seven paid staff in 1977; this number increased to fourteen in 1990.

In conclusion, most of the sites reported that the plant had both indirect and strong direct effects on fire protection. This does not mean that the city or county fire departments provided services directly for the plant but that, because of plant-related growth, such as new subdivi-

sions and apartments, a strain was placed on the existing fire departments, forcing them to hire more staff and construct more buildings.
What is irrefutable is that fire services were upgraded because of the
plants' being built.

LAW ENFORCEMENT

The terms "law enforcement" and "police" as used here encompass both
the city police departments and the county sheriff's departments. Overall, the absolute increases in police department budgets were enormous.
For instance, Spring Hill nearly doubled its budget, Marysville's increased sixfold, and Smyrna and Georgetown increased their budgets
tenfold.[6] The biggest increases were associated with the announcement,
not the opening, of the plant; the exception was Georgetown, for which
data are missing for the announcement year.

There is a fair amount of variation in the percentage increase across
time, with Georgetown ranging from a –13 percent increase to 43 percent and Marysville ranging from a 0.5 percent increase to 75 percent.[7]
No pattern emerges, however. Certainly, the announcement itself had
no discrete effect. Some of the largest increases occurred after the plant
openings, but they did not occur within a consistent time interval. As
predicted, a large increase occurred in the percentage of the budget
allocated to police activities; the exception in this case was Spring Hill.
Table 5.1 shows, for example, that in Marysville a 13.9 percent increase
occurred in the proportion of the budget for police protection in 1977
and that by 1990 police protection represented a hefty 16 percent of the
total town budget.

Numerous substantive changes occurred in law enforcement, specifically in law enforcement functions, during the stages of the economic
development process.[8] The workforce was professionalized, extra staff
and facilities were added, and changes occurred in the amount and
character of the workload.

Professionalization

The requirements for positions like police chief and county sheriff
changed, so that political acceptability by the mayor or county commissioner became less important than merit. Educational require-

TABLE 5.1. Proportion of Budget (by percentage) That Is Fire, Police, Sewage, Public Works, Planning, Recreation, Welfare, and Criminal Justice

	Fire	Police	Sewage	Public Works	Planning	Recreation	Welfare	Criminal Justice
Spring Hill								
1981	13.9	15.1	21.7	14.7	0	6.1	0	0
1989	4.2	1.6	6.9	8.2	0	0.9	8	0.67
Change	-9.7	-13.9	-14.8	-6.5	0	-5.2	0.8	0.67
Smyrna								
1977	0	1.8	1.3	6.1	0.1	0.2	0.3	1
1990	14.7	13.5	5.6	5.9	2.8	5	0.19	0.4
Change	14.7	11.7	-4.3	-0.2	-2.7	4.8	-0.11	-0.6
Georgetown								
1981[a]	2.1	9.7	0.7	21.6	0	1.5	1.1	1.8
1989	6.6	15.3	5.5	20.2	2.1	3.1	2.2	6.3
Change	4.5	5.6	-4.8	-1.4	2.1	1.6	1.1	4.5
Marysville								
1976	9.4	10.3	16.4	15.7	0.6	3	0	0
1991	16.1	24.2	1.5	10.8	0.1[b]	0[b]	9.6	16.1
Change	6.7	13.9	-14.9	-4.9	-0.5	-3	9.6	16.1

a. The figure for fire is from 1982. All other categories are from 1981.
b. The 1990 figure was slightly higher than 1991.

ments, previous experience, and objective decision making gained in importance.

County sheriff is still an elected position in many of the counties studied and generally throughout the Southeast. All chiefs or sheriffs indicated that they experienced increases in their professionalization after the plant opened. In Marysville, the chief said this occurred because security checks were stricter, a development unrelated to the opening of the Honda plant. In Columbia, the chief said that because of the increase in professionalization, the $300-per-person eight-week training course for police now cost $800. Another chief said the job of police officer had become more technical, a condition he saw as not in his control but imposed from outside. The trend toward professionalization included a shift from having a volunteer police department to having a paid, full-time staff, at least in Rutherford (Smyrna site) and Scott (Georgetown site) Counties. It appears that the plant and the associated population growth hastened this change.[9]

Staffing and Facilities

In all four communities, the police forces increased in size. For example, Georgetown had fifteen sworn officers before the plant opened in 1984 and twenty-nine in 1990. The number of communications officers rose from five to eight. Rutherford County had fourteen sworn officers in 1972 and ninety-five in 1990.

In all the communities but Smyrna, a new station had to be built. In Marysville, the police are housed in a building that was refurbished in 1985. In Smyrna, the community had to float a $4 million bond for a new jail. In Georgetown, the police expanded the amount of space in their facility; however, there was no need to add a substation.

In some communities, other capital requirements were necessary. Columbia needed ten more police cars.[10] Murfreesboro needed a 911 emergency number as well as new equipment. These costs were split among several jurisdictions.

Workload

The biggest effect on the police departments was in the volume of traffic and thus in traffic accident–related arrests, which increased enormously.[11] In Marysville, the police department kept data that could be analyzed by township. Allen, the township in which the Honda plant was located, was one of three in which the figures increased significantly: from 36 traffic accidents in 1982 to 129 in 1989. One of the two other townships was along a strip where the growth was attributed to the opening of the plant.

Several other police-related trends are significant. In at least two communities, drug-related crimes increased dramatically. In Columbia (Spring Hill), the number of such crimes went from 60 in 1985 to 268 in 1989; in Georgetown, the number went from 17 in 1987 to 178 in 1989.

It is not the suggestion here that the plant caused more drug use, although one or two respondents in one community suggested that an unexpected side effect of the increase in wealth might have been greater access to drugs. The increase in drug use could have been indicative of a national trend during this period, or due to higher levels of detection and enforcement. Finally, since these numbers were absolute, the increases could have been a function of the increase in population in these communities. In any event, the result for the police was the same: there was more unlawful activity to curb. For example, one chief reported he had four officers specifically assigned to DARE, a drug awareness and prevention program.

The number of burglaries and thefts also increased. For example, the number of burglaries in Columbia (Spring Hill) went from 32 in 1985 to 73 in 1989, and in Rutherford County (also Spring Hill) from 393 in 1979 to 504 in 1989. The total number of complaints in Murfreesboro went from 6,861 to 16,221—a 136 percent increase. In Marysville, the number of calls went from 6,600 in 1984 to 11,000 in 1989, and the number of arrests went from 1,395 to 1,658 in 1989 alone. Also in Marysville, crime reports increased from 289 in 1985 to 364 in 1989. In Georgetown, the patrol area doubled from 1984 to 1990. In conclusion, there appear to be both more demands and new demands put on police departments in the era following the opening of a plant. Consequently, there is a need for increased budgets, staff, and professionalization.

WATER AND SEWAGE

Many changes in sewage service were necessary in the period following the opening of the plant. First, as part of the initial package, each company usually negotiated and reimbursed the city or county for the lay-ing of sewage lines to the plant from the nearest main trunk line; however, the bigger question was how to handle the extra demands put on the existing system by the new volume both at the plant and at employee housing.

In terms of absolute numbers of dollars spent on sewage, the figures for each site are the sum, not the average, for all the political jurisdictions at the site.[12] Spring Hill experienced a sixfold increase, Smyrna a fivefold increase. Georgetown's sewage budget increased to twenty-three times its original size, and Marysville's seems to have dropped.

In terms of the proportionate amount of the total budgets allocated for sewage, we see a startling result, shown in Table 5.1: the proportionate amount spent on sewage *declined* over the years after the opening of the plant by almost 15 percent in both Spring Hill and Marysville. In Smyrna and Georgetown, there was an increase, but of only 4.3 percent and 4.8 percent, respectively.

The percentage increase per year varied from year to year. Sometime after the announcement or, in Marysville, after the opening, an enormous increase occurred, usually in a single year; for example, Marysville had a 1,594 percent increase in its sewage budget in 1981, and Spring Hill and Smyrna experienced large increases in the years after the plant was announced.[13] It should be noted that only infrequently are new sewage and water plants built in any community.

In summary, increases in sewage budgets seem to occur reasonably early in the economic development process. These figures do not indicate whether some of the enormous blips occurred because large amounts of federal aid were available on a onetime basis. Substantial amounts of federal aid were available during the 1970s; these subsidies, usually in the form of matching grants, no longer exist. The cost of sewage facilities for future plant sites will have to be borne by the communities or the companies involved.

Substantive Changes in Sewage Services

In many communities undergoing economic development, it is necessary to build either a new facility to handle the additional sewage or an addition to an existing sewage treatment plant. In two of the four sites, sewage stations were added. Smyrna built a pumping station, with 70 percent of the funding coming from the Environmental Protection Agency (EPA), 20 percent from Nissan, and 10 percent from the city.

At the Smyrna site, the city of Murfreesboro built a water tank and transom in 1983, of which the former was funded by the Economic Development Agency (EDA). In 1985, there was a $10 million bond issue for a sewage treatment plant that was built in 1986. A problem persists in Murfreesboro, however, because the treatment plant overloads during flooding.

Georgetown has two waste water treatment plants, one of which is used specifically by Toyota. There is only one water treatment plant used by the community, a new one. A bond was used to fund it and guaranteed that 95 percent of the capacity would be reserved for city residents, 5 percent for the industrial park.

In most of the communities, water capacity was increased significantly. In fact, each community now has a capacity well beyond the needs of its plant. In Smyrna, the capacity before the plant was built was 1.2 million gallons. As of 1990, 5.2 million gallons were being used, but the capacity was 9 million gallons with the new pumping station. The community had a water capacity that would enable it to almost double its growth. In Smyrna, the number of customers grew from 963 in 1980 to 2,212 in 1990. In Murfreesboro, the 1983 capacity was 1,699,868 gallons and the 1989 capacity was 1,807,324. In 1985, a $10 million bond issue was floated to improve water and sewer services, resulting in an increase in the number of cubic feet from 226,607 to 240,966 in 1989. The revenue the city collected from water bills increased from $2,164,866 in 1983 to $3,385,137 in 1989 and for sewage from $1,973,805 to $3,979,451 for 1989. On the other side of the coin, bad debts increased fivefold, from $7,108 in 1979 to $37,608 in 1989.[14]

The sewage and water story is not all positive. Major supply problems exist in the cities of Murfreesboro and Georgetown. Murfreesboro experiences a severe supply problem during droughts. An obvious source of water is the Cumberland River;[15] however, one small community cannot pipe in water from the Cumberland, so a group of consultants recommended that the utility district for the town of Murfreesboro become part of a regional water authority consisting of Lebanon, Franklin, Williamson County, Rutherford County, Wilson County, metropolitan Nashville, and the Saturn plant. This consortium could procure water from the Cumberland River over the long term. A short-term solution was needed, however, so a consulting group recommended Percy Priest reservoir as a source of water. Also, although it would not create any supply, repairing the dam could help conserve some water. A new steel reservoir in the area with a capacity of 3 million gallons was subsequently constructed using a federal grant.

Sewage also creates challenges for Murfreesboro. Based on present usage and growth projections, the sewage system will be overloaded in ten years. A consultant's report recommended a different treatment approach: the use of a less sensitive treatment method for ammonia removal and the conversion of oxygen aeration tanks from their old use for ammonia reduction to use in biochemical oxygen demand (BOD) removal.[16] This would triple the aeration volume. The report also recommended that the city get a ruling from state and federal environmental agencies allowing it to release more effluents.[17] There is already a consent decree in place with automatic fines; the report stated that the limits were set by a computerized model. Real conditions often vary such that the effluent levels vary as well.

Georgetown also faces a problem—tainted water. The community discovered benzene in its water in December 1989. Water from the Royal Spring—the main source of the community's water supply—has not been used since the water was found to be contaminated; the city has been using its second source, North Elkhorn. Water for the Toyota plant is supplied by Kentucky American, a private company. The city is working to find the source of the benzene and then will choose a method of treatment, which will undoubtedly be very expensive and require some construction. The money is expected to come from a depreciation fund initially, but eventually a rate increase will be necessary.

Other Changes

Ensuring that water supplies and sewage facilities are safe and adequate is central to a growth strategy; thus, sewage- and water-related issues often lead to basic questions concerning long-term planning. Consequently, the opening of the auto plants in the four communities has caused each of them "to look at the big picture" in terms of sewage and water. In Columbia, for example, consultants told the planning commission that it needed to assess the city's development fees or the city would experience a revenue shortfall. The Maury County Commission declined to levy development fees, however. In Smyrna, the community's salvation was the fact that the mayor declared that the plant would have to "pay for itself" or not be built there. The federal government underwrote the largest part of the funding for the new sewage plant. Also, the fact that the city owned the gas utility company helped increase the city's revenue. The number of gas customers in Smyrna increased from 962 in 1980 to 2,212 in 1990.

In Georgetown, the plant had its water piped in from Frankfort; however, the contamination of the groundwater supply may prove costly. In many parts of this area, the soil is such that toxic effluents released anywhere within a broad radius will taint the groundwater. Having the plant in the community will mean some changes in the big picture, including a 10 to 13 percent rise in debt, a 2 to 3 percent increase from 1989 to 1990. Georgetown can derive some comfort from its payroll tax since the revenues from it offset the costs of handling the water supply problems. In Marysville, several wells went dry after the plant opened; the city is looking into whether to build a reservoir.

In conclusion, major changes occur in the areas of water and sewage after the opening of automobile plants, including the construction of new facilities or additions to old ones. In the case of the four communities studied, these are not direct effects of the opening of the plants, but they were hastened by it. One of the benefits of such plants is that water capacity is increased beyond the levels the communities require.

PLANNING

Planning was one of the areas in which the greatest change occurred; however, most of the impact was not manifest in the communities' budgets but in the substance of the planning function. Spring Hill experienced the most radical change, followed by Georgetown.

In the communities that had no tradition of planning, the changes usually occurred in the following progression:

1. A form of laissez-faire policy exists, which means there are no zoning restrictions, no building inspections, no fees for building, and no requirements concerning use of the city or county water supply.
2. The first full-time professional planner is hired.
3. A zoning ordinance and/or a planning commission is established. (The notion of planning at this stage is somewhat controversial.)
4. A master plan is written that sets broad goals for the community.
5. Consensus exists among the mayor, council, and city manager regarding the goals of the community.

In the mature stages of this progression, the planning process is no longer controversial, although individual decisions may still evoke controversy.

In this chapter, economic development is treated as a subissue of planning. Alternatively, economic development may be a goal in its own right. Likewise, economic development is a value choice, and one that is often posited as the opposite of preservation. The four communities varied in their acceptance of economic development. Marysville has still not accepted economic development as a goal, although thirteen years have passed since its auto plant was opened. Even in the towns where there is consensus, it is inevitably a fragile one that, as Mark Schneider points out, can quickly evaporate into NIMBYism.[18]

Spring Hill

In Columbia (Spring Hill), the political culture of the relevant bodies—the political elite of the city of Columbia and the Maury County Commission—has not progressed to the mature stages with respect to planning. In Williamson County, however (at least in Franklin, the county seat), planning has evolved to the most mature and professional stage, so that there is a master plan and a consensus on goals and seven staff members are in place. The planning function had been on the books in the city of Columbia and in Maury County since 1978, but it was not until 1987 that a comprehensive ordinance created a planning department. It now has three staff members and twenty to twenty-five items to decide each month.

As part of the package Maury County negotiated with Saturn, money was made available to the community to commission studies on the projected engineering impact of the plant on the community and another on the economic impact. One report recommended a $500 water hookup fee and a $200 charge for sewer, but, as mentioned previously, the community did not approve this action and is thus living with the shortfall.

Columbia's planning department was inundated with requests to which it had to respond. For instance, in 1988, a total of 143 building permits were requested for the city of Columbia, and in 1989, there were 201 requests. This is true of other sites also. The adjacent county, Rutherford County, which is the location of the Smyrna site, experienced a similar trend: it had 215 requests for permits in 1989 and 293 in 1990. (The tax rate rose from $1.00 in 1988 to $1.30 in 1989 to $1.55 in 1990.) Most of the Spring Hill respondents concurred with the consultants' conclusion that the in-lieu-of-tax payments were falling short and forcing the community to raise taxes. Although the situation in Spring Hill cries out for the creation of a comprehensive plan, its politicians have still not agreed that it would be valuable.

At the same time, many changes have taken place. The comprehensive plan in 1987 included efforts at setting up a countywide planning function; it called for community development, consideration of levying impact fees, and tighter codes. Four major goals were established for the county and city. The first goal was to establish a comprehensive ordinance, which occurred in 1987. The second was to establish a countywide planning department to supplement the city of Columbia planning department. The third was to levy impact fees. The fourth was to tighten codes. Three of these goals were carried out. Only the impact fees were not instituted; the leaders considered them too anti-growth.

The city of Columbia, in the Spring Hill site, is still immature with regard to planning since no greater professionalization and no staff increases have occurred; there is no comprehensive planning department like the Maury County planning department. The more mature sites have also articulated a commitment to economic development in their comprehensive plans and have hired an economic development promoter. Spring Hill handles these economic development activities through the Maury County and Williamson County Chambers of Commerce.

Also included in the Spring Hill area is the city of Franklin, the county seat of Williamson, and here the planning activity tells a different story. A bedroom community for Nashville and Spring Hill, Franklin is a favorite community for Saturn executives, as is another area of the county known as Brentwood. The growth rate is among the highest in the state— 7 to 8 percent a year. In 1980, the population was 12,407; in 1989, it was 21,750.

Planning efforts have increased tremendously over the past decade or so in Franklin, which in 1978 had a one-person department and no zoning laws. As of 1990, the department had seven full-time professionals. In 1980, a twenty-year plan was drawn up, and in 1985 a zoning plan was written; in 1987, a planning and zoning ordinance was passed, the first in fifty years. In 1989, a long-term land-use plan was written. Considerable time and effort were spent in developing a computerized land-use and tax map to gather and keep data as accurately as possible.

Unlike Columbia, there is a strong consensus on planning goals in Franklin. The first of its economic development goals is to attract small businesses or light industry, primarily to generate property taxes for schools. (The current taxes are $2.15 per $100, substantially higher than nearby counties.) Another goal is to decrease the number of persons in multiunit dwellings from four out of ten to three out of ten. A large fraction of the county lives in trailer parks. Another goal is to increase historic preservation. Residents take pride in Franklin's historic village square and well-preserved downtown. The final goal is to increase recreational facilities.

In Williamson County, the Saturn plant was only one of three new factors contributing to the town's growth. In fact, in Franklin's comprehensive plan, Saturn is looked upon as having doubtful impact, although 38 percent of the plant's employees live in Williamson County. Specifically, a large proportion of Saturn's executives live in the affluent Brentwood neighborhood of Williamson County.

Unlike many other government units, Franklin does not favor annexation of the Saturn plant or any other large industrial facility because it would entail a costly upgrade of services on the annexed land in order to meet city standards.

Georgetown

In Georgetown, the opening of the plant necessitated the creation of a planning department. The first full-time planner, jointly funded by the city and the county, was hired after the plant opened. Before that, Georgetown had had a part-time planner who was also a developer and a consultant to other communities. The goal here is controlled growth. Through a survey of the citizens commissioned by the city council, it was discovered that a high proportion of Georgetown's residents ranked historic preservation as a high priority. Roughly the same percentage ranked economic development high. Preservation efforts have succeeded as downtown Georgetown has been designated a Kentucky "Main Street town" and 100 homes and buildings placed on the National Register.

Another goal of Georgetown's citizens was to protect farmland, particularly where it abutted a subdivision. A recent planning issue involved a farmer whose land lay adjacent to an apartment complex who claimed his animals had become ill after eating from the complex's dumpster. He tried to block another development unless it had a border hedge of bushes.

Georgetown has a well-established, professional, and thorough procedure for the approval of plans. The full-time planner, whose degree is from the University of California at Berkeley and who was hired following a national search, designed the approval process. It takes six weeks and involves an early and expeditious review for compliance with technical criteria to give feedback and guidance to developers. The advent of this first full-time planner is directly linked to the coming of the plant.

The citizens of Georgetown have not completely made the transition to valuing professional planning. Planning decisions are still controversial, and there is mumbling and grumbling among some members of the community over whether the standards for approval regarding development are too strict, particularly concerning the details of landscaping. Nonetheless, there is an institutionalized planning function, a direct legacy of the opening of the Toyota plant.

The Scott County–City of Georgetown Economic Development Advisory Team issued a report in 1990 that contained recommendations, based on a consensus of opinions of the community's leaders, concerning the economic development process. Many of the recommendations were progressive, even radical. Undoubtedly, the average Georgetown citizen might not concur with all of them, but they did represent what the most progressive members of the elite thought would be the right course of action.

First, the report recommended job creation via job development and diversification of the community's small businesses. The community could not count on another large industry choosing Georgetown. Second, the report recommended protecting the old homes with the "Main Street" designation and making a commitment to improving soil, groundwater, and air quality. Third, the report acknowledged the connection between education and economic development; this link is one many communities take years to recognize. The report recommended making a commitment to improve public education in Kentucky and to upgrade skills and training for all workers in the state. Cited specifically was the link between the state's low education and skill levels and its high unemployment rate. The report also recommended that Georgetown become more aggressive in introducing technology in educational settings, citing the difference between dollars spent in up-to-date business environments versus those spent in classrooms. Establishment of a business-government partnership, to be called the Education Foundation, was also recommended.

The other recommendations were less radical, such as one to develop tourism and to create a favorable climate for business. Finally, the report recommended that the community look aggressively at developing agribusiness, thus building on its agrarian roots.

Marysville

In the remaining two communities, Marysville and Smyrna, planning was not considered important; consequently, it was not as controversial on the whole as in the other two, although particular sitings proved to be controversial, as discussed later. In Marysville, planning took place on a multicounty level, as mandated by an Ohio state law. Any other planning activity was concentrated in the Office of Economic Development and jointly funded by the city and the county. We might conclude that economic development was a widely endorsed goal by the fact that this office existed. The resources to create a position of economic development officer came jointly from the city of Marysville and Union County; the position was created in 1988, however. The officer related that one of her first tasks was to create a catalog of acceptable sites for potential investors; no such listing existed before she assumed the job.

The story of the officer's first big "recruit" illustrates the fragility of her position and how little consensus existed in the community regarding economic development. A client approached her who was interested in locating in Marysville. Since the practice was to guard the identity of the client until all the details were final, the officer kept this information confidential. The client met all the necessary city zoning requirements. Subsequently, the public discovered that the proposed project was a medical waste incinerator. Hand-scrawled signs reading "Stop the Incinerator" sprang up like dandelions all over town. The controversy culminated in a public hearing before the council at which the developer and the economic development officer appeared. In a divided vote, the council passed an ordinance prohibiting medical waste incinerators inside the city limits.

This is a good example of how a pro–economic development philosophy can result in NIMBYism. In fact, individual members of the county commission called for the economic development officer's resignation, a move that would have endangered the whole effort to further economic development. At the time the interviews were conducted, the future of the economic development office was very uncertain. Similarly, there was no consensus about the direction of economic development, except that the officer and some of the city leaders thought a real estate and retail sector development strategy was appropriate. So, even though the goal of economic development as a whole is noncontroversial at this site, the specific economic development siting can and did explode into controversy.

Smyrna

In Smyrna, the planning function was greatly enhanced by an indirect effect of the plant, the emergence of a new type of community leader who strongly supported the value of planning. There are still political undertones to the planning process, for instance, in the way the chief planner is chosen; however, planning is now overseen by three professionals and a clerical worker rather than by one person as in the past. Further, the community seems to have reached a consensus concerning its major goals, which are to provide affordable housing, provide traffic signalization, enhance recreation, enforce zoning and building codes, increase revenue, maintain roads, and solve the landfill problem.

Smyrna consists of three constituent parts, each with its own distinct revenue profile: Smyrna, Murfreesboro, and Rutherford County. Because the town annexed and owns the gas company, Smyrna is managing to bring in considerable revenue. Murfreesboro did not get a cut of the in-lieu-of-tax payments but did absorb a large proportion of new residents. Consequently, it is reeling from debt. Murfreesboro's plan calls for annexation of additional land, and thus an additional tax base, as the top priority. Rutherford County's fiscal situation is best described as being neither as deeply in debt as Murfreesboro nor as rich as Smyrna.

Revenue is not the only problem planners face in the Smyrna area. Rutherford County has major landfill problems. The character of the soil is such that if toxic wastes are dumped, they seep into the groundwater. It is expected that soon the landfill will be full and then the communities in the county will have to go farther away and pay more to dump. Attempts are also being made to work out arrangements to merge into one large utility district.

Murfreesboro, especially, faces two other problems, the first of which is housing. In the $65,000 to $75,000 range, 60 out of 210 houses in a recently built subdivision had been sold as of 1990. There is a need for housing in other price ranges. The second problem is how to meet the rising demand for development with the existing revenue. This has led Murfreesboro to take four actions: to annex all property possible, to require developers to provide a letter of credit, to try to work out arrangements with utility districts to expand service (not yet achieved as of 1990), and to provide adequate commercial service areas.

In conclusion, we can see that the opening of the plant has shifted planning from a peripheral to a central function. Either the first full-time planner will be hired or the existing planning department in the communities surrounding the site radically expanded. This does not mean that planning will be any less political. Each time a battle is fought over preservation versus growth it takes place in the planning commission, zoning commission, or at city council meetings.

The emergence of planning is an immediate, albeit indirect, effect of the opening of the plant; however, reaching a consensus regarding the appropriate amount and form of economic development will be a much slower process.

PUBLIC WORKS

With respect to the absolute number of dollars allocated for public works, two of the communities have had impressive absolute increases: Spring Hill, which had an elevenfold increase, and Georgetown, where the increase was nearly tenfold. Smyrna, however, had only a modest percentage increase over twelve years; in Marysville, from 1977 to 1991, the percentage declined.

Looking at the percentage increase by year, a pattern becomes apparent. Within one or two years of the announcement that the plant would be opening, there was a jump in all the public works budgets. This is the largest or one of the two largest percentage increases in the series for all sites. Thus, most of the effects on public works budgets were felt between the announcement and the opening rather than in the year of the opening. In terms of the proportionate amount of the total budget allocated for public works (Table 5.1), the budget for each government decreased. We can thus conclude that the opening of the plants resulted not in increases but in decreases in the proportionate amount of the budgets allocated to public works.

Nonetheless, at all four sites, the elite respondents named public works as an area of public administration that was affected by the opening of the plant. The story of the bypass in Georgetown (discussed in more detail in chapter 2) illustrates this point most dramatically. The community thought it needed a bypass; however, the Toyota company did not offer funding since it had access to the interstate by way of a new slip road. Only crosstown commuters and other townspeople would be inconvenienced if there were no bypass. The city of Smyrna fared well because Mayor Sam Ridley, or "Mayor Sam" as he is popularly called, stuck to his guns. Recall that at the negotiating table the company promised to build a bypass. When the company vacillated and threatened to exit for Cartersville, Georgia, the mayor held strong. Smyrna, therefore, did not go into debt to get the road that connects the plant to the interstate. Nor did the state have to pay. Other government units in the Smyrna area, such as Murfreesboro, did not fare as well. There was a pressing need for a ten- to twelve-mile bypass, and in this case the city had to foot the bill for $20 million. It is too early to know all the effects of the plant on Spring Hill, but the state and the plant funded the big-ticket items, so at least Spring Hill, Maury County, and Columbia will not be forced to bear the cost.

In summary, the effects of the plants on public works budgets were neither simple nor uniform. In Smyrna, the company paid for everything. In Georgetown and Murfreesboro, the community had to pay. In Spring Hill, the state and the company together provided what was needed.

We can learn several lessons from these stories. First, from the community's point of view, anything not bargained for in the beginning will be difficult to pay for later. Second, if the state does not deliver on its commitment to construct roads, the community will suffer. Finally, if the company or the state does not agree to pick up the tab for a large public works project or other endeavor, the community will have to endure enormous indebtedness in the years after the plant is opened.

RECREATION

At all the sites except Marysville, the opening of the plant resulted in the opening of a new community recreation facility. And even in Marysville, Honda made an extraordinarily large donation that made it possible for a new YMCA building to be constructed.

In terms of the absolute numbers of dollars spent on recreation, Spring Hill's and Marysville's budgets increased almost threefold, Symrna's thirtyfold, and Georgetown's elevenfold. There was much variation, however, in the percentage increases from year to year. Spring Hill's budget for recreation increased by 60 percent in 1985 (the year of the announcement), Smyrna's by 96 percent in 1981 (the year after the announcement), and Georgetown's by 173 percent in 1987; Marysville's decreased by a whopping 1,121 percent in 1980.

Looking at the proportionate amount of each budget that went for recreation (Table 5.1), we see that, in general, each budget was decreased. In Smyrna and Georgetown, however, the budgets were increased, from 0.17 percent to 5 percent and from 1.5 percent to 3 percent, respectively. One reason may have been the paucity of recreational facilities before the automobile plants were built.

The interviews strongly suggest that recreational initiatives were a priority for the new residents in the communities surrounding the plants. These communities lacked parks, pools, baseball fields, golf courses, and indoor recreational facilities. The opening of the plants changed this.

Spring Hill

The opening of the plant had a great effect on the recreational options available in the communities around Spring Hill, as evidenced by a needs assessment study conducted by the county, which showed the county needed water, nature trails, and parks. Programming needs also were identified—for a softball program, for example. Each year after the plant opened, $250,000 was contributed from the Saturn fund for capital improvements. The new facilities include a pool and a park.

Use of recreational facilities in the county has increased from 200,000 to 300,000 participants, 150,000 at Mule Day alone. Mule Day is the annual summer festival that features awards for best costume and best float, a liar's contest, a pancake breakfast, a mule sale, bluegrass night, mule pulling, a checkers contest, a dance, and the Mule Day parade.

Maury County has not had a new recreation director since the opening of the plant, but there has been a trend toward professionalization of the position. The current staff includes two professionals, four maintenance employees, and one security employee, and the budget grew from $150,000 to $250,000 in the four years from 1985 to 1989.

In the part of Williamson County nearest the Spring Hill site, demands were made for a regional park; a recreational complex, including a crafts area; an indoor pool; and baseball fields. The number of participants using these facilities increased from 10,000 in 1984 to 15,000 in 1985. An estimated 3,900 to 4,000 persons visited the park in 1990. A new park is being developed in Mount Pleasant.

Smyrna

The opening of the Smyrna plant also had a major impact on the recreational opportunities available in the area. New facilities include swimming pools, two at a sports complex and two at other sites; a golf course, built in 1985; and 490 acres of parkland, including four parks and a new sports complex. The sports complex has an annual income of $400,000 through fees. Participation is very high. The newcomers to this site want city-provided programs and are not averse to paying fees.

Georgetown

In Georgetown, the Toyota company donated enough money to purchase a major office and conference facility, Cardome, which it subsequently renovated for use as a city facility. It houses the recreation department, among other departments. Georgetown and Scott County fall within the Bluegrass Development District, which includes sixteen other counties and is composed of land that is 71 percent agricultural, 23 percent forest, and 5 percent urban. Three plans guide Scott County's recreational planning: a 1985 comprehensive plan update prepared by the Scott County Joint Planning Commission; the Statewide Comprehensive Outdoor Recreational Plan (SCORP) of 1984, prepared by the Kentucky Design Assistance Team (KyDat) on the Georgetown–Scott County area; and the Master Plan for Park Facilities for Georgetown–Scott County Parks Department. These were included in a report that assessed community recreational needs. The report recommended that seven new parks be built and that funding be allocated for activities such as golf, tennis, baseball, camping, picnicking, fishing, boating, water-skiing, hunting, and swimming. The report suggested that if the community was unable to construct swimming pools, residents be allowed to use a local motel or other private facility. The report recommended increasing programming for the elderly.

The report also recommended building fourteen tennis courts, five baseball fields, five softball fields, five volleyball facilities, five horseshoe facilities, one football field, two soccer fields, one community center, two shuffleboard courts, and two croquet courts.[19] The current population base is 26,000, but the department has only one public pool. Using all three standard ways of averaging need, Georgetown–Scott County has too few pools per person.[20] Currently, the recreation department employs five full-time employees, including a dynamic and energetic director. Programs include dance, soccer, baseball, youth softball, adult softball, football, volleyball, basketball, tennis, swimming, a playground program, a special population day, canoeing, road races, fitness, biking, and racquetball.

Marysville

In Marysville, the new YMCA filled the area's recreational needs. The new building would not have been built had it not been for the contribution from Honda.

In conclusion, it should be noted that at the outset of this study the areas of largest impact were expected to be sewage, water, and education. It turns out that one of the greatest impacts of the plant has been on recreation. Interestingly, the original residents either had not been clamoring for more recreation or had been content with less organized, less spectator-oriented recreation, such as hunting and fishing. The influx of new workers and subdivisions led to major new recreational facilities and a great increase in programming.

WELFARE

It was expected that welfare budgets would be affected by the opening of the plant, especially early in the cycle of development. Astronomical increases occurred in the absolute number of dollars spent on welfare. The anecdote from the director of a chamber of commerce recounted in chapter 1 illustrates the immediacy of the effects: itinerant job seekers from California were already camped out in front of the chamber of commerce office in Williamson County, the next county over from the Saturn plant, on the Monday after the announcement that the plant would open, five years before work was available.

Once the construction phase is completed, we might expect the size of the group of job seekers to decrease; however, it was predicted based on previous research on "boom towns" that frustrated job seekers, some of them temporary construction workers, would settle more or less permanently in the area, putting a drain on the welfare system. Thus, it appears that welfare rolls are likely to swell in the period between the announcement and the opening of the plant.

Regarding the proportionate amount of the total budget spent on welfare (Table 5.1), we see that there was a moderate jump in Spring Hill and a decrease over time in Smyrna. The numbers soared in Georgetown. There was an upsurge in the proportionate amount of the budget spent on welfare in the year the plant opened and a drop the following year. Unlike Spring Hill, the proportion did not increase dramatically just after the announcement. In Marysville, unlike the other sites, an upturn was reported in the proportionate amount spent on welfare in 1983, four years after the opening.

Looking at the percentage increase spent on welfare by year, we see a clear and dramatic picture emerge at Spring Hill in the year following the announcement of the plant opening. Interviews with law enforcement, social services, and governmental officials confirmed that job seekers and construction workers swarmed into nearby communities. The percentage increase—18,471 percent—was especially large when one realizes it had been zero.

The patterns in Smyrna and Georgetown also show an upward surge after the announcement and before the opening. In Marysville, there were much bigger increases around the time of the announcement than after the opening. Combined with interview and unemployment information, these data led to the conclusion that the overall economic well-being of the Marysville area has improved greatly since the coming of the plant. It is also the case that, as one of the early sites for plants built by Japanese firms, Marysville did not attract the publicity that Spring Hill did and thus avoided the influx of outside job seekers.

The picture that emerged from the interviews was that there were no permanent welfare-related changes in the communities. In fact, although it is federally funded, welfare is a state function, so that local communities are not terribly involved. But, consistent with the idea that there is cycle of development, changes in welfare demands occurred just after the announcement or between the announcement and the opening and leveled off by the end of the cycle. These changes, caused by the influx of job seekers and construction workers, were temporary and evened out by the end of the cycle. Spring Hill, however, where little had been offered in the way of welfare before the plant, saw a dramatic increase in the number of its welfare recipients.

CRIMINAL JUSTICE

Looking at the absolute numbers spent on criminal justice, we see that there was an enormous increase at Spring Hill, Smyrna (until 1989), Georgetown, and Marysville. Percentage increases varied, with many ups and downs, but seemed to occur as a direct result of the announcement of the plant. In Smyrna, the percentage increases in the criminal justice budget were modest and consistent; in Marysville, by contrast, there were moderate to large percentage increases associated with the plant opening each year.

In Spring Hill (Table 5.1), no portion of the budget was spent on criminal justice in 1987, and the proportion rose to only 0.67 percent in 1989. In Smyrna, criminal justice represented 1 percent of the budget in 1977; it dipped slightly to 0.4 percent in 1990, after having risen to 1.25 percent in 1989.

In Georgetown, the proportion of the budget spent on criminal justice was 1.8 percent in 1981, after which it declined each year to 1.5 percent. It increased again, to 6.3 percent, in 1989 and to a high of 10 percent in 1988; thus, overall, there was an increase of 4.5 percent in the proportion of the budget allocated for criminal justice. In Marysville, the proportionate amount went from 0 percent in 1976 to 16 percent in 1991.

SUMMARY

The plants have had major public administration impacts, including the professionalization of all functions, the upgrading of ISO ratings, the investment in new trucks, equipment, and buildings for police and fire, the increase in recreation programming and facilities, enhancement in sewage capacity, and problems with water supply. These developments constitute major institutional changes and, as such, set the agenda for these communities. They also take place throughout the entire cycle of development, with many important flurries of activity occurring just after the announcement rather than after the opening. One other major and irreversible change is the legitimization of the planning function in the communities.

6 | Impact of the Plants on the Communities' Quality of Education

DURING the initial field visit, it became apparent that changes in education were among the most important developments in the communities studied; what was surprising, however, was how the schools were affected. Before the interviews with the elite, the chief issue for the schools was expected to be expanded enrollments, which would create pressure in three ways: by increasing the need for more staff, by increasing the need for new facilities, and by straining the finances of the school system. Pressure would occur because the influx of the new population associated with the plant would arrive before the community could collect additional revenue from property and income taxes.

But other changes occurred that were not predicted, for instance, in the curriculum. Sometimes the changes took the form of simple requests, such as for more music and art classes. At other times they called for a redefinition of the educational mission. In Georgetown, a vocational and technical school was conceived and built by Toyota (TMM) and the school district jointly. Another major change in the communities was in financing. Each school district must finance the additional staff to service the new staff and curriculum.

In addition, the plants affected the communities in more fundamental ways by getting education on state policy agendas. Georgetown is the best example because here the plant established education as the top item on the political agenda, leading to the biggest educational reform package in a hundred years. In a similarly radical transformation, the opening of the plants brought home the value of education for the people in these rural counties. To get a job at the plant, one's literacy level had to be higher than that of the average dropout. Finally, there was an economic incentive for obtaining an education.

A challenge of studying the impact of the auto plants on the educational systems of these communities is that there is a great degree of fragmentation in school administration. This is because school districts do not correspond to geopolitical jurisdictions, such as cities and counties; therefore, each site contains multiple school districts. This multiplicity is aggravated by two factors: the vast impact area and the fact that many small cities have an elementary school–only district and fold high school students into a larger district. Thus, there is no one-to-one correspondence between school districts and geopolitical units in the United States. For each site it was necessary to examine several school districts and summarize the main trends at that site. The data by district are available upon request from the author. What was found was that, with only a couple of variations, all the sites had common experiences.

ENROLLMENT

Smyrna. The districts for which data were gathered at the Smyrna site were Murfreesboro (the county seat of Rutherford County) and the Rutherford County system. Interviews with the superintendent confirmed the opinions of other community leaders that the middle Tennessee area had been experiencing steady growth, not all of which was due to the Nissan plant. Caution must therefore be exercised in inferring that all enrollment growth was plant-related. Both districts at the Smyrna site, Rutherford and Murfreesboro, had 48 percent rates of increase during the impact period.

In Murfreesboro, the superintendent had gathered data that made it possible to say with greater certainty how much growth was due to an increase in birth rate and how much was probably plant-related. The superintendent's study showed that of 250 new students, 50 might have been added because of the increase in birth rate. Thus, 20 percent of the increase was because of birth rate and 80 percent was because of growth. Other studies show that 60 to 70 percent of the increase was due to birth rate. Interpolating, then, these school systems would have increased by 6 percent and 9.6 percent, respectively, due to birth rate. Making a bold assumption that all other growth was plant-related, a 24 percent and a 38.4 percent increase could be attributed to the plant, respectively. Other studies have shown that 60 percent of the increase in enrollment is due to the birth rate, meaning that at the Smyrna site the plant accounted for enrollment increases of 18 to 25 percent.

Georgetown. There is only one school district at the Georgetown site— the Scott County School District, a city-county consolidated district. For the four years from 1985 to 1989, enrollment in the Scott County schools increased by 15 percent. The biggest single annual increase—9 percent—occurred between 1988 and 1989. Since the plant opened in 1988, this strongly suggests that the opening was the biggest cause of the increases in enrollment. Before the plant, there was only 1 percent growth per year. Thus, of the 15 percent cumulative increase in growth, 14 percent was due to the plant opening at this site.

Marysville. From one point of view, Marysville is the most complex site because it has four school districts: the Marysville Exempted School District, in the city of Marysville; the Fairbanks School District, in the southwest section of Union County; North Union schools, which includes part of Union County; and the Benjamin Logan School District, in Logan County. From another point of view, it is the simplest site because each district tells the same story of a statewide trend toward declining enrollments.

The Marysville Exempted School District reported a zero percent increase due to the plant. The Fairbanks enrollment dipped 49 percent over the impact period; North Union District had a minuscule increase of 5 percent over this period; and Benjamin Logan had a 4 percent decrease over the same period. Therefore, at the Marysville site as a whole the enrollment effects due to the plant were nil.

Spring Hill. Of the workforce at the Spring Hill site, approximately 30 percent live in Maury County and about 30 percent live in Williamson County. Maury County has one school district, and Williamson County has two. The county seat and largest town in Williamson (Franklin) includes the Franklin Special School District (kindergarten to ninth grade) and the Williamson County District, which oversees the higher grades.[1]

It was estimated that each Saturn employee had 1.6 children and that approximately 33 percent of the Saturn employees lived in Maury County in 1990.[2] The total original projected workforce size was 5,000, and approximately 33 percent of that number equals about 1,667. That figure times 1.6 yields 2,672 people; however, only 1,500 new pupils were enrolled up until 1990. Thus, the actual figure was not as high as one might have expected. It should be noted that in 1990, when the measurement was taken, the plant workforce was not as large as had been anticipated.

Another factor also influenced this district. The state of Tennessee had mandated a change in class size to a target of 23, down from the previously mandated average of 26 for lower elementary schools, a target of 25 to 26 for upper elementary schools, and a limit of 30 for high schools.

The total increase in enrollment in the Maury County schools from 1985 to 1991 was 2,420, a 27 percent change. The other school system in the impact area, Franklin Special School District (Williamson County), estimated that as of January 1990, just 225 of its 33,500 pupils were identifiably children of Saturn employees. The projection was that there would be a full 480 such pupils by January 1991. The superintendent credited the growth of the school enrollment to four factors, only one being the Saturn plant. The other three were the opening of an American Airlines facility nearby, the attractiveness of Franklin County, and the low unemployment rate.[3]

FACILITIES

Smyrna. After the plant opened, it was necessary to build two new schools in Murfreesboro. In 1987, a $7 million school for a thousand pupils opened; in 1990, another new school opened for another thousand pupils at the same cost.

Georgetown. Facility improvements completed during the impact period included a $2.7 million renovation of Garth Elementary School; a $1 million renovation of Georgetown Middle School; a $1 million renovation of Scott County Middle School; and construction, for $3.5 million, of Northern Elementary School. The major facility that has been added is Scott County Technical School.

Marysville. In terms of physical facilities, in 1990 the Marysville Exempted School District had to put on a new tax levy to raise the needed $14 million for a new high school. The Fairbanks School District has not needed extra facilities over the impact period. In fact, two new buildings were sold. In the North Union schools, no new physical facilities were built during the impact period, but in 1985 the junior high was remodeled. In the Benjamin Logan School District, changes took the form of plans to open a magnet elementary school in the former middle school by 1991–92. The intended focus of the magnet school was math and science.

Spring Hill. Two factors besides Saturn caused the need for more facilities at Spring Hill: the state-mandated order that class sizes be smaller and the mandate for special education classes, which have only three to fifteen children.[4] A new elementary school was built in the fall of 1990, with there being a need for two other schools. The community was scheduled to build a new high school before the Saturn announcement. Saturn donated forty acres of land for a new high school in Maury County; this high school was built between the announcement and the opening of the plant.

The Franklin Special School District was remodeled and expanded in 1984. In 1986, a new elementary school was built for $3.8 million. Two other buildings were constructed: an elementary school, which opened in the fall of 1990, and another school for the northern part of the district, which opened later. The total cost of the two schools was $6.2 million. There is also a $2 million bond for a Franklin middle school conversion and renovation. These projects total $12 million in bonds.[5]

In the Williamson County schools, six new buildings were erected since 1984. The superintendent did not attribute all these changes to Saturn, stating that other growth factors—the new American Airlines facility in Nashville and a planned new beltway and shopping center—could also be responsible. In the Murfreesboro schools, there is a much clearer connection between the plant and the changes.

STAFFING

Smyrna. In Murfreesboro and Rutherford County districts, major increases in staffing occurred over the impact period. The teacher to pupil ratio in Murfreesboro was 22 for kindergarten through third grade, 22 for fourth grade, and 23 for fifth and sixth grades, compared with state-mandated ratios of 25, 28, and 30, respectively.

Georgetown. Twin demands were caused by increases in enrollment and the establishment of Scott County Technical School, the latter putting more staff demands on the high school. From 1985 to 1989, the number of teachers rose from 242 to 280, a cumulative increase of 16 percent over five years. Further, a qualitative change took place in the type of superintendent who was in charge. Previous superintendents had been good old boys, whereas the current superintendent is a highly professional person with excellent credentials who was recruited from outside the state and the region.

Marysville. There has been an increase in the Marysville Exempted School District of 23 staff over the thirteen-year impact period, or an average of 1.6 staff per year. The Fairbanks School District is in the process of adding 2.5 more staff persons. The North Union District went from 80 persons at the beginning of the impact period to 90, an increase of about 8 percent. But even more than the opening of the Honda plant, the state's changing requirements are putting great demands on school staff. This was reported across the four Ohio school districts.[6]

Staff increases during the impact period have been linked to changes in the state's curriculum requirements. In fact, enrollments in these districts have been declining.

Spring Hill. In Maury County, the projection is that there will be an increase in staff as a result of the opening of the new elementary school; however, another important factor may be the state law mandating smaller class sizes and special education classes. From 1985 to 1989, a total of 132 new positions were created in Williamson County schools.[7]

One interesting feature of the district is that the superintendent is now an elected official. Neither educational experience nor a Ph.D. in education is a requirement for the position. The election of a superintendent is considered an extremely unreformed method of selection of a supervisor. Usually the local school board appoints a superintendent from qualified candidates after a merit-based countrywide search. It is more common for a superintendent to have a Ph.D. in education or administration and extensive teaching experience. The current superintendent has a master's degree in business and primarily a business background.

According to the superintendent, the Franklin Special School District has hired ten new teachers. Upgrading is occurring throughout Tennessee, and the state is requiring in-service training. The new elementary training center will house ninety teachers.

CURRICULUM

Smyrna. In Murfreesboro, the superintendent described the Nissan parents as supportive and said that they have brought a new optimism to the schools. There have been few curricular changes attributable directly to the Nissan parents except an Extended School Program (ESP) for children of working parents.

Most of the innovative curricular changes that have occurred in the Smyrna area involve the Rutherford County schools. Many new programs have been started since 1979, including programs in drug education, teacher support, English as a second language, preschool parenting, peer counseling, in-school suspension, dropout prevention, alternative schools, elementary guidance, Skills Training for Enhanced Potential (STEP), Adopt-a-School, the Business Education Partnership (Rutherford County Chamber of Commerce), a program for gifted students, and a shadowing program (a mentoring program whereby a professional at Nissan acts as a role model for high school students).[8]

The STEP program is sponsored by Nissan. It involves after-school vocational training sessions for high school students at the Nissan Training Center. It allows them to study hydraulics, pneumatics, programmable controls, and robotics for academic credit. STEP has been cited by national and state educational officials as a model program and was nominated as Tennessee's entry for the best program for national recognition in vocational education.

The Business Education Partnership, begun in 1989, has spearheaded some curricular changes. Sponsored by the Rutherford County Chamber of Commerce, it is designed to "promote and support innovative collaborative programs to foster a better understanding of both education and business concerns." Its first award went to the Nissan Corporation for the advancement of science education. Corporate contributions have been used to buy science films for Rutherford County schools. Finally, Nissan has had an impact on curriculum and on revenues through such generous donations as a fleet of Nissan Sentras to the drivers education program.

Georgetown. The Georgetown site's curriculum has changed in two dramatic ways. A 30 percent increase occurred in the number of people applying for GEDs through the Scott County–Georgetown consolidated schools because, according to the interviews, many locals failed the literacy part of the plant's employment requirements. In addition, a vocational school (Scott County Technical School) was opened. Its mission is to prepare the citizens of Scott County for employment and to provide employers in a multicounty area of central Kentucky with trained employees. To achieve this, a curriculum had to be designed to meet the needs of both the students and local employers.[9]

The school, which is designed to serve both secondary and post-secondary students from several counties, will be located adjacent to Scott County High School. Funding will come from state and local sources. There will be an attempt to avoid duplication in the curriculums, and the school will meet state accreditation standards. The school will provide both generic training and specific skills building, with an emphasis on high technology. The target population served by the technical school will include: regular high school students; "at-risk" high school students; undereducated adults who lack a high school diploma or need basic academic and technical skills to be employable; and unqualified adults who have career aspirations for certain jobs but lack the requisite training.[10]

The technical school will address both students' and employers' needs. The students, many of whom are dropouts, require the academic and technical skills that will make them employable. As laid out in the curriculum design report, the need for technicians to repair and maintain machines seems especially critical in a high-technology environment; students will therefore be required to have generic skills and the ability to learn on the job.

Employers will continue to need workers skilled in accounting, general clerical skills, data and word processing, and secretarial skills, as well as in drafting, electricity, electronics, mechanical, and maintenance jobs. Computer skills and general education are necessary for employment in this new era.[11] Thus, high school and postsecondary education courses will include computer application, science, math, supervision, English, and leadership training.

The establishment of a technical school is a major step for the Georgetown community. Combined with the opening of the plant and the concomitant job opportunities, it will mean, in the words of one respondent, "There's something to keep our children here."

Marysville. One of the communitywide innovations since the opening of the Honda plant is the International Family Center, a pleasant meeting place where Japanese and Americans can share their cultures. It is not run by the schools but was mentioned in the superintendent's interview as an educational resource for the community. Curriculum areas that have been added as a result of the plant are English as a second language and a latchkey program. Other developments have come about because of changes in the state law. Also, a superintendent's advisory committee, the Business Advisory Committee, has been established to address curricular issues and requirements.

The major identifiable curricular changes in the Fairbanks School District have been the addition of drug programs and the opening of a vocational school. As the district becomes more populated with two-career families and more blue-collar workers, as noted by the superintendent, the need for day care has grown. Sixty percent of the students in this district go on to college.

In the Benjamin Logan District, the main change in curriculum is a new focus on math and science and on computer literacy. No major changes were made to the curriculum in the North Union District. A drug awareness program was started, but it was unrelated to Honda's opening its plant. A young authors program was begun with help from Honda.

Spring Hill. The process of change has just begun in Spring Hill, but the large influx of people from outside the area is bound to result in changes in the school system. Initially, people begin to serve on school boards and to become active in civic affairs. Some newcomers are already involved in parent-teacher organizations. The expectation is that over the long haul the newcomers will become a source of school-related expertise.

A survey taken among parents of children in the Maury County schools showed general satisfaction with the curriculum. Although Saturn employees come from forty-five states, 40 percent are from Michigan. There was some dissatisfaction among the migrants with arts, music, speech, and extracurricular physical education activities. Tennessee does not fund the arts. They are considered an "extra," particularly in the elementary schools.[12]

According to the superintendent of the Franklin Special School District, no great curricular changes have occurred since Saturn opened its plant because the curriculum is already "progressive"; however, the district is considering two innovations due to the new growth spurt. The first is to institute a program called Before and After School Care (BASK). The second is to initiate year-long school combined with BASK and a new recreation program. If there were year-long school, there would be 180 days of classes and four tracks. Each student would have forty-five learning days followed by fifteen days off. The recreation department would bus the children back and forth on their days off. The number of children that could be accommodated is four tracks' worth, but staff would be needed for three tracks since at any given time one track of children would be in the recreation program.

The superintendent cited three advantages to year-round school. It reduces total teaching staff through longer work years or, more precisely, it stabilizes it even when there is increased enrollment. Second, it prevents burnout. And third, students who are deficient in their studies can use the recreational break for remedial instruction.

A specified grant approach is used to facilitate new resources for innovations in curriculum. This program was used to set up science laboratories, for example. This new program was chartered in 1988 and is headed by Harold Pryer, president emeritus of a local community college. It will support such resources as mini-grants for teachers and recognition awards.

Williamson County. The superintendent defers to an advisory board for suggestions or demands concerning the curriculum. There have been demands for more music and art classes in the public schools and particularly for teachers trained in these two areas.

A recent innovation is the Before and After School Care (BASK) program, which was begun in the fall of 1990. Through this program, the school provides day care at the school on a fee basis for the children of working parents. The idea for the program came from a mother who approached the superintendent. What began as a volunteer pilot program has now become a permanent paid service staffed by district employees.[13]

FINANCES

Usually plants place new obligations on community schools in the form of capital expenditures for facilities, new staff, and curricular changes; however, incoming revenue often offsets these outlays indirectly through increases in property taxes as a result of higher property values and directly as a result of in-lieu-of-tax payments made to the communities by the company and earmarked for the schools. In addition, there is normally an increase in property values of at least 30 percent in the wake of the plant opening that reaps revenue without a tax rate increase. The picture is further complicated because, using various formulas, the amount received in increased local funding will cause a proportionate decrease in the state's funding.

One superintendent complained that his constituents expect too much. He stated that when citizens read in the paper that the company has contributed a certain amount to the school district, they expect a tax decrease. Another superintendent claimed that the public needs some education on this point. It needs to understand, for instance, that a 5 percent inflation factor in a budget means an additional $600,000 is necessary to provide the same programs and services.[14]

Another factor that determines a school district's finances is whether the district is predominantly residential or industrial. Many jurisdictions zone with an eye to preserving a suburban character only to have their school districts discover that it takes many houses to equal one industry's tax contribution.[15] A final factor is the escalation in real estate prices itself. Although the rise may result in more property taxes with no increase in the tax rate, the increase in prices is a two-edged sword. The effect of real estate speculation is that the district often reels under the weight of new land purchases because the district must buy property at the new higher price.

Smyrna. Murfreesboro did not get any in-lieu-of-tax support directly from Nissan, just its share of Rutherford County's. Of the total Murfreesboro budget, 56.9 percent comes from local sources, 5 percent comes from federal budgets, and 37.7 percent comes from state sources.[16] The state's proportionate contribution to Murfreesboro is a different story. It dipped slightly from 40.5 percent to 39.9 percent over the eleven-year period from 1975 to 1989. Looking at Rutherford County, the total revenue figure for the schools increased by 228 percent from 1978 to 1989. Significantly, state contributions declined over this period—to 47.8 percent in 1989.

Georgetown. The annual budget for Scott County schools was $8 million in 1985. By 1989, it had risen to $12 million. It is worthwhile to examine the breakdown of the incentive package.[17] As mentioned in chapter 2, a substantial amount of money went for training. Out of a total package of $125 million, some went to site improvement, some to a planning center, and $61 million in state, federal, or local money went to training.

Marysville. Seventy percent of the funds for Marysville Exempted School District comes from real estate taxes.[18] The average state expenditure is $3,800 per pupil. Of this amount, the state aid per pupil is $2,700. Marysville averages $4,000 per pupil, so it is slightly above the state average. There is $12 million in the budget, of which $8 million is Honda-related. Four million dollars is directly Honda-related; however, this is a gross, not a net, figure.[19] In addition, the Honda Foundation has supported the Marysville Exempted School District. According to educational administrators, Honda has also been a good citizen and has helped the schools. It has also contributed money to establish a day care center.

The financial base for the North Union District at the Marysville site increased from $3.5 million in 1977 to $6.5 million in 1990. The Benjamin Logan District experienced a hefty increase of 20 percent in 1980–81. During most of the years between 1977 and 1986, there were double-digit increases. The amount of revenue projected to come from Honda to this district by October 1991 was $2.5 million. This is a gross, not a net, figure since the state's contribution to the district will be reduced proportionately to the gain in local revenues, according to the state's foundation formula, or school funding formula. Only Fairbanks reported no revenue or other impact as a result of the plant. In the future, the Benjamin Logan District and other government units will expect to see some revenue from Honda. In 1994 and 1995, the abatement ceases, so taxes will begin to flow in.

The single most consequential education-related effect at this site was reported by the North Union District, in which the percentage of college-bound students dipped from 60 percent to 35 percent from 1979 to 1980 and then went back to 60 percent within a year. It appeared for a short time in this district that human capital theory was being refuted: instead of future workers staying in school to increase their human capital, they left school in pursuit of high-paying factory jobs.

With the exception of Fairbanks, the plant had a generally positive impact on the finances of the districts surrounding Marysville. This positive financial picture, combined with steady or declining enrollments, meant local schools had more resources to fulfill their needs and were not stretched to the maximum by burgeoning enrollments.

Spring Hill. Revenue from sales taxes went up during the period while the plant was being constructed. In 1990, the city of Columbia proposed a tax rate increase. The revenue in 1984–85 was $15 million; in 1989–90, it was $30 million.[20] All the school district superintendents reported that

Saturn kept them informed of the numbers of employees who had children so they could plan for the increase in enrollment.

The Maury County schools had an increase in revenue of 95 percent during the impact period. According to the superintendent, no money was earmarked for education in the in-lieu-of-tax revenue received from Saturn. Saturn contributed a forty-acre site for a new high school and leased the school district an additional ten acres for $1. The company also donates resources through the Adopt-a-School program.

Real estate speculation is raising costs for the Spring Hill site (particularly Maury County). If real estate prices escalate by 30 percent or more of their original price, what happens when a school district needs to purchase land to accommodate swelling enrollments? This dilemma was illustrated by an example given in a superintendent's interview. Land was purchased for $5,000 in 1980, but when the district needed to buy just one acre in 1989, it cost $40,000. This made Saturn's gift of the forty-acre piece of land for the high school very important.

In Williamson County, a 27 percent increase in enrollment occurred over the impact period; however, since employees were just beginning to arrive in 1990, the increases may be even greater over time. A sampling from 1989 revenue sources illustrates that revenue from county taxes represents approximately half the county's total revenue. No revenue has accrued from licenses or permits. State education funds amount to almost half the total budget; other state revenues, charges for current services, and local revenues amount to an inconsequential fraction of the total of $31,943,039. Also, $469,632 of federal funds is received through the state, as is $9,000 in direct federal revenues.

Because of its special legal and statutory status, the Franklin Special School District is in a unique situation; it is empowered to either reduce or raise the tax rate. The revenue sources for this district are property taxes, city special school taxes, and county taxes. Thus, the district has a degree of autonomy in its finances that is not typical. Overall, the budget for education for this site nearly doubled from 1983 to 1989. One can see that city/special district taxes represent one-third of this budget. Both amounts are substantially smaller, however, than the state's $4,040,146 proportion of the education budget. In terms of debt, a total of $12 million was incurred in the form of bonds being floated for new buildings. This helps put this reserve figure in perspective.

The site's financial picture is therefore complicated and difficult to summarize. Usually more revenue flows in after a plant opens. Although this revenue makes a large contribution to operating expenses, capital expenses such as construction of new buildings are the biggest single financial encumbrance. The money for these is raised by floating a bond or by raising a tax levy—in other words, by going directly to the voters.

AGENDA SETTING

At all four sites, other changes that occurred during the impact period affected the quality of and budgets allocated for education. In Tennessee, for example, state laws changed, affecting class size, and in Ohio, curricular changes went into effect. Nonetheless, in each case, the plant seems to have had an independent, irreversible, and important effect on education. Kentucky is the best example. It moved toward instituting the "biggest educational reform package in one hundred years," according to a University of Kentucky scholar and observer of the local scene. The plant was credited with spawning it.[21]

In short, the opening of the plants put education on the public's mind and on political agendas, as a result of a changed public attitude toward the importance of education. Education took on new value in the eyes of the citizenry. When the Toyota plant opened in Kentucky, it was flooded with applicants who were high school dropouts. These applicants had been convinced that there was no return to staying in school; however, now an education made the difference between being hired and not being hired by Toyota. There was a 30 percent surge in Georgetown–Scott County registration for GED classes in one year. The governor who succeeded Governor Collins and the legislature became convinced that the state needed a strong educational system either because of the value of education for its own sake or as an economic development tool.

In Kentucky, the plant genuinely set the educational agenda not just for the county, the city, or the region but for the entire state. After Toyota opened a plant in their state, the link between education and economic development became clear to the public and to political leaders.

This phenomenon did not occur uniformly, however. In Marysville, for example, the scene was played out quite differently. Before the plant opened, it was assumed by the public that one had to go to college to get a high-paying job, and about 60 percent of the high school graduates went on to college. When the auto plant opened, however, the young people quickly learned that employees without college degrees were earning eighteen dollars an hour. Consequently, the percentage of the district's high school graduates who went on to college dropped to 35 percent. As of 1990, the figure was back up to 60 percent. This was clearly an unintended effect of the plant. In Marysville, the effect of the plant appeared to be in the opposite direction from that in Georgetown and the other sites.

In Murfreesboro, already a university town, cultural center, and bustling tourist area, the plant did not have the pronounced effect on agenda setting in education that it did at Georgetown. For example, in Murfreesboro, the plant may have been more of an influence on business-educational partnership efforts and vocational programs at the site. Of course, the other factor in Tennessee was the state law mandating class size limits.

SUMMARY

Education is one of the areas most affected when a new plant opens in a community. There is usually an increase in enrollment, however, with no extra revenue, unless the district is considered within the impact area and has negotiated in-lieu-of-tax payments. At three of the four sites, enrollments burgeoned. Such radical increases put these sites in a triple pincer: not enough space, not enough staff, and no revenue yet. Only the Marysville, Ohio, site experienced drops in enrollment, and these were part of a state trend.

The building of new facilities probably poses the biggest problem to districts because new structures require long-term capital investments. Since taxes are abated, concerned districts should negotiate in-lieu-of-tax payments at the front end to cover the increases in enrollment.

The most momentous change heralded in this chapter was that the citizens of these communities "discovered" the value of education. This was driven by a recognition of the link between economic development and education. To quote an economic development report, "Scott County's Economy in Transition": "Basic skills are the basic development issue."[22] Citing a national trend, the report states that high school graduates increasingly do not have the literacy skills required for most jobs. Only 25 percent of new entrants into the job market will be qualified for three-quarters of the new jobs.[23] The report states that 90 percent of the applicants to Lexington Community College, for example, must take remedial math courses and 40 percent must take remedial reading and writing.[24] Furthermore, local employers have reported that Scott County high school graduates lack both the literacy and socialization skills necessary to hold down a job.[25]

Another challenge to the community is that nationally jobs require higher credentials; whereas literacy once meant the ability to add, subtract, and read, it now means the ability to solve problems. Jobs that once required a sixth-grade education now require a high school degree; those once requiring a high school degree now demand college or advanced professional degrees. As Reich points out, workers with college or advanced professional degrees are being hired for the good-paying jobs, exemplified in the extreme by the salaries of jobs requiring symbolic-analytical skills—that is, a combination of "technical, problem-solving and communication skills" not traditionally part of Scott County's economy.

Rural areas historically have venerated manual labor, such as farm or factory work, over academic or cerebral work, which was viewed as a luxury. The opening of the auto plants jolted the citizenry in these rural communities into rethinking this attitude. This excerpt from the Scott County report citing Peter Drucker's 1977 quotation exemplifies the change: "The substitution of knowledge for manual effort as the productive resource in work is the greatest change in the history of work, which is, of course, a process as old as man himself. Education has moved from having been an ornament, if not a luxury, to becoming the central economic resource of technological society."[26]

The recognition of the links between education and economic development led to three changes. First, the citizens of Georgetown and of the other rural communities have realized that education is important. In the words of the report, "It will be more and more difficult to separate working and learning in the career of Scott Countians." Second, education and lifelong training have been linked to the ability to attract and retain industry.[27] Third, most industries and communities have a shared interest in developing skills beyond the traditionally provided academic and vocational skills so as to ready citizens for jobs and to help them retain them as these jobs change.

In Georgetown and Spring Hill, which had the most rural environments, these realizations were pronounced and had profound effects. In Smyrna, the change took the form of creative business and education partnerships, such as STEP, an after-school applied skills program sponsored by Nissan, Business Education Partnership (cosponsored by the Rutherford County Chamber of Commerce), Rutherford In-School Suspension Program, a dropout prevention program, Rutherford alternative school program, and the shadowing program. Ironically, in Marysville, the plant had the opposite effect, at least temporarily. The plant's high wages led to an exodus from the high school. Ohio historically has had a very strong educational system, however, so its graduates were able to meet the literacy requirements.

In each of these communities, the plant was catapulted and elevated to a role in the global economy where academic and educational skills are rewarded. This is noteworthy considering that many economists, such as Thompson and Thompson, argue that automobile plants do not increase the ratio of professional-technical workers to all employees.[28] Auto plants dominated by low-skill employees are a thing of the past. Now production and maintenance employees are expected to participate in decisions, supervise robotic equipment, and have literacy, computer, and personal skills.

In the words of one resident of the Georgetown site quoted in "Scott County's Economy in Transition" in the *Lexington News Reporter* in 1990, "Local businesses don't fear Toyota. But people have had to aim much higher because of it." Further, the elite and the public generally considered the curricular changes to have moved the community in a progressive direction. The changes in staffing and physical facilities were viewed as benefits as well.

There were some costs, however. In districts one district away from the plants' jurisdiction, the costs have been enormous, since there were no in-lieu-of-tax payments negotiated for the schools even when these payments were negotiated in the immediate districts. This problem led one community to recommend a school-business partnership to raise revenue for the schools. The increase in real estate prices was a two-edged sword for the schools in these communities. Even though a district would garner more revenues because of the escalating prices, school officials had to pay 30 percent more when purchasing property for the new facilities, thus raising the burden on taxpayers.

7 | What About the People?

HOW DOES the "person on the street" view the plant? To explore this matter, a telephone survey was conducted in July 1992 of residents from each site's impact area. For the purpose of the survey, the impact area for the Spring Hill site was the city of Columbia, Williamson County, and Maury County; for Smyrna, the city of Smyrna, the city of Murfreesboro, and Rutherford County; for Georgetown, the city of Georgetown and Scott County; and for Marysville, the city of Marysville, Union County, and Logan County. The sample included 150 residents from each area, drawn from the residents of these cities and counties who had telephone numbers.[1] In general, the wording of the survey was kept the same for the public as for the elite except where the pretest indicated that a change was warranted.

CHARACTERISTICS OF THE SAMPLE

Only 5 percent of the sample was employed at the plant; an additional 4 percent had a spouse who was employed there. Four percent had a son employed at the plant, and 2 percent had a daughter. Less than 1 percent had parents who were plant employees, and 15 percent had more distant relatives who were employees. Finally, less than 1 percent of the respondents were ex-employees. Thus, based on the broadest definition of family member, approximately 30 percent of the sample was linked to the plant through a family member. Even more, 58 percent, had friends who were plant employees.

Fifty-eight percent of the respondents had been born in the impact area, and 20 percent had lived there "most" of their lives. Thirteen percent answered "no" to a question about whether or not they had moved there in the "last few years"; 6 percent said they "came for the job"; and 1 percent "came for spouse's job."

Thus the respondents, like the populations of these communities, were primarily homegrown. Their average age was 44 years; 49.9 percent had at most a high school education, and 49.9 percent had attended at least some college. In terms of partisanship, 30.2 percent of the sample identified themselves as Democrat, 29 percent as Republican, and 31 percent as Independent. Twenty-four percent were from the Spring Hill area, 26 percent from the Smyrna area, 26 percent from the Georgetown area, and another 24 percent from the Marysville area.

PUBLIC'S VIEW OF THE PLANT

Three questions were used to measure the public's satisfaction with having the plant in the community.

Was the Incentive Package Justified?

The question "Is the incentive package justified?" could be answered in one of five ways: "justified," "leaning toward justified," "mixed feelings," "leaning toward unjustified," and "unjustified." In the Smyrna and Marysville areas, a majority of the respondents thought the incentive package was "justified," but in the other two areas only a minority had this opinion. When the results for the two positive responses are combined, however, the picture looks different;[2] then the percentage saying it was justified is 64 percent for Spring Hill, 57 percent for Georgetown, 70 percent for Smyrna, and 64 percent for Marysville.

Does the Public Want Another Plant?

Another way of measuring satisfaction with the plant is by asking whether the respondents would want another large-scale industrial plant in their community. Respondents in the Marysville area most favored this idea; there, 71 percent were strongly in favor of having another plant. Respondents in the Georgetown area were the least enthusiastic; only 32 percent said they strongly favored the idea. The percentage in Spring Hill was also quite low: 48 percent. Smyrna respondents were moderately enthusiastic, with 56 percent saying they strongly favored another plant.

Combining the percentages for the two positive responses ("Favor" and "Favor, but no more than one additional plant siting"), it is apparent that in three of the impact areas slight majorities would want another plant in their community: 56 percent in Spring Hill, 53 percent in Smyrna, and 56 percent in Marysville. In Georgetown, only 38 percent favored the idea.

Thus, satisfaction with the incentive package does not necessarily result in the community wanting another plant. Perhaps this is because the public recognizes that there are both drawbacks as well as benefits to having one. The traffic and tax situation, for example, may be as bad as the community can tolerate. Or the community may be tilting toward a limited rather than an unfettered growth philosophy.

Attitudes toward having another large plant may also reflect a community's overall attitude toward economic development. Clues to a community's views on this issue can be discerned from two questions. One question concerns the type of plant people want, if they want one at all. The other concerns how much the community favors growth at any cost, controlled growth, or little or no growth. An overwhelming 79 percent favored controlled growth. Only 16 percent, however, said they wanted another large industrial plant. The modal response, given by 40 percent of the sample, was that they wanted "small and diversified businesses"; 8 percent said commercial businesses; 4 percent said real estate; 10 percent said service industries; and 12 percent said other. This suggests that the public in these communities defines economic success less in terms of "capturing a big plant" and more by the degree of diversified smaller businesses in the community.

Is the Community Better Off?

Both of the questions so far focused on specifics related to the plant. The first tapped respondents' views on tax abatements, whereas the second captured more specific views on economic growth. The third question provides a more general gauge of how satisfied the public was with the plant. It asked: "Overall, do you think the community is better off, much better off, about the same, a little worse off, or much worse off with the plant?"

Only a minority of the respondents in each area said they were much better off with the plant. Marysville residents seemed the most satisfied; nearly 50 percent said their community was much better off. In Smyrna, 35 percent said the community was much better off. The lowest levels of enthusiasm were in Georgetown and Spring Hill, which were both 33 percent. When the "much better" and "somewhat better" categories are combined, however, support climbs to between 78 percent and 84 percent feeling the community is better off in all four sites.

BROAD IMPACT OF THE PLANT

Respondents were asked their views on several areas of potential impact, including jobs, new businesses, traffic, government, and new government programs. Some questions were asked in the form of "Is X an impact?" Others were posed as "Was Y a benefit?" Others were asked in the form of "Was X or Y a cost?" Thus, the respondents were not forced to assume the author's or other scholars' preconceptions of whether an impact is a cost or a benefit.

Table 7.1 indicates the percentage of the public in each impact area that identified an item an impact. As one can see, the majority of respondents in all the areas were enthusiastic that jobs were an impact and to a lesser degree a benefit. Note that in Marysville an overwhelming 97 percent of the respondents said that the plant had an impact on jobs. Looking at the other economic impacts—business as a benefit, industry as a benefit, and commerce as a benefit—we see that a very high

TABLE 7.1. Percentage of Respondents Stating, "Yes, each of these growth issues is an impact," by Site

	Smyrna	Georgetown	Marysville	Spring Hill
Broad impact				
Brimjobs[a]	90%	88%	97%	62%
Brimbus	78	88	80	69
Brimtrff	70	96	87	75
Brimgovt	42	50	40	51
Brimprof	33	23	19	17
Brimdecn	36	48	44	37
Brimprog	44	52	39	22
Benefits				
Benjobs	89	78	93	53
Benindus	82	79	86	61
Bencomm	81	79	74	61
Benknow	49	51	52	40
Bencap	82	80	84	83
Costs				
Costtax	49	56	48	50
Costpoll	43	22	24	13
Costsserv	23	20	19[b]	28
Costwages	45	37	57	20
Costrst	86	92	92	87

a. The abbreviations for these variables are explained in Table 3.4, page 79.
b. There were as many "don't knows" as "yes's" for the cost of social services.

percentage in each area agreed that these were secondary and tertiary benefits. The respondents definitely thought the plant had a positive economic impact.

In the area of government, the plant was thought to have led to increased professionalization of public-sector jobs, and might have had a broad impact on decision making and on government programs. In only one area, Spring Hill, did the majority of respondents (51 percent) think the plant made a difference in their government. This is an important finding. Clearly, a plant's impact on community government is more visible to the elite than to the general public. The impact was perhaps more visible or tangible in Spring Hill because a new city hall was built after the plant opened. Only a small minority of the public in the four impact areas thought that public-sector jobs had become more professionalized, and only about 30 or 40 percent thought that decisions were being made differently. And only in Georgetown did even a bare majority (52 percent) think the plant led to there being new government programs.

What about the impact of the plant on pollution and traffic? At least in these four areas, pollution is what Matthew Crenson would call a "nonissue."[3] The proportion of respondents who said pollution was a problem varied from 13 percent in the Spring Hill area to 43 percent in Smyrna. Objective evidence showed that pollution was indeed a problem in the greater Nashville area and the counties adjacent to Spring Hill and Smyrna.

To summarize Table 7.1, there was little variation across the sites in the respondents' definitions of the benefits. The least enthusiastic group was at Spring Hill, where only 53 percent identified jobs as a benefit; however, 62 percent said "jobs were an impact." Although this percentage is lower than at the other sites, it is still surprisingly large considering that the plant hired no locals for blue-collar jobs.

One benefit the public did not generally acknowledge was the new knowledge in the community. In Spring Hill and Smyrna, 40 percent and 49 percent, respectively, said the community benefited in terms of knowledge. Very few people cited the impact on government and focused instead on the plants' economic impact—in the areas of jobs, commerce, and capital. With the exception of taxes and the cost of real estate, costs were generally not acknowledged, although 86 to 92 percent of the respondents said that real estate costs were higher because of the plant. To find out how the people truly felt about each impact, it is necessary to look at the qualitative information divulged in their open-ended responses.

Jobs

Many of the respondents in Spring Hill were anguished over how few jobs went to locals. Although 62 percent acknowledged the plant's impact on jobs and 53 percent said jobs were a benefit, the majority of open-ended remarks regarding jobs were negative, for example, "Saturn did not hire local people," and workers "came from GM in Flint." Some respondents grudgingly stated that "maybe," "indirectly," jobs had been created or "satellite jobs, which are a lot lower wages than Saturn." Further indications of the respondents' views on the plant's impact on jobs were revealed in the question on whether they would want more large or small industry in the future: "As long as they hire local people," "either one as long as they bring jobs for Maury Countians," and "everything under the sun just so people can get jobs."

By contrast, in Smyrna, the picture concerning jobs was overwhelmingly rosy. Of fifty-one open-ended responses, forty were positive. People said Nissan "created over 6,000 jobs for the plant—about half in Murfreesboro." Others echoed the sentiment of this respondent: "Five thousand jobs open at Nissan plant alone." One person, though, worried that Smyrna ran the risk of becoming a company town, saying Nissan was "the only source of jobs in town." Other negative comments included the following: "Nissan had their own people come into the plant," "You had to know someone to get on," and "Family members have jobs," in reference to Nissan's alleged practice of nepotism.

In the Georgetown area, the closed-ended answers were overwhelmingly positive; however, the open-ended responses portray a more mixed picture. The sixty-nine open-ended responses were equally divided between positive and negative. The positive respondents made comments such as "All satellite plants came with Toyota and hired people"; the plant "attracted new people to Georgetown"; the plant "created jobs within a fifty-mile radius"; and "Locals got jobs." The negative comments revealed a great deal of savvy and precise information, for example, "of 4,800 employees, only 280 were from Georgetown." Another complaint was about the "too strict job requirements to get a job at the plant." Finally, a more equivocal response was; "Jobs were offered to people all over, not just this area."

In Marysville, 97 percent said jobs were an impact and 93 percent said jobs were a benefit; the qualitative responses paralleled this enthusiasm. To quote one grateful resident: "If it weren't for Honda, we'd be in a depression."

Industry and Commerce

Among the secondary and tertiary effects, the plants attracted new satellite industries to their areas and attracted, helped retain, or revitalized commercial concerns such as small businesses, particularly in the retail sector. In all four areas, the open-ended responses concerning industry and commerce were positive.

Typical positive responses were: "There are 100 industrial plants in Kentucky because of the plant" and "There are jobs like housing, retail, trucking, and railroad." The most unusual responses came from a resident of Spring Hill: "I think General Motors is waking up to Saturn quality and pride," and another who said, "The plant was a quality challenge nationally within the American automobile industry."

People were not as positive concerning the plants' impact on commerce, but generally the same pattern emerged. The feeling across the sites was that the plants spurred commercial activity, particularly new businesses, new malls, supermarkets, and restaurants. In Georgetown, the plant had a major effect on restaurants; over a quarter of the open-ended responses were about this aspect of life in the area. Some of the elite had commented that few premier restaurants existed. There was one excellent restaurant, however, named Elijah's, after the famous Baptist minister who founded Georgetown. The restaurant, which flourished with the advent of the plant, was located in a historic brick home and served superb food.

Most of the comments concerning commerce in Georgetown were positive and focused on the plant's "multiplier effects." But there were negative comments as well: "Smaller local businesses are being overrun by larger ones," and "Strip centers have risen; businesses have been closing." One respondent mentioned there had been an "increase in grocery stores, especially chain stores, [which] hurt independents." And, as in Marysville, some respondents were concerned that Georgetown could become a one-industry town: "All new business is Honda related."

Capital

As is apparent in Table 7.1, the person on the street in Spring Hill and in Georgetown shared the view that one benefit of the plant was that it brought an influx of capital. The majority of the open-ended responses in all four impact areas indicated that capital was flowing in because of the plant, although Spring Hill and Georgetown residents were less enthusiastic in their qualitative remarks than those in Marysville and Smyrna. For example, one perturbed Spring Hill resident stated, "I think it [the plant] is a minus due to what we had to give in some ways." Another said, "The offset the county paid on taxes offset any new income." Another commented: "It cost the farmer too much to bring this company in." The Smyrna residents demonstrated a more uniformly positive feeling concerning the influx of capital, evident in their use of terms such as "economic revival." An isolated respondent noted how precarious the situation was: "If Nissan stopped selling, this would be the world's largest junkyard."

Some negative respondents in Georgetown said, "Locally, [the plant] has hurt Georgetown business. Took it all to Lexington," or "Everyone goes to Lexington so it [the amount of capital] is about the same." In Marysville, the vast majority of residents who gave open-ended responses were very positive, represented by comments such as "Would have been a depressed area without the plant." One recurrent worry was articulated here and similarly in the other areas: "Honda employees don't spend their money here in Marysville."

Knowledge as a Benefit

Looking at the closed-ended responses and excluding the "don't knows," 71 percent said that knowledge was a benefit of the plant; however, the general public did not feel as strongly as the elite that the imported expertise was a good development. Thirty percent did not answer "yes" or "no" to the question of whether new knowledge was a benefit. When the closed-ended responses are examined (Table 7.1), only 40 to 52 percent of the respondents in the four areas, with Marysville being the highest, thought knowledge was a benefit.

According to the qualitative information, respondents in Spring Hill did not view new knowledge as very important. In Smyrna, however, most of the qualitative responses were positive; in particular, growth in such aspects of community life as the Girl Scouts and Jaycees was mentioned. References were also made to "medical expertise," "volunteerism," and "the program where they go into the schools and speak." One negative comment was that "Nissan is encouraged to keep to themselves—concern over unions."

In Georgetown, the open-ended responses were primarily positive, with typical comments crediting the plant with improving "Little League," "United Way," and the "Chamber of Commerce," as well as "new management concepts and robotics" that have been introduced at the plant. Respondents also pointed out that the company was responsible for a new seat belt safety program in town. Among the negative comments were these two: "Most of the big-shots live in Lexington, where they are involved," and "As far as politics and religion, they stay out of it." The latter comment, also expressed by the elite, reflected the idea that Toyota supported local causes as long as they were uncontroversial.

Marysville's citizenry felt that new knowledge was important, summed up by the comment that "the newcomers have constructive ideas." Of the ten open-ended responses, all but one was positive.

Government

As can be seen from Table 7.1, the majority of the citizenry in all four areas did not think the auto plants had a major impact on local government. The first government-related item was meant to measure the plant's general impact on government, for example, in the area of structural changes or reforms. The second item concerned the plant's impact on public-sector jobs, such as whether a certain educational level was now required to be a police officer or firefighter and whether merit rather than political criteria was used to select sheriffs and fire chiefs. The third item asked whether or not the decision-making process had changed, that is, whether decisions were now made more formally. The fourth item asked if there were new government programs and, if so, what they were.

At all four sites, the respondents mentioned a rich variety of programs that had been started in their areas after the plants opened. Although the plant had just opened in Spring Hill, people credited (or blamed) it with bringing new government programs to the area. One person mentioned that new drinking laws—for instance, liquor can now be sold by the drink—accompanied the opening of the plant. Another person said that economic development was being pursued more vigorously in the area because the plant was there. Other respondents mentioned that improvements had occurred in education and that roads had been built and new drug prevention programs created because of the plant.

Half the Smyrna sample provided open-ended responses concerning the plant's impact on government services. Perhaps the response was so large because the site was mature and a plant's impact on government services usually is seen in the latter years. The plant's greatest impact was in the area of recreation: a recreation center, a park, ball fields, and tennis courts were constructed after the plant was opened, and more recreational programs and softball teams were started. The citizens of Murfreesboro pointed out that there were more recreational opportunities for Smyrna residents but not for them.

Some respondents in the Smyrna area thought government-related decisions were being made more formally. They also mentioned that a new county courthouse, new schools, a new center for children in need, and new training programs, such as in English as a second language, had been developed. Nissan was also credited with helping to get a quicker county ambulance service and "getting schools and libraries built."

Almost all the respondents in Georgetown answered the open-ended questions about the plant's impact on the government. The largest number of respondents (one-third) mentioned the plant's impact on recreational services, the fact that parks, a community center, a golf course, and a youth center had been built. "Toyota donated to recreational programs," said one. Respondents thought education was the next most important government-related impact. They cited the increase in GED enrollment; planning, health care, and chamber of commerce activities; improvements in police, fire, and ambulance services; and city council–sponsored events, such as "the Fourth of July fireworks."

In Marysville, only about a third of the sample provided open-ended responses to questions concerning the plant's impact on government services, and these emphasized the plant's contributions to the community's cultural life, such as the "foreign club to socialize," the "friendly friendship center," "activities to help Japanese to integrate into community and schools," "more international relations programs to learn about each other's culture," "teaching Japanese at our school," and "exchange-type programs." One respondent mentioned "the orchestra for the school." Several respondents mentioned that recreational programs had been created since the plant opened, including conservation programs, senior citizen programs, and recreation programs for youth, as well as a pool and a park.

People in Marysville credited Honda with some miscellaneous changes that were not direct results of its opening the new plant, such as "the new postal office." Two respondents mentioned that new roads had been built. Two persons correctly noted that the town's new economic development programs were a function of the plant's being opened. Other respondents attributed such miscellaneous changes as the development of a tricounty action committee, nutrition and environmental programs, and housing construction to Honda.

Taxes

The increase in taxes was more of a concern to the public than to the elite. Based on responses to a closed-ended item that asked "Have taxes been a cost of the plant coming?" on average, 51 percent of the public in each area, compared with 38 percent of the elite, thought the opening of the plant led to higher taxes. Fifty percent of the public in Spring Hill thought taxes were a cost of having the plant in the area; the figures were 49 percent for Smyrna, 56 percent for Georgetown, and 48 percent for Marysville.

The auto companies were viewed as the cause of the higher taxes for several reasons. First, the formidable tax abatements granted to the auto companies were well publicized and controversial. Second, at the mature sites at least, the citizenry was probably acutely aware that taxes had gone up. Third, the opening of the plant was a big event and widely heralded, so it became an obvious target to blame for all sorts of woes, including increases in taxes. Two sage respondents noted, however, that "taxes would probably have been higher had Nissan not been," and "yes, they did rise, but Honda was not the reason."

In Spring Hill, nearly two-thirds of all the open-ended responses by persons interviewed indicated that higher taxes were a cost of having the plant in the community. One person stated: "Ever since they talked about Saturn coming, taxes went up." A typical remark was that taxes are "a lot higher—a 9 percent sales tax." But some citizens denied that the plant had anything to do with the tax structure: "Not in my area; taxes go up anyway," or "Taxes were artificially low." Yet another respondent remarked: "I'm not sure [the increase in taxes] is due to the plant."

Such responses were made more frequently in Spring Hill, where people were more unsure of their feelings about taxes than at the other sites.

The respondents in Smyrna, Georgetown, and to a certain extent Marysville provided some astoundingly sophisticated insights concerning the overall impact of the plant on their communities, such as this from a Smyrna resident: "It will take another twenty years to find out what this plant's impact will be." That response supports a key premise of the theory of the cycle of development—that the full effects are not known in time period 1 but only after a site has completed all eight stages.

Many respondents presented rival hypotheses for why their taxes went up. It is "due to new real estate development as a result of Nissan coming," said one person. Another respondent blamed "mismanagement of government," not the plant. Two respondents said the impact was uneven: "County taxes have increased, city taxes have been reduced," and "Those living closer to Honda had to pay more but not me."

In general, the responses concerning taxes were less intense in Marysville than in the other areas. Typical was this one: "Taxes have doubled over ten years." Others indicated that taxes would have gone up regardless of whether the plant was in town. Or, "Yes, [they did rise], but Honda wasn't the reason."

Pollution

The closed-ended responses indicate that people at all four sites were in a state of denial concerning the plants' impact on pollution. The objective fact is that two counties in the vicinity of metropolitan Nashville had high levels of air pollution and were within the impact area of the Smyrna and Spring Hill plants. At the more mature sites, people appeared to be both more perturbed or better informed about the risks of pollution, although still denying that it was a plant impact.

Based on the closed-ended questions, only 13 percent of the respondents in the Spring Hill area thought pollution was a problem. Similarly, in Smyrna, most of the forty-one open-ended responses indicated the respondents did not think the plant was causing pollution. Interestingly, other Smyrna responses indicated a very high information level: "There has been illegal dumping, but it hasn't been proven yet." Another said there was "substantial pollution. Tennessee is rated the third worst in the U.S.A." And this comment: "The plant is the highest polluter in the county." Relying on direct observation, another respondent said there was "minimal pollution. I live within sight of the plant." Another mistakenly said, "Nothing about it mentioned in the paper."

What these comments may illustrate is that, unless there is obvious controversy, pollution is an "invisible" problem, especially compared with traffic, for example. Respondents knew there was a traffic problem without reading about it in the paper. Several people who denied there was a pollution problem seemed eager to point to culprits other than the plant: "The plant was environmentally concerned, but an increase in population caused pollution." More sophisticated respondents acknowledged that "the plant has not been here long enough to [cause a pollution problem]." Another person stated, "Locals are not aware of it yet; politicians are short-range thinkers."

Recall that on the closed-ended questions, 46 percent of Georgetown residents said pollution was a problem. On the open-ended questions, a high proportion of the responses mentioned either water supply or water quality as having been affected by the plant. The spring, the primary water source, had been tainted, then closed in the area, so the people's concerns were well-founded. One person referred to a "sickening smell; solvent in the air." Several others expressed concern about land use, specifically "waste disposal, landfill is now closed," and that "the best farmland is being taken for industry."

In Marysville, the public already saw pollution as a serious concern, as evidenced by the sixteen out of twenty open-ended responses that indicated it was a problem. One citizen was convinced the plant was "putt[ing] out acid rain. I don't care what people say," he said. "I live close." Others reported seeing "dust and particles in the air" and that smoke was "coming out of the smokestacks at the Honda plant." Another found solace in the fact that the "plant is so far away from a populated area." This was an interesting comment since it indicated that the respondent thought air and water pollution honor geographic and political boundaries. One person commented that "garbage from the plant goes into the landfills," a major environmental concern. Again, the respondents at the more mature sites of Smyrna and Marysville thought pollution was more of a problem. The comments by these respondents were also more sophisticated.

Wages

In rural or agricultural communities with only scattered light and nonunionized industry, wages may rise overall after a large auto plant opens in the area. Workers view the increase in wages as a benefit, but small businesspersons or other industrialists may view it as a cost. If a respondent says, "Higher wages are not a cost," he or she could be saying that the wages have not increased or that the higher wages are a benefit. The following statement is typical: "Wages have gone up, but I don't know if I consider that a cost." Even among those who said the higher wages were a cost, many commented, "Factories are paying more to compete with Nissan," and "They're only higher for suppliers and the plant."

In the Spring Hill area, only 20 percent of the respondents said the higher wages were a cost. Of the fourteen open-ended responses, only one indicated this was a problem. In Smyrna, by contrast, 45 percent of those answering the closed-ended questions thought wages were a cost; of the thirty-seven open-ended responses, twenty-three held the opinion that higher wages had been a cost.

The picture in Georgetown was less positive. Only a minority of the respondents who answered the closed-ended items thought the higher wages were a cost; results for the open-ended questions were similar. Two typical responses were that wages "increased at the plant, but not in other areas of the community," and that "jobs people can get are at minimum wage except at Toyota."

Of the four sites, only in the Marysville area did a majority of the public (57 percent), when answering the closed-ended item, say that the higher wages were a cost. Summarizing the qualitative or open-ended answers there, we see that seventeen of the thirty-two respondents giving open-ended responses thought the increase in wages was a cost, not a benefit. Typical of the "benefit" responses were the following: "Wages have increased, but that is a benefit." Other responses were: "Wages have increased, but only for the Honda employees," and "As far as I know only the plant and the company supplying for them have been affected." Citizens' attitudes obviously differed depending on whether they were employees or businesspeople and on where they lived.

Real Estate

Respondents at all four sites viewed the increase in the price of real estate as a cost of having a large plant in their community. Based on responses to the closed-ended questions, 85 percent of the total sample thought the increase in real estate prices was associated with the plant. The "spin" people put on this depended on whether they were property buyers or sellers. Obviously, owners or those about to sell were more pleased than those about to buy. Some respondents noted that real estate prices had "dramatically" increased or "doubled" or "tripled" or went up "25 percent to 50 percent." Others said a "$35,000 house now costs $55,000 or $60,000," and "my home increased by 25 percent." There were few distinctions from site to site in respondents' comments concerning the increase in real estate prices. The cost of real estate soared everywhere initially but then dropped, although not to the level it had been before the plant was announced.

Social Services

The general perception is that having a large plant in a community puts a strain on social services because flocks of job seekers, real estate speculators, and other transients come to the area, stay after their temporary jobs are over or fail to find employment altogether, then enter the public welfare system. Further, concomitant with the other changes in the community, there are often increases in divorce, drug use, and emotional problems requiring counseling. This phenomenon was first identified in the interviews with the elite.

Only a small minority—approximately a quarter of the people in the overall sample—thought the cost of social services had risen because of the plant. No clear pattern emerges from the qualitative information. At Spring Hill, one person noted that her daughter had been laid off, which suggested bad times after the first euphoric welcome, while another claimed that "we have the smallest percent unemployment in state." The most sage comment was by one respondent who said, "Not yet; it may be later if they [the auto plant] have a layoff." In Smyrna, the dominant feeling as indicated by the majority of open-ended responses was that the cost of social services was not higher.

In Georgetown and Marysville, half the open-ended responses concerning social services were negative and half were positive. Statements from Georgetown citizens—that the plant increased "demand for child care," "guys marrying girls and not paying for child support," and "youth getting in trouble"—all point to social instability. Marysville respondents echoed these sentiments, citing the "divorce rate, drugs, domestic violence" and the fact that "welfare clients are attracted to the area" as reasons for their view that there had been an increase in the cost of social services.

Infrastructure

The public was definitely enthusiastic about changes in the town's infrastructure that occurred as a result of the plant. A typical remark was that the plant meant a "health service, two new malls, new airport, roads, forty other companies to support the plant." Smyrna residents were the least vocal about infrastructure changes, probably because the area already had a diverse industrial base and a growth rate of 6 percent a year even before the plant opened. But even in Smyrna improvements were made that could be linked to the plant: "The county ambulance service is quicker," one respondent said, and, most important, "Highways leading to the plant have been improved." Some respondents, especially in Murfreesboro, grumbled about their higher taxes.

In Georgetown and Marysville, the infrastructure improvements linked to the plant were viewed as rather substantial. A Marysville resident acknowledged that the "sewer and water line was developed by Honda," and a Smyrna resident was happy that the town had a new "exit off the interstate." One Georgetown resident credited the plant with having the "highways, roads, and bridges replaced," and another credited Toyota—incorrectly—with having the bypass built. (In fact, the city of Georgetown financed it.) Finally, a Spring Hill resident was glad about "a new city hall, a new school, and a fire department."

ISSUES AND PROBLEMS: IS THERE A COMMON AGENDA?

In the agenda-setting literature, a problem or issue is defined as something everyone is talking about. The next question is whether issues or problems are universal across the four sites or unique to each site. Although it is common for the elite to identify an issue as a problem and quickly legislate in an effort to "fix" it, it is also common for an issue to be on the systemic agenda before the formal government agenda. If economic development occurs in predictable universal stages, one would expect the same set of issues to be considered problems across all sites. Was this, in fact, the case?

Table 7.2 lists all of the issues and problems respondents identified as such, the percentage of respondents in each area who named these issues, and the issues' ranking.[4] As can be seen in Table 7.2, respondents

TABLE 7.2. Problems and Issues That Respondents Identified, by Rank Order and Percentage of Responses

	Smyrna		Georgetown		Marysville		Spring Hill	
1	Real estate	61%	Traffic	96%	Traffic	87%	Traffic	87%
2	Traffic	60	Real estate	80	Real estate	74	Streets	80
3	Higher taxes Housing School bonds	57 57 57	Housing	79	Housing	70	Real estate	75
4			Streets	67	School bonds	68	Housing	70
5			Higher taxes	62	Streets	66	School bonds	65
6	Annexation	52	Water	52	Higher taxes	57	Higher taxes	59
7	Streets	45	Annexation School bonds	48 46	Annexation	53	Annexation	48
8	Sewage Cost of wages	40 40			Cost of wages	48	Cost of wages Water	32 32
9			Cost of wages	46	Water	36		
10	Water	38	Sewage	44	Sewage	30	Sewage	30
11	Other bonds	22	Pollution	26	Other bonds	24	Pollution	16
12	Pollution	35	Other bonds	18	Pollution	23	Other bonds	11

Note: Problems (i.e., more than 50 percent response rate) common to all four sites included traffic, real estate, and housing. School bonds, roads, and taxes were common to three sites; and annexation (only two had not been annexed) was a common problem to two sites. Water was only a problem for the Georgetown site. Fewer than 50 percent of the respondents for all four sites rated sewage, wages, pollution, and other bonds as being problems or issues.

at all four sites mentioned three problems: traffic, real estate, and housing. An increase in traffic is one of the costs of economic development; at three out of the four sites, it was considered the number one problem. The high cost of real estate was also among the top three problems mentioned at all four sites. Housing, specifically a shortage or a mismatch between demand and supply, is also considered a universal problem associated with economic development; it consistently ranked third or fourth on respondents' lists of plant-related problems. Therefore, three of the twelve problems respondents identified not only were mentioned by respondents at all the sites but ranked equivalently high as well. The three issues or problems mentioned at all the sites are all related to "creature comforts." They are tangible and discernible by the average citizen no matter what the person's walk of life. Everyone experiences traffic problems and is aware of increases in real estate prices, whether the person is a buyer, seller, or renter.

Table 7.2 shows that respondents at three sites identified three other issues as problems: school bonds, roads, and taxes. Only in Georgetown did respondents not see school bonds as an issue. This may have been because the school district there had already been consolidated by the city and county, thereby preparing the community for the coordination and expansion necessary when the population increased because of the plant. The company also made a large contribution toward the construction of the new vocational-technical high school, Scott County Technical School, and to the construction of a robotics center at the University of Kentucky.

Only in Smyrna did respondents not see roads as a problem. This was probably because Nissan funded a bypass and a road in anticipation of the traffic problems it would create after the plant was built.

One would have expected that respondents at all the sites would have identified taxes as a problem, but at Spring Hill the respondents did not think this was the case. This may have been because Spring Hill was the least mature site and because taxes back-load, that is, they become an issue in the last stages of the economic development process.

At two sites—Spring Hill and Marysville—respondents identified annexation as a problem. Again, the public appeared well-informed. In Georgetown and Smyrna, annexation had been successfully carried out, and consequently the respondents did not identify it as a problem.

The criterion for determining whether something was identified as a problem was if 50 percent or more of the respondents called it such.

In Table 7.2, these problems are ranked by site; in Table 7.3, they are ranked for both the elite and the public. Among the nonissues—those less than 50 percent of the respondents considered problems—were pollution, wages, sewage, and other bonds.

Turning to the patterns by site, not surprisingly, some differences emerged across sites in how people felt about having a large auto plant in their community. Smyrna residents seemed relatively positive; although respondents named real estate, traffic, taxes, housing, school bonds, and annexation as problems, the percentages were considerably lower than those for the other sites. Sixty percent of the people in Smyrna thought traffic was a problem, for instance, whereas in Georgetown, Marysville, and Spring Hill the figure was 80 to 90 percent.

There were some surprises in how concerned people were about the issues. Spring Hill respondents should have been very concerned about the plant given that the public viewed the incentive package unfavorably. In fact, respondents indicated that they felt equally strongly about at least a couple of issues as respondents at other sites. For instance, 65 percent of the Spring Hill sample thought school bonds were a problem, giving it only the second-highest ranking for this issue. Spring Hill

TABLE 7.3. Problems and Issues Cited by Community Leaders and the Public, by Rank Order and Percentage of Responses

	Leaders (N = 65)		Public (N = 584)	
1	Traffic	97%	Traffic	78%
2	Real estate	94	Real estate	74
3	Housing	85	Housing	69
4	Roads	79	Taxes	61
5	Higher taxes	71	School bonds	59
	School bonds	71		
6			Roads	58
7	Annexation	70	Annexation	51
8	Other bonds	62	Wages	42
9	Water	61	Water	40
10	Wages	57	Sewage	36
11	Sewage	52	Pollution	22
	Pollution	52		
12			Other bonds	19

respondents identified fewer problems than did those at other sites, however: five, versus six for Smyrna, six for Georgetown, and seven for Marysville. Only traffic, real estate, housing, taxes, and roads were named by more than 50 percent of the sample in Spring Hill.

One would have expected that Smyrna-area residents would report the fewest issues since the town cut the best deal with the auto company, but respondents identified six, the same number as respondents in the Georgetown area. Smyrna respondents did feel less intensely about their issues, however. Thus, only 60 percent said traffic was a problem, compared with 96 percent in Georgetown and more than 80 percent in both Spring Hill and Marysville. Likewise, only 57 percent of the people in Smyrna identified housing as an issue, compared with 79 percent in Georgetown; at 57 percent, Smyrna respondents tied with Marysville for the lowest figures for taxes. The lower figures for Smyrna may reflect the fact that it negotiated the best package of the four sites. It could also be that its problems had subsided by the time of the survey, which was at the end of the town's cycle of development. Or perhaps because Smyrna had been in a growth corridor for a comparatively longer time and was not as rural as the other sites, respondents did not "blame" the plant for its problems.

VIEWS OF THE ELITE VERSUS THE MASSES

Based on the survey findings, we know that there is a core set of problems that at least 50 percent of the respondents at all the sites thought was plant-related.[5] We also know that 50 percent of the elite at each site identified a set of problems. How do their perceptions compare?

At all four sites, the elite identified real estate, traffic, and housing as issues; at three sites, school bonds and annexation; at two sites, wages, water, and sewage; and at one site, taxes, roads, and pollution. Clearly, there are similarities in what both groups of respondents perceived as problems. Specifically, at all the sites both groups focused on tangible problems that affect individuals' comfort—traffic, real estate, and housing.

As can be seen in Table 7.3, the public viewed traffic, housing, the cost of real estate, taxes, school bonds, and roads as the most important problems. The most important problems for the elite were traffic, housing, the cost of real estate, roads, taxes, school bonds, annexation, other bonds, water, wages, and pollution. Thus, both the public and the elite ranked traffic, housing, the cost of real estate, roads, taxes, and school bonds similarly.

Table 7.3 indicates that the elite (the community leaders) and the general public were consistently concerned about the same issues or problems. Nonetheless, there are some differences. For example, based on the survey findings, the public considers only seven issues as problems, whereas the elite thinks twelve issues are problems, although only 52 percent identified pollution and sewage as such. The fact that a higher proportion of the elite identified these issues as problems is consistent with the notion that the elite has higher levels of information. For instance, 62 percent of the elite thought "other bonds," meaning all bonds for capital except school bonds, were a problem, versus 19 percent of the public; 52 percent of the elite identified sewage as a problem, compared with 36 percent of the public.

The public is just as likely as the elite to recognize the economic impacts of a large plant on a community but much less likely to acknowledge the plant's impact on the local government. Only public-sector employees or applicants for public-sector jobs and members of the elite are likely to notice subtle but significant plant-related changes in the government, for example, professionalization of public-sector jobs; the average citizen will notice only major changes, such as that a new city hall or county courthouse has been built. The average citizen may not realize that there are higher educational requirements for police officers and firefighters; however, he or she is likely to notice the plant's impact on jobs (a once unemployed neighbor is working) or on commerce (a new Wal-Mart has opened).

Other differences emerged as well. The public was more likely than the elite to see roads as a problem and less likely to identify sewage and water quality or supply as problems. In fact, in no impact area did more than 50 percent of the public think sewage was a problem.

The elite at two sites thought that higher wages were a problem, but at no site did the public think so; also, only in the Georgetown area did the elite consider annexation a problem. As the reader may recall, this was one of two sites in which annexation of the plant site occurred, and it was as a result of the mayor's patience and bargaining skills. It may be that the elite considered it a problem only until the mayor negotiated the annexation. In fact, Toyota agreed to the annexation voluntarily.

Pollution is of minimal importance to both the leaders and the public. As can be seen in Table 7.3, 52 percent of the elite and only 22 percent of the public in the Marysville area identified it as a problem, but it still ranked low relative to other problems, tying for seventh out of seven. As with pollution, average citizens did not view the cost of other bonds as a problem, and at only one site did the elite identify it as such. Higher wages are more likely to be named by the elite than by the masses. This may be because members of the elite are more likely to have an employer's perspective and therefore would identify higher wages as a cost.

It is notable that the elite and the masses agree about the importance of such creature comforts as traffic, pollution, and roads. There was strong agreement between the leaders and the public on traffic, with both groups citing it as the top problem. Roads are of equivalent importance to members of the elite and to the masses: 79 percent of the elite mentioned it, versus 58 percent of the public.

Members of the elite clearly notice the plant's impact on the local government more than the masses do. Only about 20 percent of the public said that having the plant in their community affected the government, whereas the majority of the elite said it did. Members of both the elite and the public were more likely to perceive the plant's impact on the economy than on the government; however, more of the masses identified the economic impacts than did the elite.

IS ECONOMIC DEVELOPMENT UNIDIMENSIONAL?

One question that remains unanswered is whether the public perceives the impact of a large plant unidimensionally, for instance, in only economic terms. Table 7.4 displays the results of a factor analysis that addresses this question empirically. The reader will recall that the factor analysis for the *leaders* of the four impact areas indicated that they thought of the plant as having three dimensions. The first dimension is short-term political and short-term economic impacts, such as on job creation; the second is secondary economic impact on industry and commerce, plus some broad government impact and, to a lesser degree, some broad impact on the way decisions were made; the third is longer-term impacts, evident in increases in the community's knowledge base and government programs and in the professionalization of public-sector

TABLE 7.4. Factor Analysis of Three Key Dimensions of Economic Development as Reported by the Public at All Four Sites

	Overall Economic Development (factor 1)	Pure Government (factor 2)	Creature Comforts (factor 3)
Broad Impacts			
Brimjobs[a]	.58[b]	−.03	−.08
Brimbus	.54[b]	−.04	.17
Brimtrff	.18	−.05	.35[b]
Brimgovt	−.04	.64[b]	.04
Brimprof	−.24	.44[b]	−.01
Brimdecn	−.03	.60[b]	0
Brimprog	.19	.41	−.07
Benefits			
Benjobs	.64	−.02	−.10
Benindus	.62[b]	−.05	.02
Bencomm	.55[b]	.06	0
Benknow	.34[b]	.19	0
Bencap	.47	.07	.27[b]
Costs			
Costtax	−.22	.06	.46[b]
Costpoll	0	−.02	.29[b]
Costsserv	−.06	.08	.31[b]
Costwages	.36[b]	0	.44[b]
Costrst	.18	−.01	.04
Eigen value	2.7	.87	.58
Variance explained	.77	.24	.16

Note: N = 600
a. the abbreviations for these variables are explained in Table 3.4, page 79.
b. Statistically significant.

jobs, as well as in such costs as higher taxes, pollution, and the increased need for social services.

Now turning to the public, instead of the leaders, the public thinks of economic development as composed of three distinct dimensions, each having more than economic impact. The variables that load high on factor 1 are broad impact on jobs, the benefits of jobs, industry, commerce, knowledge, and capital, the cost of wages, and broad impact on professionalization of public-sector jobs (in a negative direction).

Note that the economic variables that load high on factor 1 include both the plant's primary or short-term economic effects, on jobs, for example, and the secondary and tertiary impacts, that is, the long-term impact on new industry and commerce. Also note that the benefit of new capital loads high on factor 1. Thus, factor 1 in Table 7.4 has been labeled an "overall economic factor." By comparison, members of the elite named immediate or short-term economic impacts such as jobs and capital on factor 1, and secondary and tertiary impacts such as business, industry, commerce, and two of the government variables on factor 2. Also, the cost of the higher wages variable loads high and is positive and significant on factor 1, although it loads even higher on factor 3. This means those who identify broad economic impacts (primary, secondary, and tertiary) also think of higher wages as a plant-linked cost. Note that none of the government variables, except broad impact on professionalization, were particularly strong on factor 1. One inexplicable finding is that the benefit-of-knowledge variable loads high on factor 1 for the public.

All the government-related variables, but none of the economic or sociocultural variables, loaded high on factor 2. Thus, this factor is referred to as "pure government" in Table 7.4. This factor seems to capture government impacts primarily, so that broad impact on government, professionalization, decision making, and programs all load very strong and the economic variables are virtually invisible. This result seems to indicate that the people who see economic development as an economic process do not see it as having an impact on the government.

Factor 3, which for the elite contained long-term sociocultural changes, contains traffic, benefits of capital, and higher wages as a cost, and in general appears to encompass more of the creature comfort costs for the public. Specifically, the six variables that load very strong (and significantly) on factor 3 are traffic, capital as a benefit, higher wages as a cost, higher taxes as a cost, more demand on social services as a cost, and more pollution as a cost.

Like the elite, the public views the plant as more than an economic phenomenon; however, for the masses, the three factors are different than for the elite. Among the masses, the people who notice government impacts are not tuned in to economic impacts and vice versa. Also, for the public, factor 3 contains a litany of creature comforts, some of them of long-term concern, such as pollution, the cost of social services, higher wages, traffic, and the benefits of capital. For both the elite and the public, these longer-term costs loaded high on factor 3.

In conclusion, the general public views the process of recruiting and opening a large plant as more than an economic process bringing more jobs into the community; however, those who see it as an economic process do not see the political impact and vice versa. Those who recognize it as an economic process see the primary effects of having more jobs but also that there are secondary and tertiary effects on business, industry and commerce, the benefit of capital, and the cost of higher wages (factor 1). Those who view the plant as having a solely economic impact do not tend to see its broad impact on government, decision making, professionalization, and programs. Then there are those who see their creature comforts being impinged upon; for them the plant's greatest impacts are in the areas of traffic, wages, taxes, social services, and pollution. Although both the elite and the public stated that pollution was a nonissue, it emerges as part of factor 3 for the public, along with other perceptible costs for the public.

DETERMINANTS OF THE PUBLIC'S ATTITUDE TOWARD THE PLANT

This chapter began with a discussion of whether the public viewed the incentive package as justifiable, whether it thought the town should recruit another large company, and whether it thought the community was better or worse off with the plant. Respondents at different sites were more or less enthusiastic regarding these questions. One important question was not addressed, however: Can the differences in attitude be explained by individual-level variables?

Individual Correlates

What characteristics would one expect to be good predictors of a person's attitude toward the incentive package, the prospect of another plant being opened in his or her community, or the effect of the current plant on the community? Age, income, education, race, gender, partisanship, economic status, whether the individual is a native of the area, which impact area the individual lives in, as well as whether a family member, a member of the individual's extended family, or a friend is a plant employee might all be important variables.

Hypotheses

We would expect that the younger the respondents, the more enthusiastic they would be about the prospect of economic development. We would also expect that the higher the income and education levels, the more positive respondents' attitudes would be toward economic development in general and toward the plant in particular. We would expect party identification to be important; thus, because of their business interests, that Republicans would be more in favor of the plant than Democrats. We would also expect natives to be less enthusiastic than transplants because of the natives' fears that having the plant in their community would bring about significant changes; natives are generally more protective of their lifestyles.

Race and gender also need to be included as demographic controls. We hypothesized that professional and other white-collar workers would favor the plant more than blue-collar workers because of their philosophical bias toward economic development. This hypothesis was not tested, however, because missing data were too extensive for the occupational status variable.

The next control—economic stakes—requires some amplification. One would think that beneficiaries of the plant, that is, employees or relatives of plant employees, would have positive attitudes toward the incentive package, toward the idea of having another large plant, and toward the plant in general. Few of the persons in the sample actually had jobs at any of the plants in their impact areas; however, survey items captured whether members of the immediate family were employed at the plant (the variable is called Dimmfam), whether members of the extended family were employed at the plant (the variable is called Dibigfam), and whether any of the respondents' friends were employed at the plant (the variable is called Difriend). Thus, economic stakes are defined rather broadly. The hypothesis was that respondents who had economic stakes in the plant would more likely have positive attitudes toward it, as defined by these three variables.

Looking at Table 7.5, the correlation matrix of all the demographic variables combined with these three attitudes toward the plant, we see that the pattern is as predicted: natives opposed the package (this is a significant finding); people who had immediate or extended family at the plant favored the package significantly. Having friends at the plant

TABLE 7.5. Matrix Correlation of Demographic Variables and Attitudes Toward the Plant

	1.[a] Versions		2.[b] Diaddition	3.[c] Dincentive
	Doverpos	Diover 2		
Dinative: A native is a person who answered "Yes, born here" or "Yes, lived here most of my life." The people who answered that they just came for jobs, whether their own or a spouse's, were coded as not native.	-.08 (575)	-.07 (575)	.09 (575)	-.17** (575)
Dibigfam: Is a member of an extended family, including parents, siblings, grandparents, cousins, uncles, and aunts, employed at the plant?	.20** (575)	.12* (575)	.08 (575)	.12* (575)
Dimmfam: Is a member of the immediate family, including siblings, mother, and father, employed at the plant?	.13* (575)	-.09 (575)	.07 (575)	.15* (575)
Difriend: Is a friend employed at the plant?	.19** (575)	.13* (575)	0 (575)	0 (575)
Diage: Age	-.05 (575)	-.01 (575)	0 (575)	.02 (575)
Gender	.06 (575)	0 (575)	-.11 (575)	-.04 (575)
Diptyid: Party identification (Republican or Democrat)	-.20** (575)	-.20** (575)	-.06 (575)	-.31** (575)
Diincome: Income variable; either below or above $30,000	.12 (575)	.10 (575)	-.07 (575)	.13* (575)
Triincome: Below $30,000; $30,000 to $59,000; or above $60,000	.10 (575)	.10 (575)	-.04 (575)	.15** (575)
Race	-.08 (596)	-.06 (532)	-.06 (578)	.01 (546)
Occupatdi: Occupation, either blue- or white-collar	.07 (307)	.07 (347)	-.10 (382)	.08 (356)

Note: The prefixes di = dichotomous and tri = trichotomous.
a. "Overall, do you think the community is much better off, better off, about the same, a little worse, or much worse off with the plant?"
b. "Does the public want another plant?"
c. "Is the incentive package justified?"
*Statistically significant at the .05 level.
**Statistically significant at the .01 level.

had no effect on whether respondents favored the package. Further, age, gender, and whether the respondent was in a white-collar or a blue-collar occupation had no noticeable effect on whether he or she approved the incentive package.

Income had a positive and significant effect, so that persons who earned more than $60,000 a year were particularly enthusiastic about the prospect of the plant. Partisanship was also significant; generally, Republicans felt more positive toward the plant.

What variables correlate with wanting an additional industrial plant in the community? The correlates with the community-is-better-off variable are as follows: native was negative but not significant; income was positive but not significant; Republican was positive and significant; age, gender, occupational status, and income were not significant. The economic stakes variables were positive and significant in predicting attitude toward the overall impact of the plant.

Results of Multivariate Data

As much as the simple correlates tell us, they do not indicate which relationships will prevail when put in a model with the other variables as controls. Simple models were developed and used to predict what the public as a whole thought of the incentive package, having an additional plant, and the overall impact of the plant (see Table 7.6). Since the data were cross-sectional, the R^2 was modest. Nonetheless, the results were interesting. Using all the variables in a model, several of the individual variables as well as site-linked variables were significant. Of particular interest was the relative importance of the site-related factors as opposed to the individual-level predictors.

The basic model includes site, native status (Dinative), status of whether the immediate family works at the plant (Dimmfam), status of whether an extended family member works at the plant (Dibigfam), income (Income), party identification (Party), and race (Race). First, some preliminary analysis had to be done about which site behaves differently than other sites in terms of each of the three dependent variables. The reason the Spring Hill site variable is used for the first model involving the overall benefit of the plant is that respondents there had different feelings regarding the overall benefit of the plant than respondents at the other sites.[6] Residents of Spring Hill were less likely to think that the plant had a positive impact on the community. Georgetown

TABLE 7.6. Models Used to Predict What the Public Thought of the Incentive Package (Dincentive), Having an Additional Plant (Diaddition), and the Overall Impact of the Plant (Doverpos)

	Variables[a]	Coefficient	Standard Error	Significance
Doverpos	Dibigfam	.69	.32	.03
N = 547	Difriend	.68	.23	.004
Prob chi^2 = .00	Dinative	−.63	.30	.04
Pseudo R^2 = .13	Diptyid	−.13	.06	.02
	Site is Spring Hill or not	−.13	.26	
	Constant	1.30	.61	.03
Diaddition	Dibigfam	.40	.20	.06
N = 496	Difriend	.27	.19	.14
Prob chi^2 = .00	Dinative	−.48	.21	.03
Pseudo R^2 = .05	Diptyid	.75	.05	.10
	Site is Georgetown or not	−.74	.21	
	Constant	.09	.27	.74
Dincentive	Dibigfam	.91	.27	.001
N = 500	Difriend	.31	.22	.16
Prob chi^2 = .00	Dinative	−1.00	.30	
Pseudo R^2 = .09	Diptyid	−.20	.05	
	Site is Georgetown or not	−.54	.23	.02
	Constant	2.24	.36	

a. Abbreviations for these variables are explained in Table 7.5.

residents had distinctive feelings regarding having an additional plant and toward the incentive package; therefore, the Georgetown site variable was used in the two respective models using those two dependent variables.

As can be seen from Table 7.6, certain individual-level variables remained strong predictors of whether respondents would have favorable attitudes toward the plant. If the person had a family member or friend who was employed at the plant and if the site was other than Spring Hill, he or she was likely to think the plant had had a favorable impact on the community. Democrats were less likely than Republicans to think the plant had had a favorable impact.

What does the model indicate regarding the public's opinion toward having an additional plant? Natives were significantly less likely to want an additional plant. Respondents who had an extended family member who worked at the plant were significantly more favorable toward the idea of having another plant than were those with friends who worked at the plant, but the latter was not a statistically significant relationship.

Party affiliation was not significant. Which site the respondent lived near was important, so that those in the Georgetown area were significantly more opposed to having an additional plant than were respondents in other areas.

What about the public's attitude toward the incentive package? If a member of the person's extended family were employed at the plant, and if the person were Republican, then he or she was significantly more likely to feel the package was justified. Having a friend who was employed at the plant was not statistically significant. Natives were strongly against the package. Finally, those in the Georgetown impact area were significantly less likely to think the incentive package was justified than were those in the other three areas.[7]

What Do the Results Mean?

If site-level variables had not been important in predicting respondents' attitudes, then the demographic characteristics of a community alone would be enough to predict residents' attitudes toward having a large plant in their community.[8] In fact, site makes a difference.

The meaning of "site" is complicated and multidimensional. Independent evidence from chapters 2 and 4 suggests that the leadership of a community plays a critical role in how a large manufacturing plant affects the community and, consequently, in how the residents react to the plant. The incentive package also varies by site, as do infrastructure needs. Moreover, the skillfulness of the bargaining team that negotiates the incentive package and the particular way the plant affects the community are also site-specific. In short, not all of the public's attitudes are determined by their individual characteristics.

SUMMARY

This chapter has addressed a number of key findings. First, in each of the four impact areas studied, the public felt strongly that the automobile plant had had a major impact on the community. Given that the impact was diffuse and that only a minority of the sample worked at one of the auto plants, it is noteworthy that people acknowledged the impact. Second, the public was acutely aware of the plant's economic impact but did not acknowledge such government impacts as the plant's effect on the way decisions are made, in professionalizing public service jobs, and in creating new government programs, although respondents correctly attributed certain government programs to the plants, especially in the areas of recreation, planning, and zoning.

Third, having a large plant affects what both the elite and the public view as community issues. Both groups viewed traffic, real estate, and housing as plant-related issues or problems. Both groups also viewed roads as important issues, although the public thought of roads as somewhat less of a concern. Taxes were important issues to both groups as well, although the public ranked taxes as more important than the elite.

There were some similarities and a few differences in the issues the masses and the elite viewed as least important. The issues both considered important were pollution, sewage, higher wages, water, and non-school-related bonds. The main differences were ones of magnitude, with fewer of the public noticing impacts than the elite. Fifty-two to 62 percent of the elite thought the preceding were plant-related problems; yet less than 50 percent of the public did so. So one major difference is that the elite tends to be more sensitive in perceiving something as a problem.

Fourth, differences clearly existed across sites. For instance, Smyrna-area residents did not have the same intensity of feeling toward the plant as did respondents from Spring Hill, Georgetown, or Marysville. This could have been because Smyrna was already a mature site, that it had negotiated the best package, or that it had been undergoing a steady growth prior to the plant for several years. The evidence points most strongly toward the fact that it was because Smyrna negotiated the most favorable package, a finding that suggests that residents at sites that least need the plant may feel there are fewer plant-related problems than residents of other sites. Parenthetically, this finding indirectly supports the notion that communities vary in bargaining power and that some (like Smyrna) are in better bargaining positions.

Fifth, by and large, across all four sites people felt their communities were better off with the plant than without it. They also feel the incentive package was justified.

Sixth, people's views on the plant's impact on the community tend to mirror reality rather accurately. Both the elite and the public tended to agree on what the major issues were, although members of the elite were more likely than the public to report that an issue was a problem.

8 | Political and Cultural Transformation

THIS CHAPTER explores the way in which the politics and culture of communities change after the opening of a large manufacturing plant. In this context, political transformation means changes not just in the leadership or in the political parties in the community but in the way the government does business. These changes are not short-term; in fact, in the short term, some are immeasurable. Nor are they random; they happen in predictable sequences and occur because two parties exist where before there was one, because new leaders emerge with new characteristics, and because new ideas are put forth. At each stage of economic development, there are manifestations of political change. This chapter documents this process. These changes affect the entire political system; if political power had been centralized, it becomes decentralized. In combination, these changes also induce a change in the political culture.

In this context, cultural transformation is defined as a fundamental change in values or in the way the community sees itself. There may be a general expanding of horizons for the community as a result of it being thrust into the national spotlight, the emergence of hope and pride, more arts and cultural activities, and, ironically, doubtfulness. In addition, the lifestyle may change from rural to more urban, and concurrent with growth, the population may diversify, the community may polarize into a "we/they" division as a result of the influx of outsiders, and unions may arrive on the scene as a topic of discussion, sparking change.

The material for the section on political transformation was drawn from interviews with the elite, comments from members of the general public, and background material and public documents. Unless otherwise noted, the data for the analysis in the section on cultural transformation come almost entirely from the public opinion data; quotations are from individual respondents.[1] In general, the cultural changes were most noticeable to the general public, whereas the political changes were more perceptible to the elite.

There appear to be several commonalities in the political events that take place in communities undergoing major economic development:

1. There are more actors in the political arena, and decision making becomes more decentralized.
2. The new leaders are more likely to be outsiders, to have more education, and to be eager to professionalize the public sector.
3. The transformation of the political leadership from good old boys to the new regime does not progress at a steady rate; there are setbacks and sudden surges.
4. Although the community's power needs to be centralized to equalize the bargaining power of the company, political regimes that were centralized before the plant eventually become more decentralized.
5. Negotiation continues between local community leaders and the company over resources that were not initially obtained for the community.

The following progression outlines the stages in the political transformation:

1. Announcement. Good old boys; small number of leaders; centralized power; informal decisions; one party.
2. Plant opening. Replacement of one or two key leaders.
3. Transition. New breed of leaders; new programs (planning); professionalization.
4. Middle to long term. Use of merit in hiring; more formal decision making; new actors.
5. Transition to maturity. Second party; decentralization.
6. Maturity. Consensus that economic development is a goal; complete turnover; new way of doing business (formal); professionalization.

POLITICAL TRANSFORMATIONS

Typically, before the plant announcement is made, a tight group of political actors is in power. The political situation in Smyrna illustrates this point. There the mayor, Sam Ridley, headed a strong city hall machine. As chapter 4 and the siting literature tell us,[2] centralization of power within the community is a huge advantage in bargaining with a large corporation like an auto company, in which power is centralized, even unitary. The company may not welcome the sight of new leaders who have not known each other for years, not shared values, and not worked together informally. Mayor Ridley personally worked to convince Nissan to open a plant in Smyrna, but Mayor Jones of Spring Hill, Tennessee, tried to annex the land on which the plant was built and ultimately argued against recruiting the plant in his political campaign. And in Marysville, spearheaded by the election of a new-breed politician, Tom Kruse, the former Mayor Knuckles and his camp started to disintegrate after the auto plant opened, although Knuckles and his followers neither recruited nor resisted the plant.

At all the sites, the auto companies were careful not to have their executives and middle managers participate in politics, become active in controversial political activities, or take political positions. Rather, the companies became involved in what one community leader described as "warm and fuzzy" activities—the United Way and educational sponsorships and donations, for example. The new political actors in town are more likely to be the new chief of police, fire chief, superintendent of schools, chief planner, and others who are hired after the plant is opened, using new criteria that emphasize the importance of professionalism.

Old-guard business leaders are sometimes ambivalent about the plant because it brings about a change in the way business, as well as government, is conducted. Decentralization may appeal to some citizens because it appears to be more democratic than centralization, replacing a set of older actors with new faces and breaking up the power hold of a small set of actors. However, decentralization may impair quick action on decisions. The new actors are more beholden to the company than were their predecessors. Thus, the presence of new actors, although it looks more democratic in that there is a change in the cast, may mean a greater commitment to economic development in general and the plant's interests in particular. In effect, there is some debate over economic development or not, but the new-guard leaders are overwhelmingly enthusiastic.

As stated earlier, a sea change occurs in the politics of these communities; a new politics emerges. Among some of its characteristics are a change in the elected leadership and appointed offices, the birth of a second political party, changes in government structure and the emergence of proposals to consolidate the city and county governments, and the emergence of planning as an important function.

Emergence of New Political Leaders

The turnover in political leadership usually begins at the time of the first election for city and county positions after the plant opens; typically, within three elections, substantial change has occurred. The key actors who step down or are defeated at election time are the members of the city council and of the county commission, the mayor, and the head of the chamber of commerce. The person in the last office is often appointed, not elected, and is fairly easy to oust. Other important jobs experiencing turnover are the chief of police, the fire chief, the head planner of the city or county planning commission, and the superintendent of schools.

Political change occurs in three ways. First, it may occur because of turnover; incumbents may resign or be defeated by challengers. Second, leaders may change their behavior in response to demands of the public or the auto company. Third, the values of the new leaders may be different from those of the old guard, resulting in changes in the political culture. Most of the political change at the four sites occurred in either the first or the third way. There were one or two examples of the second type of change—responsiveness to ensure political survival. In Marysville, for example, the leaders introduced and passed an ordinance banning the siting of a biomedical waste incinerator within the city limits in response to public pressure after first approving an economic development officer's recruitment efforts.

Turnover per se does not always constitute change. Thus, it might result in a different face but the same value system. This is particularly likely to happen in an insulated community. What is needed for actual change to occur is for the leadership to become fundamentally different. Only at mature sites such as Smyrna did such a total transformation take root completely.

At the two "middle-aged" sites, Georgetown and Marysville, there has been turnover in the office of the mayor but not in the county government. This is not unusual. County governments are the slowest to change and tend to represent the most rural elements of a community. They also tend to be less in favor of economic development than city councils, for example.

What are the hallmarks of the old political culture? The leader tends to be a good old boy or girl in terms of values, to be a native, born and reared in the town or county, to be less enthusiastic about economic development than about preserving the character of the town, to have a less-than-average education, meaning he or she was self-educated or schooled at the hometown college, and to be parochial rather than worldly. The new leader, on the other hand, tends to be a professional; from outside the county or state; in favor of economic development; well educated, having attended a college outside the county or state; and worldly rather than parochial in outlook.

The chair of the county commission at one of the sites epitomized the old-style leader. He was an affable and intelligent man whose main pursuit was farming rather than politics. He was expected to do his job full-time and was compensated at a salary of $40,000 a year. He took off one morning a week to attend a hog auction, where he sold his livestock. One of the other leaders is illustrative of the new type of community leader, although she is not currently an elected official. An officer in the local League of Women Voters publicly criticized the commissioner for taking one day off a week to sell his livestock at auction while on a full-time government job, alleging conflict of interest. The commissioner thought these charges were not justified and was stunned by his critic's rudeness since he thought his commitment to the auction did not inter-fere with his ability to perform his duties. Having been a friend of his critic for years, he took her criticism as a personal insult. Such conflicts exemplify the classic value clash that can occur between "unreformed" leaders and the "new" political leaders. The two groups of leaders do not know how to interpret each other's behavior. They speak a differ-ent language.

The mayor of Georgetown, Tom Prather, and the mayor of Marysville, Tom Kruse, personify the new leader. Prather is young, magnetic, and glamorous and has considerable political ambition. He has had many loyal followers and was able to marshal the forces of the city council and county commission to speak to one another and solve their mutual prob-lems. Recall from chapter 1 that through extraordinary patience and bargaining skills, Mayor Prather was able to negotiate annexation of the plant to the town of Georgetown, thereby bringing profit and payroll tax revenues to the city and to Scott County. The companies usually prefer to locate on unannexed land, outside any town's jurisdiction. Prather also professionalized the planning function.

Although the mayor and his appointees, including a police chief, fire chief, and water director, are thoroughly modern, reformed good-government types, the Scott County Commission has not undergone a complete change. The county commissioner, or "judge" as he is known in these parts, is a close political friend and former mentor of Tom Prather. He and others describe the commissioner as a new-guard type, and he probably meets the criteria in that he has had a formal education; however, his rural constituency prevents him from being a truly progressive new-guard leader.

Mayor Tom Kruse of Marysville is another example of a new-guard leader. He is a Democrat who was easily elected in a solidly Republican county. Although the election was technically nonpartisan, this was still quite a feat. He removed some of the tight group of good old boys who for years had dominated town politics but retained certain of the old guard in appointed positions, particularly those who commanded "pull" on the council and who were professional in their outlook. Annexation has also been on Mayor Kruse's agenda, although by law annexation of some contiguous land between the plant and Marysville has to be achieved first. Kruse, who runs a dry cleaning establishment, was schooled outside the area and earlier held a bureaucratic position with the state of Ohio. Having been stung by the ravages of partisanship, he has been eager to build bridges across party lines.

As in Georgetown, Marysville's political transformation has not been complete. This explains why in chapter 2 both Marysville and Georgetown were labeled time period 7 rather than 8 (completely mature) as Smyrna was. In Marysville, the mayor exemplifies the new guard, but the county commissioners represent a mixed group of old and new guard. The mayor has adopted a strategy of inclusion, complete with incorporating the experienced and trusted members of the government, either city council members or mayoral appointees.

Although Marysville has had its auto plant longer than any of the other communities, the leadership there has not completely turned over and the town has not undergone a complete cultural transformation; in fact, based on the interviews, it appears as though a turnover at the mayoral level followed by replacement of key mayoral appointees would wipe out all the new guard in town. One indication that economic development was not a firmly rooted idea in Marysville is the way in which the controversy surrounding the medical waste incinerator threatened the future of the entire economic development office.

Although the four sites share certain general characteristics, the details of the process of political transformation were different at each site. The least mature site, Spring Hill, has not undergone many of the changes that have occurred elsewhere. The fact that controversy was still erupting at the time of our visit in 1990 was a sign that the site was in the early stages of political transformation. After an abortive attempt to annex the land on which the plant is built, Mayor Jones used the plant as a campaign issue and ran against the plant.[3] Thus, a new guard had not taken over except in professional positions such as the head of planning for Maury County and for the city of Columbia. There are two chambers of commerce; one was in transition, having recruited a head from outside the state who was an enthusiastic booster of economic development, and the other in a nearby county resembles somewhat a traditional old-guard organization. Chamber members have dinner once a week and dub themselves "the committee of last resort," reminiscent of something out of early community power studies, such as Floyd Hunter's study of Atlanta.[4]

The irony in Smyrna was that the machine credited with recruiting the plant was dismantled by it. When the Smyrna respondents were asked who was responsible for the plant being in their community, they unanimously answered, "Mayor Sam Ridley." His regime was so tightly knit that it could accurately be described as a machine. After the plant was opened, the mayor was charged with conflict of interest for sending city cars to his own car dealership for servicing. While under indictment, he ran for reelection against five other candidates and won with 60 percent of the vote. After being convicted, he appointed his twin brother to take his place for the remainder of the term.

One of the issues that aroused the ire of the citizens of Smyrna was the town club, which required a public subsidy to sustain it. In the words of one respondent, Smyrna is a "working-class town" where the subsidy of a country club was viewed as a case of the middle class and working class subsidizing the rich.

Opposition to Mayor Sam was further set in motion after he and his brother "excused their own utility bills," that is, charged themselves the no-use rate. A member of his opposition who worked in the city utility department got wind of the situation and spread the word; subsequently, a group of citizens came to every city council meeting wearing T-shirts with the word "Watchdogs" emblazoned on them to let the mayor know he was being watched. The movement to pass a new city charter also was less a reform movement than an attempt to prevent the mayor from appointing council members for remainders of terms due to midterm resignations or retirements, thus ensuring the incumbents an advantage at election time.

Smyrna as a city was less reformed than the surrounding areas that make up the Smyrna site, such as Rutherford County and Murfreesboro. The Rutherford County Chamber of Commerce at the Smyrna site is headed by a major booster of economic development and of Nissan. The nearby city of Murfreesboro also has its share of boosters. During the years after the plant was sited, the Rutherford Planning Commission and the Rutherford County Chamber of Commerce underwent major cultural changes, which included the appointment of a new talented, dynamic, and innovative leader named Ralph Vaughn. Another way the new-guard leaders in Smyrna were close to the company and different from the old guard is that many in the local government and in the chamber were married to employees of the plant. Thus, although the permanent aspects of political culture change are not yet complete, Smyrna has progressed to the eighth stage of development; the turnover in the elite has occurred, but the permanent change in the attitude of the community, referred to as political culture, is still evolving.

Parties

All four sites are in areas dominated by one political party. Smyrna is in middle Tennessee, which includes Nashville and the surrounding rural areas. Historically, it has been Democratic at least in local politics. In his policy positions on issues, Mayor Sam Ridley was a Democrat in the southern Democratic tradition. Middle Tennessee has had its more liberal pockets, such as Murfreesboro, which is the county seat and home of Middle Tennessee State University and a music, arts, and sports festival. Local politics were still predominantly Democratic at the time the middle managers and executives from Nissan arrived on the scene, but there is now evidence of a viable Republican party. The newcomers, of managerial rank, are responsible for a Republican party in local politics.

The impact area for Spring Hill includes both Maury and Williamson Counties. Maury is a typical rural, predominantly Democratic county. Williamson, with its county seat Franklin, is a bedroom community for executives from Nashville and thus almost entirely Republican. After the plant opened, Williamson County engaged in a long-term planning exercise designed to increase the number of multifamily rental units and units for lower-income families. One would expect the new diversity in the county's population to result in a shift toward more of a two-party system, which it did. Therefore, previously one-party counties had to adjust to the advent of a second party that was started by the newcomers. Similarly, in Maury County, the leaders and the public observed the beginning of another breed of Democrat, which was not surprising given that most of the new Spring Hill blue-collar workers were more pro-union, liberal, and northern, rather than southern, Democrats.

Both the town and the county around the Marysville site had been solidly Republican, but after the plant opened a Democrat was elected, albeit in a nonpartisan election; however, the county governments of Logan and Union remain rural Republican Ohio mainstays. By contrast, Georgetown and Scott County had clearly established Democratic party traditions. Mayor Tom Prather was the grandson of an earlier Mayor Prather, a Democrat during Franklin Delano Roosevelt's presidency; but here again, with the influx of professionals, middle managers, yuppies, and developers, the area has become increasingly Republican at the local level.

New Ideas and Radical Changes

The influx of newcomers with diverse backgrounds and values stimulates the community to such an extent that a mix is created similar to the policy primeval soup described by John Kingdon.[5] There may be efforts to get the state to make greater investments in the region's public education; recognition that planning is necessary; attempts to annex the plant site; proposals to consolidate city and county governments (Georgetown); efforts to change the charter of the city government to achieve procedural changes; and efforts to increase economic development activity by hiring a full-time economic development officer.

Since several of these ideas were covered previously, the discussion here will focus on the efforts to consolidate city and county governments and to change the city charter. City-county consolidations are rarely proposed and even more rarely passed. The reasons are simple: although a community may achieve economy of scale when merged, the incumbent actors (the mayor and the county commissioner) have nothing to gain from the merger and everything to lose. Notably, the consolidation referendum in Georgetown had the backing of the city government, the county government, the mayor of Georgetown, and the county commissioner. Recall that the mayor had worked long and hard to get the city and county to cooperate regarding the consolidation and that he was a friend of the county commissioner. Development interests, particularly those of one big developer, defined the debate in terms of stopping "big government" and paid for television ads to that effect. The proposal to consolidate was defeated by a large margin. The defeat is probably not the last chapter of this story. As Kingdon suggests, ideas have to percolate.[6]

The other radical innovation was put forth in Smyrna and involved the charter proposal to change the city charter to require elections if a post is vacated midterm. Although it may have looked like a "good government" proposal, its goal was to curb the mayor's power. In this case, the proposal passed. Also during Mayor Sam's tenure, a professional city manager was hired to help upgrade the city government. Yet, although the rest of the country would have considered hiring the city manager evidence of professionalization or reform, in Smyrna the move was associated too closely with the old regime since Mayor Sam made the appointment; the proposal to change the charter and have a different method of selecting a city administrator, therefore, gained steam and ultimately was passed. These examples illustrate how the new people affiliated with the plant are responsible not only for new faces but for new ideas as well.

Planning

Prior to the plant, the community saw the ideal of planning as an unwarranted government intrusion, if they thought about it as necessary at all. City planning becomes more important after the opening of the plant. The sudden growth that occurs after the plant is opened catapults planning from a peripheral, often disdained, role to a central and necessary function. The turning point occurs when a full-time professional planner is hired. This is the first sign that the community takes planning seriously. Planning usually becomes controversial since much is at stake for both developers and citizens. Georgetown is a good example of a community in which the planning function was upgraded and rationalized, but not without controversy. Appointed by Mayor Prather, its new full-time planner, a University of California at Berkeley graduate, caused consternation as she quickly set in place a set of formal procedures for the review of proposals. Developers had become used to a more casual approach.

One of the most lasting impacts of the plant is that there are plural ideas that are introduced into the community. If there had been one way of doing things before, now there are several. In most settings, this pluralism leads to the elite becoming more progressive and more in favor of economic development and to the growth of a second party. Ironically, these changes decentralize power. If the community was highly concentrated before the plant, it becomes decentralized, at least in the short term. Then, aided by another process of transformation, the new guard attempts to solidify its base by appointing like-minded, professionally trained boosters of economic development to key positions. All the while, new political ideas and radical innovations percolate in the policy soup of the community, as Kingdon would say.

CULTURAL TRANSFORMATION

Broadening of Horizons

A community's culture is defined as the set of values or mores the citizenry has in common. In the cases of the four communities studied here, undeniably urban and rural cultures came together. In the case of three sites, one culture was Japanese and one was American; in the fourth case, northern urban and southern small-town American cultures were combined. There is a notion from studies of American-Mexican culture that suggests that over time the resulting culture is a convergence of the two.[7]

Recall that cultural change occurs in two ways: as a result of a community being in the national spotlight and developing a sense of hope and pride and ultimately doubtfulness, and as a result of the introduction of a more urban lifestyle.

Being in the National Spotlight

"How we gonna keep them down on the farm once they've seen Japan?"[8] This sentiment captures how introducing a large automobile plant into a community can expand citizens' cultural horizons. In many cases, the national media coverage surrounding the plant siting peaks at the time of the announcement. Such publicity is easy for an outsider to overlook but difficult for a local to forget. One respondent proudly stated that the plant "spotlights middle Tennessee." A resident of Kentucky proclaimed, "The plant put Scott County on the map."

Initially, publicity was generated by the intense bidding war. When the announcement was made that the auto plant would be built, reporters from the *Wall Street Journal* and the *New York Times* swarmed over the town like locusts. The press heralded the five-cent cup of coffee available at a Columbia, Tennessee, restaurant and the election day tradition in which the local winner treats everyone to free food at that restaurant.

At first, the local folk were flattered by all the attention. By the time our research began, however, the elite was weary of interviews by outsiders. In fact, one Georgetown leader, expressing her fatigue, asked, "How is your study different from all the other studies?" Besides fatigue, a degree of suspicion had crept in, prompting one respondent to say testily that he was taping the interview so he would not be misquoted.

Hope and Pride

Having a large auto plant in their town brought great hope to the residents of each of the four communities. As one leader in Marysville said, it would "let young people stay and raise families here." The citizens obviously recognized the tangible benefits of economic growth, as illustrated by statements such as "Tax money helps the community," and "Seven members of my family are employed by Honda." Coexistent with this was the idea that a successful partnership had been created between the community and the auto company: "There is an attitude in the community of acceptance of Toyota; it differs from the experience in Detroit."

Similarly, there was a feeling that the community was undergoing a renaissance, as illustrated by the Spring Hill respondent who said, "Spring Hill is alive. Youth can learn new ideas. People are talking more." Another Spring Hill resident said, "[The plant] has upgraded their [the residents'] class to middle." Then there were endorsements, such as the Spring Hill resident who said: "I think everyone's views toward everything has changed for the better."

Hope and pride were expressed in many ways; one respondent from Georgetown announced proudly, for instance, that he "got [his] GED." Another Georgetown resident remarked that "local people have moved from old houses to new since the plant came." Two other people from Georgetown remarked that "[the plant] moved from being a small town to a richer better community," and "The new people who are coming in are interested in better education. The plant is a breath of fresh air." "People and government are proud of the company," a Spring Hill resident proclaimed. One person even attributed the opening of the plant to divine intervention: "We church people have been blessed with the coming of the plant." Another person said, "The plant has been a positive. It has given a better image to this part of the South." Describing the pride in partnership, one person said, "The plant was a positive example of what the company and the community could do together in harmony or partnership."

Cultural Uplift

Many respondents remarked that their community had been upgraded. "People are going to work. We were too much of a welfare community before," a Georgetown resident declared, and a Marysville respondent asked rhetorically, "Where would all these people be without Honda?" Many remarks mentioned the increased number and variety of cultural offerings in the community, particularly curricular changes in the schools. Residents claimed that the plant "made an impact on charitable causes, cruisers for the police, money for the parks," brought in "more cultural things," and had "cultural benefits." One respondent said, "Toyota brought a golf course," supporting the argument advanced in chapter 5 that one benefit of the plants was that directly or indirectly they supported the construction of more recreational facilities.

Another type of cultural upgrade occurred as a result of the link created between local citizens and the new international community. One respondent pointed out that "our town has a sister city in Japan and cultural contacts with the Japanese"; this is true of several of the cities. A respondent from Marysville indicated that "having Japanese kids in our schools [helps the children] understand cultural diversity." Another person remarked on the "intermixture of cultures and [that a] beautiful new elementary school" had been built after the plant opened. A Marysville resident stated that "people have become a little more worldly because of the [plant's] programs." A Georgetown area resident noted that he moved to the community because "Toyota is helping to improve the school system." Another Georgetown person said, "The [plant] was a positive impact on services, school, quality of government, and opportunity for citizens."

Residents of Georgetown and Smyrna, respectively, commented that "Toyota is supposedly putting money into schools and there's public day care" and that "the increase in day care could be linked to the plant." By any yardstick, the availability of public day care was a major change for communities of this size and sophistication.

Citizens in Georgetown also mentioned that Japanese was being taught at the local university. Referring to Georgetown College's curriculum, a resident said, "It has made [the] university more aware; more arts being offered." More surprising, a Smyrna resident commented on the "overall positive attitude of people toward Japanese methods of manufacturing."

Quality-of-life differences were also noted, in the "quality of government," for instance, and the "greater opportunity for citizens." Some individuals defined the differences in economic terms, saying that people "have upgraded their class [to middle] due to an improvement in their quality of life." Viewing the plant as an economic magnet, one respondent acknowledged that "there have been a lot more medical people who have come to the area." "Grocery stores, restaurants, roads, bridges have been built," chimed in a Georgetown resident. A Marysville resident described the improvements by noting that there were "more management and engineering type people in the area." A person from Smyrna put it this way: "The plant brought wealthier and more educated people; resale value is good in this area."

Smyrna residents tended to emphasize the plant's economic effects, while those in Spring Hill emphasized the cultural, perhaps because locals were not hired for front-end jobs at the plant. Georgetown respondents were particularly aware of Toyota's value in "community involvement." At all four sites numerous respondents commented that the plant brought restaurants and "Japanese culture into the town."

Doubtfulness

Even with all of the positive feelings, however, residents of all four communities harbored doubt just below the surface. Why? Because they figured the bubble would burst. After all, the daily news was filled with reports of plant closings. Such worries were not surprising in Marysville and Georgetown, both of which were somewhat depressed before the plant; however, the comment of one Smyrna resident that "as long as [the plant] stays stable, families have a good source of income," indicates that at least some people were worried there as well.

One Marysville respondent expressed concern that the town could become too dependent on the plant: "The plant may make the community reliant on one source or one economy." As reported in chapter 7, doubts also surfaced in the citizens' responses to the question concerning whether they would want an additional industrial facility in their community.

Loss of Rural Lifestyle

"We have opened our eyes to see that we are no longer a small town." As expressed in this comment by a Marysville resident, a common theme among respondents was that the opening of the plant was a turning point for their communities and that life would never again be the same. A Spring Hill resident declared, for example, "There is more crime now than before plant," and another said the plant was responsible for there being more "bars and restaurants."

The change in the physical environment was the most obvious evidence of the loss of a rural lifestyle. A Spring Hill resident claimed that the plant "spoiled the rural demeanor of the area," and, in the words of one Georgetown resident, "This is no longer an oasis; it is a fast-food strip." A Smyrna resident said the plant "tore up a lot of land and built a lot of houses that are empty." Another Spring Hill resident complained that it "bulldozed lots of virgin land—lots of timber pasture lands gone." A Smyrna resident complained, "We have such large areas of concrete and buildings, lost land." Continuing to remark on the physical impact, other Smyrna residents commented that "sometimes too many people coming in can overdo" and that the plant "takes up lots of extra land space." Yet another Smyrna resident decried the fact that "commuters use city services but live outside the city." A Georgetown resident had a similar complaint: "Our farmland has been sold to the plant; our country is no longer a country." Two Smyrna citizens echoed this glibly, one of whom commented on "the loss of land," the other that he "left the big city to get away from it and now it's here again." A Georgetown resident cautioned, "We need our trees. Be careful!"

Other citizens complained that their communities were getting too big. One said, "I don't like largeness." Another described the town as "busting at the seams," saying it had "lost [its] small-town atmosphere." Another respondent put the size problem this way: "Population is almost a disadvantage."

Other respondents commented on what they perceived to be urban ills. One person remarked, "Grocery prices have gone up two or three cents an item." Another summarized the urban ills as "crime, speeders, and fights." A Spring Hill resident claimed that "the crime rate has tripled." A Smyrna resident cited "overcrowding and racial problems similar to large cities."

One Marysville resident complained that "we paid for a pressurized water valve for the plant," while another said, "We got the highest water cost in Ohio and the real estate also." City living was an annoyance to one Georgetown resident because "gas is wasted in traffic." "There are less jobs and more traffic," noted another Georgetown citizen. "It's impossible to get through town."

Based on their comments, it appears that the residents of these four communities believe there are both costs and benefits to having a large plant in their area but that in the final analysis the pluses outweigh the minuses. As one Georgetown resident said: "We're very pleased with the new jobs. The positives outweigh the negatives." Another Georgetown person thought of how seeming costs could be benefits: "Building new roads is a cost to local government, but it brought more business." A cynical person in Smyrna realized there was "no free ride; schools and other government services cost more," whereas another resident of Smyrna said the community should strike a balance and that he was "in favor of carefully measured growth." A Georgetowner expressed another view: "Community hasn't grown for years, but growth also has problems."

Continuing in the vein of urban ills, a Marysville respondent was concerned about the increase in property values, claiming, "Government has gotten more revenue." Another person from Smyrna pointed out the "positive effect [of the plant on jobs], negative for population growth." Another Georgetown resident summed up his feelings in no uncertain terms: "I wish the plant was not there." More typically, residents felt ambivalent: "Traffic has increased, but that is okay if the plant is beneficial to the people," and "Traffic is horrible; we have more choices now, though."

Many of the urban ills the respondents were concerned about, such as the higher divorce rates and real estate prices, are familiar problems to residents of medium-sized and large towns but were unfamiliar to residents of these small towns and rural communities. One respondent from Marysville summed up one of the differences in lifestyle when she said, "The plant people are always in a hurry." The costliness of living in a city was also on people's minds. A complaint from Georgetown was that "smaller businesses are being replaced with big chains." A comment from Marysville stated that there was "too much traffic and too many people with no respect for other people's property."

Another person summed up the changes in the lifestyle in Marysville as a function of "overspending"; another commented on the "consumer credit counseling necessary for the 'Hondamoids.' They don't handle money very well." Another person summed up this problem of over-spending as "the Honda syndrome."

Some of the changes tore at the fabric of local society. A Marysville respondent commented: "My wife is an attorney. There are more di-vorces taking place, more stress on marriages." A Georgetown resident said fiercely, "Keep Toyota in Japan, and keep U.S. companies in the States." A resident from Smyrna lamented that "just when retirees want to live in the country, this area has turned into suburbia." One of the most damning comments was made by a Georgetown resident: "They located a plant too close to a city that was not ready for growth."

In the residents' minds at least, the scope of the changes in their towns was enormous. The elite in one location cited "liquor by the drink" as a major impact of having the plant, a reference to the passage of a county-by-county referendum that revoked a ban on selling liquor by the drink. The referendum never would have passed in these Bible Belt communities before the influx of outsiders.

Adjusting to the Diversity and Change in Population

"It's not just more people—it's different people." This comment sums up the feelings of town residents to the increasing mix of people from varying backgrounds moving in to their communities. A person from Smyrna said: "There are more different religions and people of differ-ent backgrounds." There were negative comments as well; someone in Marysville, for instance, said the plant "has brought in some good people and some undesirables."

According to residents of Spring Hill, the dominant group their town had to absorb was "Yankees," and in the view of several residents they were not an easy group to absorb. "Northerners have an attitude. They are angry and harsh people. Their kids are more violent," said one area resident. Another resident of Spring Hill captured the sentiments of many: "These northerners are ungodly rude." Others disagreed, like the Spring Hill person who said, "[The new] people are nice."

Another respondent from Georgetown said the change in population amounted to "construction and factory workers from Kentucky, Indiana, Ohio, and Texas." A Smyrna resident echoed, "People coming from everywhere: Detroit, Kentucky, short and far distances." Other comments from Spring Hill pointed out that the diversification was not just based on geography. One respondent said that "there were more urban and middle-class people. There were also more Catholics," as well as more "business-type-looking people than before." The influx of new people also meant there were "more different religious people of different backgrounds," as one Smyrnan said, and "different people, bigger churches, schools, more people in congregation." Another said that some of the new workers "come from small towns in [the] South and management comes from Michigan."

Several respondents in Smyrna mentioned that there were now "Laotian people," people of "diversified cultures," as well as "more Asians in the area," so that "people are more aware of Asians." Except for Spring Hill, there were far more Japanese. Many Smyrna and Georgetown residents commented that there were "lots of Japanese here now." Another Smyrna respondent said that there were "more people from foreign countries coming in and people from the North," as if the two groups were from equivalently alien cultures.

Some of the respondents suggested that there were specific economic implications to having so many strangers in their midst: "People are becoming greedier. People are collecting welfare and costing the government money." A Spring Hill resident stated resentfully that the plant "brought a lot of people into the community without money. Had to give credit to strangers."

Clearly, respondents had mixed feelings as to whether the diversification of and increase in population was a good or a bad development. One Smyrnan saw these changes as positive and part of a larger process of sophistication, saying, "The population increase means a diversified way of life, different religions, different places to eat." Two typical statements in this vein were from Smyrnans: "There's a better attitude toward Asians since the plant came," and "There's a tolerance to outsiders and an acceptance of the make-up of the community."

Others had a less generous reaction bordering on the xenophobic. One Smyrnan said, "Lower-class people came from Detroit and Texas [and] often would end up on welfare." Two angry residents from Georgetown and Smyrna, respectively, said, "A lot of Japanese people cut us out of jobs," and "A lot of foreigners have taken over." A Marysville resident said there was "a certain amount of antagonism toward Japanese."

Some residents felt there had been a loss of culture associated with the influx of the newcomers, a sentiment embodied in this comment: "[The plant] changed the southern character of the community." A Smyrna resident echoed this feeling, saying the newcomers had a "different standard of living. Family traditions and values are leaving." The following two comments were made by Georgetown residents: "It's a different culture than what our town was used to since W.W. II," and "People had to adjust to Japanese coming in; difficult for some veterans."

Some residents were concerned since the average age of the employees of the three Japanese plants is well below the average age of workers in the American automobile industry. A "young group of people from different parts of the country are coming in," said one person who summed up the observations of many. But at least one respondent, from Marysville, noted the good side of the influx because of the "younger people, businesses stay open longer."

Polarization

Not surprisingly, given the radical transformations occurring, the four communities became polarized into several groups: residents versus immigrants; lower-class versus middle-class; Yankee versus southerner in Spring Hill; and Japanese versus American in Georgetown and Smyrna. As expressed by a Smyrna resident, one core notion was that the outsiders were predatory: "People are coming from surrounding counties and are getting the plant jobs." Someone from Georgetown echoed this feeling: "Too many local people [are] out of work that can't get a job at Toyota."

Further evidence that the natives may have had to struggle with the idea of accepting outsiders comes from the findings reported in chapter 7 that the natives were significantly less likely to think the package was justified, less likely to think the community was better off with the plant, and less likely to want another large industrial plant in their community.

The class schism evolved from a recognition that the income levels of some residents had risen while those of others had been left behind.

Residents were also concerned that, though newcomers were paid a lot, they were not a better class. One Smyrna resident commented that the newcomers were "better paid " than the locals. Another Smyrna resident lamented that "there are illiterate people making $40,000–$50,000 a year, and they cannot read and write." The tension between the two groups bordered on class conflict. Regarding this issue, one Smyrna person said the plant led to a "higher social class population," and another said the plant "made a lot of people rich overnight." A Smyrna person said that the "change in the make-up of the area has gone to higher middle class instead of low income." Another person put it this way: "More well-to-do people now. Sexual harassment on the job"—an interesting juxtaposition of two seemingly very different issues.

Those who felt left behind also voiced their concerns, like the Spring Hill resident who said, "Developers build $100,000 homes people can't afford," or a Smyrna resident who declared that "low-income people are struggling to get by." Another person pinpointed the problem: "There are a lot of $4-an-hour jobs but not enough higher-paying jobs." One Georgetown resident was angry over this irony: "The plant raised prices of real estate, and people cannot afford to buy homes." A Smyrna resident, who obviously felt left out, summed up his and others' feelings: "The people that continue to suffer are the poor because everything [prices] continues to go up."

The "U" Word: Unionization

Although only one of the four auto plants was unionized (under the Saturn–United Automobile Workers [UAW] agreement), unionization has begun to rear its head for the first time in these southern or otherwise conservative communities. One distinct characteristic of this issue is that no one speaks about unions but they are very much on everyone's mind. Attempts have been made to unionize workers in Marysville and Smyrna, and these union elections have brought the issue to the fore periodically. Smyrna had a union election in 1990, but to the great relief of most of the elite interviewed, the union was defeated. One local head of a chamber of commerce, referring to the defeat of the UAW as the bargaining agent, noted that the Smyrna vote "sent an important message" to the rest of the country. The message, in this leader's view, was that unions were not welcome.

In the Spring Hill area, several small manufacturing concerns scattered across the county have been organized by unions in the paper, textile, and chemical industries. The Nissan vote in Smyrna, however, was of a different magnitude. Nissan was the largest employer by far in the region, the next being Middle Tennessee State University. Not surprisingly, the prospect that the largest employer would become unionized made the business leaders anxious. Furthermore, the UAW was viewed as stronger and more militant than the unions in other industries. Finally, the UAW was traditionally associated with Detroit, Michigan, an area of the country that was not regarded favorably by Tennesseans. Sprinkled throughout the interviews with both the elite and the general public were comments like "We do not want to be a little Detroit."

The leaders were much more explicit and vehement than the general public in voicing their feelings toward unions. They seemed to find the concept of unions loathsome because it was alien and the reality even more loathsome because of what they believed it would mean for the business climate, such as strikes, alienation, and image problems. Members of the public were less judgmental, preferring to think of unionized workers as simply alien or different. Among the more vitriolic comments was one a Smyrna leader made when asked why Smyrnans preferred to have a Japanese rather than an American automobile plant in their community. He leaned over and, in a Godfatherlike whisper, said, "Because the Japanese automobile industry is clean." In the context of the interview, the research team construed "clean" to mean "nonunion."

SUMMARY

The physical and economic changes brought by the plant pale in comparison to the permanent mark that cultural and political transformation leaves. A Georgetown resident summarized this transformation saying, "The plant came in like a whirlwind and after it settled we were all better off." Thus, some of the effects of the whirlwind of change may be disconcerting, particularly urban ills like traffic, crowds, and crime. The short-term effects may be destabilization for the longtime natives. All of a sudden, there is a Catholic church, a second political party, a change in political leadership, liquor by the drink, and Yankees or Japanese in a town that was once sleepy and stable.

What remains as permanent? Much of the change is permanent. Take the political change, for example, which follows this sequence. First, there is turnover to the "new guard," then the new guard's appointment of like-minded professionals in bureaucratic positions: fire chief, police chief, full-time planner, and full-time economic development officer. These persons implement policies that represent a new culture, involving a change from good old boys (or girls) to sophisticates, that is, professionals who were educated outside the area who have a higher educational level, who have a broad worldview, rather than a narrow, parochial view, and who are economic development boosters. Turning to the cultural transformation, it is a mélange of sweet and bitter. The community is thrust into the national spotlight and is filled with hope and pride at the future, and there is generally an increase in the community's alternatives. However, there are doubts in people's minds. They know that what goes boom can also go bust. The more transcendent and permanent change is the change from the rural small-town lifestyle to a more urban lifestyle. This transition from proto-urban to urban is not complete, but its direction is irreversible. Such hallmarks of the change to proto-urban are the annoying urban ills, such as traffic, crime, and crowds; the newfound diversity, which is permanent, be it the advent of Japanese or the advent of Yankees; the "we/they" differentiation or class polarization; and the simmering but invisible question of unionization, which the coming of the plant brings to the fore.

9 | Economic Development as a Policy Choice

ONE WAY to view economic development is as a policy choice made by a community; in fact, the community makes a series of decisions in which each one dictates the following one in an ever-narrowing range of alternatives. This sequence of decisions, which more resemble what Richard Cyert and James March describe as sequential decision making and satisficing behavior rather than maximizing behavior,[1] comprises two stages: first, the community chooses to develop or to preserve its traditional character. If the decision is to develop, the next step is for the community to decide to recruit a large industrial firm or to nurture the growth of small employers from within. If the decision is not to develop, subsequent decisions hinge on how best to do that.

The choice is not always made rationally, at least not in the sense of assessing all the alternatives and choosing the best for the community. Rather, the community displays a bounded rationality, similar to that described by the Cyert and March school.[2] There is also a need at this point for community leaders to develop what Bryan Jones and Lynn Bachelor call the "solution set" of the community leaders.[3] The choice to develop or not develop may not even be a conscious one. A community may suddenly be thrust into making a decision to accept or reject being the home to a large industrial plant without having the time to carefully consider the consequences. In three out of four of these sites (everywhere but Smyrna), the plant came as a surprise to the community, although the relevant state had wooed it.

WHY GREENFIELD SITINGS?

The three policy choices facing a community are to avoid growth and stay the same, to promote growth by bringing a large company to town from the outside (the so-called greenfield siting), and to promote growth by generating growth in small businesses. Being a greenfield siting has been the preferred choice of communities for several decades. The siting of a large plant can be a stimulus to the local economy. A plant means not only more jobs and expanded industry but increased political prestige as well. The choice is not without opposition, however. Businesspeople or other locals may fear that the plant will put upward pressure on wages and cause the breakup of their political power.[4]

From the employer's perspective, the greenfield siting has a lot to offer because the plant is located outside town or city limits. The company, therefore, is not restricted by local zoning ordinances. Further, land is cheap, labor docile, and transportation inexpensive.[5]

Politics Versus Economics

More than economics, political factors often determine a community's decision to pursue economic development. Over the last thirty years, the allure of jobs has meant that community leaders try to aggressively woo large industrial recruits.[6] Recently, there have been citizens' outcries at the size of the incentive packages given by communities to companies. Examples of such revolts are the Georgetown groundbreaking, where Ralph Nader, the unions, and citizens protested the size of the package; the Spring Hill election in which the mayor, seeing that the citizens' disgruntlement was sufficient to elect him, ran "against the plant." Beyond the four cases studies here, we can observe the Flat Rock, Michigan, election, in which the incentive package was controversial enough to defeat the mayor who brought it.[7]

Researchers are beginning to address the way town leaders can shape the destinies of their communities and either tame the legal and political controversies surrounding greenfield sitings or succumb to them. Michael Pagano and Ann Bowman, for instance, brilliantly elucidate the importance of local political leadership in shaping and fulfilling a community's vision and changing its face during a major economic development event, such as a focus on a certain image or face for the city.[8]

It should be noted again, as was developed in chapter 4, that the power relationship between the company and the community is largely unequal, particularly in terms of information and time. There is certainly not a level playing field, by a long shot. However, there is some encouraging news from the results in this book. There was a large amount of variation across the sites in the degree to which the community can negotiate a good deal, which is very encouraging from the point of view of the hubris of the community.

ASSUMPTIONS AND POLICY RECOMMENDATIONS

This section examines the economic assumptions behind the political move by community leaders to recruit a large company. Based on the experiences of the four sites, these assumptions are compared with reality. From there, it is possible to generate a list of recommendations to help a community avoid the common pitfalls of greenfield sitings, which is the policy choice taken by the communities in this study.

In general, the leaders of a town make the following assumptions about the impact of a large plant on their community: locals will be hired at the plant; the benefits from the plant will exceed the costs; commercial activity will be generated; the revenue flow will be even and steady, making the plant lucrative; and the effects of the plant will be felt when the plant opens, not when the plant is announced.

Contrasting the reality of the impacts of the plant to the preceding assumptions and responding with recommendations is the next task. The remainder of this chapter summarizes the major impacts of a large plant on a community. Each key finding is followed by recommendations of ways the community can deal with those impacts.

The Plant's Impact Is Diffuse and Regional. The community officials invited to the table to negotiate the in-lieu-of-tax payments are those heading the county or city where the plant is located, not those of the government units adjacent to the plant. Because of the speed of traveling on interstate highways and the decline in employment opportunities in the agricultural and manufacturing sectors of rural communities, however, the plant is likely to attract employees who will have to commute one or two hours each way.

• State economic development offices should attempt to provide better economic projections of the plant's actual impact area and should include leaders of more jurisdictions at the negotiating table based on projections about the average hiring radius of most plants in greenfield sites and average commuting distances in the area. Alternatively, the state could set up a plant impact fund from plant revenues to offset costs incurred by communities due to the plant's impact.

• In conjunction with the manufacturing company, the leaders of the county or city where the plant is being sited should attempt to reach an agreement about what counties and jurisdictions are within the impact area.

Lack of Time and Information Minimizes the Power of the Community. There is usually little time to conduct research on the plant's projected impact once the announcement of the siting is made. In fact, often the negotiating process begins within a day of the announcement.

• Leaders of the community should consider asking the employer to wait a month or two after it has made its decision before announcing it. This would help remedy the time deficit that the community has compared with the company in terms of research efforts. Unfortunately, this is difficult to do because members of the news media press the company for its decision; secrecy can be maintained, however, as Disney demonstrated when it purchased huge tracts of land in Orlando.

Secrecy has the added advantage to both the company and the community of controlling the land speculation that usually follows the plant announcement. In the case of the Toyota plant siting in Georgetown, Kentucky, the state made a costly error by committing to buy the land for the plant from farmers and other property owners and did so right after Toyota made its announcement. Real estate speculation was rampant in the weeks just after the announcement, causing an enormous increase in the cost of the package to the state, since the value of the land shot up. On the other hand, the company is only one of the actors. A governor who wants to claim credit for bringing the plant to the state also may be eager to announce the plant to impress the citizenry with his or her economic prowess.

• To solve the information imbalance, the community should negotiate to have impact studies done by engineers or economists. This commitment can be built into the package, as was done between Saturn and the governments of Maury County, Williamson County, and the city of Columbia. As Spring Hill illustrates, however, nothing can guarantee that a community will adopt the recommendations of the consultants. In this case, the community declined to implement the development fees recommended in its consultants' report. Finally, because of the time involved, this recommendation applies more to slow-track than to fast-track plants.

• Whenever possible, bargainers from other communities and studies of comparable communities should be made available.

• The community should negotiate to include "reopeners" in its agreement with the company; that is, it should be allowed to renegotiate the contours of the package if additional information becomes available.

The Time in Which to Solve Growth-related Problems Is Much Shorter Than Under Normal Growth Conditions. Without the plant, the usual problems associated with development, such as increases in traffic or in the demands for schools, are typically solved in, say, ten or twenty years; with the sudden influx of population, however, the community is pressured into solving these problems in three to four years.

- Communities should attempt to front-load payments from the company to the community by negotiating aggressive in-lieu-of-tax payments, for example, or should arrange ways to allocate revenue evenly across the impact period to spread out the plant's fiscal impact and create greater financial stability.

Planning Becomes a Central and Politicized Community Function. The change from a laissez-faire approach to making planning a central function in the community can be a tortuous one because much is at stake in each of these planning decisions, and they can become politically charged. Long-term planning needs to be done concerning a range of issues that affect areas both within and beyond the borders of the city and county in which the plant is located. Ohio's law bears some scrutiny in that it calls for multicounty planning bodies to coordinate planning on a regional basis across several counties. The problem is that, say in the Honda site, the three-county state-designated planning zone in which Marysville falls does not correspond to the counties in the precise area of the Honda plant's impact. Based on findings from the Economic Development Advisory Committee report in Georgetown, coordinating planning across multiple jurisdictions is highly recommended. There is no institutional memory since this is the first large plant. The planners and city and county officials need to record what worked and did not—a sort of data bank for planning.

- If a community is anticipating significant economic development, it should hire a full-time planner. A stable and professional economic development office with an institutional memory can be a very helpful tool in this endeavor.
- The focus of the planning process should be on the regional impact, particularly where sewage, water, and landfill demands are concerned. Invite all parties who may be affected to the negotiating and planning table.

Issues Often Arise That Were Not Anticipated at the Negotiations. Anything not negotiated at the beginning is very difficult or impossible to get later on; however, there are a variety of strategies at the community's disposal, each with its advantages and disadvantages.

The community quickly realizes that the burst of growth that occurs after the plant is built will incur costs in new schools and new infrastructure. It may also realize that the deal it negotiated for in-lieu-of-tax payments was not based on complete information. Chapter 4 specifies that the first round of negotiations occurs between the state and the company. The second round, the negotiations over in-lieu-of-tax payments, occurs between the community and the company. The third round occurs continually between the company and the community over the subsequent stages of economic development.

The community may employ various strategies designed to increase the amount of revenue available to it to offset the negative impact or drain the plan may have had on the local economy. Among the strategies a community might try out in the second and third rounds of negotiation are annexation; levying profit and payroll taxes; taking over ownership of utilities; imposing a sales tax or garnering general growth-related revenue, such as increased property taxes from new housing; development fees charged on a per lot basis, such as $150 for sewage and water per new lot; and negotiating a commitment from the company to buy its supplies, particularly construction materials, locally, thus guaranteeing a flow of sales tax revenue. If the community fails to negotiate one of these strategies in the second round, it may try again in the third round.

1. Annexation of the land on which the plant is built can be a revenue plus or minus for a community. On the one hand, annexation often means that a city must provide a level of services it currently does not have to provide to the area, such as sewage lines and water service. On the other hand, if the land is annexed, the community can garner revenue from payroll or profit taxes.

   Three out of the four communities in the study (Smyrna, Georgetown, and Spring Hill) pursued annexation, and it was achieved in Smyrna and Georgetown. Just after the announcement, Mayor Jones of Spring Hill tried quietly to gain support for the idea; later he did so more publicly and confrontationally. The citizens were not unified behind him and, in the second attempt, some showed up at a public hearing to voice their concerns. Nonetheless, there is strong evidence that in Smyrna and Georgetown annexation worked very effectively as a revenue enhancement device. For instance, Smyrna has, as of 1990, absolutely no debt and did not in the 1980s. By contrast, Murfreesboro, which did not annex the plant site but did bear the brunt of the community's population explosion and overflowing schools, went into significant debt after the opening of the plant.

Many states require that annexed land be contiguous. Companies usually locate the plant outside the jurisdiction of the nearest small city in what has been referred to as "geopolitical limbo."[9] In Marysville, for instance, the political leaders thought it would be advantageous to annex, but the land between the town's limits and the plant contains the second-largest employer in town, which did not want to be annexed.

The decision to site outside city limits appears to be a conscious one, although no interview data confirm this. What is certain is that with the exception of Nissan in Smyrna, the companies studied resisted the idea for obvious reasons. Being annexed would mean the company would be subject to payroll or profit taxes if the city had them or were to pass them in the future. Also, annexation would bring the plant under any zoning regulations the city had. In Smyrna, Nissan asked that the land be annexed because, in the words of a company representative, it wanted to "talk to one person," the one person being Mayor Sam. For the company, dealing with the fragmentation between the city and the county was even less attractive than annexing the land on which the plant was sited and consequently having fewer players with whom to have to negotiate. This was unusual, perhaps unique.

In Georgetown, the mayor had such formidable negotiating talents that he was able to annex after the plant was sited. Consequently, Georgetown was not affected by the revenue pinch that afflicted other communities during the later years of the development cycle. Because the city, rather than a private company, also *owned* the gas utility, annexation meant the city could pass a tax on gas and collect revenues in this way.

2. A profit tax is a tax levied by a city or county on the profits earned by companies within its juridiction. Although it is an effective way to garner revenue, for obvious reasons it is not welcomed by business. If the land on which a plant is built is not within town limits, this strat-

egy needs to be combined with annexation to achieve the desired results of extra revenue. This is what was done in Georgetown. To the credit of Mayor Tom Prather, Toyota agreed to annex the land on which it was building, making the plant's employees subject to payroll taxes and the plant subject to profit taxes. Furthermore, and this was a testimony to both the mayor's excellent bargaining skills and Toyota's good citizenship, Toyota waived its right to have a hearing regarding annexation, a step that could have delayed the flow of revenue by quite a while.

A payroll tax is a tax on those employees working within a particular jurisdiction, whether or not they reside in that city or county. Profit taxes are similar to payroll taxes except that they are levied on a firm's profits. For the first two years a plant is in operation, it is not profitable. Although a profit tax is an effective community strategy for enhancing revenue, there is a gap between the time a plant opens and when it starts to show a profit. In Georgetown, for example, the plant opened in 1985 and was annexed in 1988; revenue from payroll taxes started flowing into the town in 1988, but profit tax revenues did not flow in until late 1988 or early 1989. Further, payroll taxes are levied on all employees, regardless of where they live. In that way, they differ from income taxes, which are assessed at the point of residence.

3. One effective strategy a community can use if a large plant is being sited nearby is to buy a utility. Smyrna, for example, owned the natural gas utility, but in 1995 the Nissan Company in Smyrna announced it would build its own power plant. Georgetown managed to purchase privately owned Georgetown Water Company. In this case, ownership was a mixed blessing, however, because the local water supply was tainted with benzene, and it has and will continue to cost enormous amounts of time and effort to clean it up. At the time the interviews were conducted in 1990, Georgetown was having to pump in water through pipes from a nearby community as a stopgap measure. The water department was in the process of considering whether to clean up the spring or to construct a reservoir. In fact, the water to the plant was not supplied by the city of Georgetown but by a private water company. Notwithstanding this exceptional case, ownership of the utility did not lead to revenue enhancement as it did in Smyrna.

4. Sales taxes can be a very useful source of income for communities undergoing significant economic development. There is considerable

state-by-state variation in the way sales taxes are distributed back to the counties and in the equity of the formulas that are used to distribute them. Sales taxes are a substantial source of revenue when the economy is booming, but the coffers reflect it when the economy is languid; however, the revenue-enhancing activity generated in the community by the influx of consultants, engineers, architects, construction workers, and the "advance team" of the company is substantial.

5. Development fees are levied once against land developers to cover the administrative costs of providing sewage and water to a lot that was previously outside the service area. They are an important means for generating revenue during the frantic, highly speculative period right after the announcement is made that a large plant is to be built. Development fees were levied effectively at the Spring Hill site after the plant announcement, when there was a flurry of activity as developers attempted to secure building permits and schedule zoning hearings. Many of the proposed projects never came to fruition, but they required an investment of time by the respective planners from Columbia, Tennessee, and Maury County, Tennessee. The development fee is a way for a city or county to recover its costs of assisting developers with development plans that go nowhere.

In the words of an economic development officer of one community, water and sewage are the "two guns of economic development," meaning that they are two absolute requirements of any company building a plant in a greenfield site. It is the provision of sewage and water that gives the community leverage. Control over these essential services provides an opportunity for a community to enhance its revenue or cover the costs.

6. Many communities assume that the company will buy locally, only to find out that construction materials are being imported from outside the town, the state, or even the country. In the case of the four communities studied here, only one had an agreement with the company that all materials for the construction of the plant had to be purchased in the county. According to interviews with the community's leaders, this arrangement made an enormous financial difference to the community, since the company needed to purchase thousands of dollars' worth of raw materials.

Alternatively, the community may require the company to hire a local company to do the construction or to hire local construction workers. None of the four communities in this study had such an agreement and, consequently, all of the construction workers were from outside the area.

- Communities should try to annex the land on which the plant is sited, thereby allowing them to levy a payroll or profit tax. Companies also may benefit from this arrangement because it enables them to deal with a single government actor rather than with several leaders who are part of a fragmented structure.

A Plant's Impact Is Diffuse, so That Government Responses Are Often Fragmented.

- In many areas, a regional response to the plant is desirable. This may mean consolidating city and county units or, at the minimum, coordinating the planning function for several counties or a city and a county.

Plant-related Revenues and Expenditures Do Not Follow an Incremental Pattern but Rather Have a Roller-Coaster Effect on Small Communities.

- Communities need to do more on their own to even out the flow of revenue. In the early stages of negotiations, they should ask for a payment schedule and be sure payments are as equal as possible.

The County Adjacent to the Plant Often Experiences Much of the Impact but Collects Little or No Revenue.

- Include at the negotiating table representatives of a broader group of counties than just the one in which the plant is located. Perhaps obtain a commitment from the company where the plant is located that once at least 20 percent of the plant employees live in another county, that county will be eligible for an in-lieu-of-tax payment. This may strike the reader as a very naive suggestion, but it may be possible to get the company to agree to it if the state exerts pressure to do so. Obviously, the county in which the plant is located will not rush to invite another county if the assumption is that the more the second community gets, the less the first one gets. The leaders of the county where the plant is located may feel the home county has everything to lose and nothing to gain from inviting another interested party to the table.
- Try to negotiate an agreement with the company to return to the table after a specified number of years after the plant has been open. This is similar to a reopener agreement in labor negotiations.

State Governments Play an Important and Controversial Role. A plant has a long-term impact on a community, yet the state's role in the economic development process, like that of a broker, is short-term. The problem is that the elected officials who recruited the plant may not be in office later on, when both the long-term negative and positive effects are felt.

- Local communities should push to secure appropriate state resources, such as roads or bypasses, as long as these resources are necessary, and try to get enforceable commitments that the state or the company bears the primary commitment for providing these services. One technique for doing this is for the community to ask the company for items that the community wants. A stable and professional economic development office with an institutional memory can be very helpful in this endeavor.

There Is Variation in the Bargaining Skills of the Chief Negotiators. For instance, several community leaders suggested that Mayor Sam Ridley had a clearly pronounced conviction that "the plant would pay for itself." Consequently, Smyrna had a fundamentally superior position in terms of revenue and debt relative to the other sites.

- A community should strive to have a fairly tough bargainer but also do its best to ensure that the company does not decide to build its plant somewhere else. If that occurs, a high political price will be paid. Resources to pay out-of-town bargainers and to conduct impact studies should be made available. Such information is essential, since the prospect of being the home to a large plant is a once-in-a-lifetime opportunity for many small to midsized communities.

The Plant's Impact on the Community's Educational Resources Is Clearly Enormous. The sudden, radical increases in enrollment that occur after the plant is built put communities under triple pressure: not enough space, not enough staff, and no revenue yet.

- Invite the school districts in the area to the table to negotiate an in-lieu-of-tax payment, some of which should be earmarked for education. Typically, it is only as a result of the generosity of the company that the school districts receive any money from the company to offset the plant's impact. Consideration should be given to the company or the state reimbursing affected districts for increased costs due to swelling enrollments, additional staff, and new buildings, as the federal government does for school districts near military bases.

The Presence of a Large Plant in the Community Greatly Affects the School Curriculum in Ways That the Superintendents Generally Considered "Progressive." In Kentucky, for example, the percentage of students enrolled in high school equivalency programs soared.

- Districts should be prepared for an influx of nontraditional students or dropouts seeking to acquire the credentials they need to get hired at the plant. This may result in a fundamental change in the mission of the local public school system.

There Is a Time Lag Between When a Community Needs Increased Revenue and When the Additional Revenue Flows In. Tax districts that are primarily residential are at a particular disadvantage because the tax revenues from homeowners are proportionately so much lower than those collected from businesses.

- Districts that are primarily residential should pursue a strategy of attracting light industry and small businesses to garner money for their schools.

Conclusion

THIS BOOK has discussed the changes that occurred in four small, rural communities after each was chosen as the site for a large automobile plant: Nissan's plant in Smyrna, Tennessee; Toyota's in Georgetown, Kentucky; Honda's in Marysville, Ohio; and Saturn's in Spring Hill, Tennessee.

This book has argued that economic development is a process that requires more than just a static cost-benefit analysis. Rather, it requires both a new conceptual framework and a new evaluation methodology.

The author has provided a new framework in the form of the stages of economic development notion (Figure 2.2) and in the idea that economic development sets the agenda for these communities for years to come. A key finding is that economic development is not idiosyncratic or a process unique to each community but a multistaged process that is both universal and generalizable. Another key finding is that a plant begins to have a significant impact on the community in which it is located not when it opens its gates but long before, when the siting is announced by the media.

Predictably, in the initial stage after the plant announcement, there is an influx of outsiders to the community, including transient consultants, job seekers, construction workers, and other temporary workers. Typically, there is also extensive real estate speculation. Among the mid- to long-term events and changes that are likely to occur are a turnover in leadership, an influx of permanent residents, increases in traffic, new strategies for increasing revenue through the passage of school bonds and other bonds, and an attempt (often the second) by the city nearest the plant to annex the land on which it is located. Finally, over the long term, new government programs are likely to be established and the attitudes and behavior of community leaders and citizens transformed.

As the findings of this study point out, a community that becomes the site of a large plant undergoes more than just economic changes, although only fewer of the leaders of the four communities identified political or cultural effects than identified economic effects. Nonetheless, even the leaders recognize that economic development is a three-dimensional process consisting of short-term political and economic costs and benefits, including increases in the availability of jobs and capital, in the demand for social services, in wages, and in taxes; secondary or medium-term effects, such as the creation of new businesses, new industry, and new commerce, government changes, and an overall increase in wages; and long-term sociocultural impacts, such as increases in pollution, in taxes, in the professionalization of public-sector jobs, in new government programs, and in knowledge coming into the community. The leaders who conceived of economic development as involving short-term economic and political factors, such as embodied in the first factor in chapter 3, were not the same leaders who strongly associated with the medium- or long-term economic or political effects, nor those who strongly associated economic development with sociocultural impacts. In short, economic development is a complicated, multidimensional process. This finding is one of the more intriguing of the study.

What do members of a community expect when they recruit a large plant? Most definitely, they expect the plant to generate jobs; in fact, it not only creates jobs and concomitant commercial activity but it is a catalyst for fundamental changes in the community's politics and culture. Sleepy, agrarian communities may become dynamic, urbanized towns or cities with more traffic, crime, and higher-priced real estate. Many in the community consider these to be "urban ills," but for most of the residents the negatives are offset by the newly gained sense of efficacy, the progress, the economic vitality, and the feeling that the plant was like a magnet attracting commerce and business.

The hope that the plant will bring jobs is generally fulfilled. Even Spring Hill, the one community where leaders and citizens felt disappointment and almost betrayal because the plant did not hire locals, still showed reductions in its unemployment rate. Further, the other economic expectations—that the plant would attract capital and satellite industries—were fulfilled. Although a large percentage of the community leaders said that commercial activity was forthcoming, they expressed disappointment that the communities had not become retail or commercial centers as soon as hoped. Residents, they pointed out, still commuted to large nearby cities.

In the case of the four communities studied, each plant transformed the community by forcing problems to the forefront and thus influencing the political agenda. Furthermore, the leaders at the sites generally identified the same issues as problems, nine out of twelve of which have been named in the literature on growth. Across the sites, the three most important problems the leaders identified were the increases in real estate prices, the increases in traffic, and housing. At three of the sites, the leaders thought school bonds were a problem. At only one site was pollution named as a problem, although objective data indicated it was. In general, the leaders were very happy the plants were in their communities.

The general public tended to notice the effects of the plant less than the elite did and, perhaps for this reason, had less rosy views toward it. The general public also was more aware than the elite of the plant's impact on the government, although the public was very aware of the plant's effects on the economy. Only a small minority of the public considered the higher wages that resulted from having the plant in their community a cost, whereas a higher percentage of the leaders felt this way. This is understandable since the person on the street was more likely to be a plant employee and the leaders were more likely to be business owners.

The plant-related problems identified by the general public were similar to those named by the leaders: increases in traffic, housing, increases in the cost of real estate, taxes, school bonds, and roads; increases in traffic, housing, increases in the cost of real estate, taxes, and school bonds topped both lists. Members of the general public were less likely than the elite to identify roads as a problem, and they thought sewage and water supply and quality were less of a problem than the elite did; in fact, at no site did the public think sewage was a problem. There were also issues important to the elite that the public did not consider important, such as higher wages.

The public, like the elite, viewed economic development as multidimensional. What did the plant's impact mean to the public? The public saw the plant as meaning broad positive impact on the community's breadth of knowledge, supply of capital, and wage levels. The public does not view the professionalization of the public sector as positively associated with the plant.

Also, in contrast to the elite, who conceived of all short-term factors as one dimension called factor 1 (primary growth), be they economic or political variables, the general public primarily saw one primary dimension as encompassing overall economic impacts of the plant, be they short- or long-term (see chapter 7 for greater detail). The three dimensions of economic development for the public were

1. An overall economic factor.
2. An overall political factor (with no sociocultural or economic impacts.
3. A factor that embodies many of the day-to-day creature comfort impacts, including traffic, capital, higher wages, higher taxes, increased demand on social services, and pollution.

Overall, certain sectors of the public perceived the plant as more directly affecting the economy, some viewed it as affecting the political culture, and others viewed it as meaning an increase in discomforts associated with urban living, such as traffic, higher wages, higher taxes, and pollution. Thus, the public tended to divide itself by group based on the sector of the culture the residents thought was most affected by the plant, while the elite's views were organized temporally by the impacts over the short term, midterm, and longer term. Also, the economic impacts of the plant were more pronounced to the public.

One of the most interesting findings was that the impact of the plant was diffuse rather than concentrated. The plant affects many small communities and several counties, not just the town and county where the plant is located. Typically, representatives of the community in which the plant is sited are not included in the early stages of the bargaining for the incentive package; rather, the state and the company thrust the terms of the package upon it. In three out of the four communities, the leaders were quite angry with the state and the terms it had agreed to.

During the bargaining over the amount the company will pay in lieu of taxes, the representatives invited to the table are from the government entity where the plant is located, thereby leaving out many representatives of affected jurisdictions. Based on city and county budget analysis, these communities clearly had lower revenue and higher debt over the period of time between the plant announcement and plant opening than did those that were represented.

The fact that the plant's impact is diffuse makes it harder to study. Likewise, it makes coordinated planning among communities for investments in such items as the infrastructure more difficult but all the more necessary. Once again, the community's response to the plant's advent is decentralized and fragmented, and the company's voice, in making its demands, is concentrated and unitary, creating imbalance and making the community vulnerable.

The conventional wisdom put forth in much of the scholarship on political economy, urban studies, and policy is that a community is vulnerable compared with a corporation and the state. In fact, the most vulnerable cities get the worst deal.[1] Is the community destined to be hopelessly vulnerable? This author, based on the findings here, is more optimistic than others who have suggested that cities or communities are inherently limited, relative to corporations.[2] Clearly, the community is vulnerable but not totally powerless. It has choices, and it can establish clear criteria for what it will take to break even. If it does not want to go into debt if the company does not provide the resources necessary to break even, this may mean that the community's bargainers will have to walk away from the table. Sam Ridley, the mayor of Smyrna, was prepared to do this even at the threat of losing the deal for Smyrna to another community, Cartersville, Georgia. But sometimes, as Lynn Bachelor points out, even when a state or community has clear-cut data on what it will take to break even, it may give in because, given the region's economic situation, the jobs are irresistible.

The community can also protect itself by employing a variety of strategies, including annexing the land on which the plant is built, imposing a payroll and/or profit tax, buying one or more of the utilities, levying development fees, and requiring the company to buy materials locally. The recommendations to the communities are laid out in chapter 9. The budgetary and revenue data in chapter 4 demonstrated that communities that are successful at using these strategies are rewarded with increases in revenue and strong revenue-to-debt relationships. Of the four communities that are the focus of this study, Smyrna has been the most successful at using these strategies, followed by Georgetown. Annexation turned out to have great advantages in both these cases.

As Judd and Parkinson, Fainstein, and Michael Pagano and Ann Bowman state,[3] the future of a community can be guided by the leaders; towns with strong leaders who foresee the importance of using such strategies as annexation fare far better during periods of economic development than towns where the leaders sit back and passively accept the companies' offers without aggressively negotiating.

Clearly, the plants had an enormous impact in the areas of public administration: police, fire, sewage, water, public works, recreation, welfare, and criminal justice. In all the communities except Spring Hill, the proportionate amounts of the budget that went to the fire, police, and recreation departments were vastly increased in 1990 compared with before the plant was opened. Perhaps the most permanent and dramatic of the changes in the areas of public administration was the professionalization of public-sector jobs. The move in all four communities to the use of merit-based criteria and of national searches for public-sector employees was an enormous and irreversible change. Of course, one of the hallmarks of a reformed city, rather than an unreformed city, is a professional governmental workforce.

In addition to this, another profound political change is the emergence of a new political leader, a new guard, which replaces the power hold the good old boys, or girls, of yesteryear previously had on the community. The new-guard leader is more likely to be educated outside the community, more in favor of economic development, and more worldly in outlook than the previous generation of leaders.

Based on the findings discussed in this book, a community undergoing the process of economic development can determine its own destiny, at least to some degree. Strategies like annexation and other rather simple yet profound actions like hiring an astute bargainer, perhaps a professional, can translate into revenue for the community.

Although the four communities in this study did not start from the same base, they experienced similar aches and joys. Thus, there is a generalizable cycle of development with various time stages following a certain order. Many of the problems faced by these small communities are common to growth: increased cost of real estate, traffic, and the preeminence of the planning process, for example. Thus, growth—and the management of growth—may be much more universal, across both rural and urban settings, than previously thought. This suggests that the potential for blending the findings of urban scholars and those who study rural problems is alive with possibility.

What the majority of the community thinks it is getting when it recruits an automobile plant is jobs. But the process that is set in motion is much more complicated and multidimensional than that expectation suggests; in fact, nothing less takes place than an economic, political, and cultural transformation that will span ten to twelve years. It is a transformation that permanently and irreversibly changes the character of the community, a process so profound that, in the words of one Georgetown resident, it took his town from the "nineteenth to the twenty-first century."

Appendices

TABLE A.1. Mean of Factor Scores

	Factors		
	Primary Growth	Secondary Growth	Sociocultural
Elected	.46	.20	.14
	(.09)	(.56)	(.25)
Not elected	−.26	−.18	.07
	(.29)	(.26)	(.31)
Old-style leader	−.40	−.27	−.10
	(.36)	(.30)	(.40)
Professional leader	.20	.13	.05
	(.20)	(.23)	(.20)
Business (N = 6)	.59	.22	−.26
	(.11)	(.30)	(.22)
Not business (N = 20)	−.08	−.04	.02
	(.23)	(.25)	(.25)
Economic Development (N = 7) [a]	.58	.24	−.36
	(.10)	(.28)	(.15)
Noneconomic development (N = 18)	−.14	−.16	.06
	(.25)	(.25)	(.28)

Note: Numbers in parentheses indicate standard error of mean.
[a] The mayor was coded as an economic development person in these four communities because that was the role the four mayors actually played in them.

METHODOLOGY

The data for this book come from four different sources: elite interviews; documents in the public domain or provided by the leaders interviewed, for example, a publication of the chamber of commerce or a school board or planning commission report; budgets for the cities and counties in the impact area; and public opinion gathered through the random survey conducted at all four sites of 600 respondents, 150 at each site. Details of how each of these data sets were developed are provided below. Upon request to the author, the detailed questions asked of the elite and the public can be provided to the reader.

The Elite Data Set

Funding to obtain these data was provided by the Economic Development Administration grant #99-07-13727. In the grant proposal, under the principal investigator Dr. Lou Ferman, several institutional areas were listed in the presumed order of importance in terms of impacts: schools, recreation, water and sewage, public works, welfare, planning, police, fire, criminal justice, and welfare. The head or director of each of these functions for each jurisdiction within the impact area for four sites was interviewed. An "institutional version" of the survey was developed to be administered to these directors. It contained many of the same questions as on the functionary survey, including length of time person has held this position; previous position the person has held (either government bureaucrat, elected official, small business or commercial, industry position, service sector position or educational position); and status as native of the area or not. The broad impacts included governmental impacts such as a broad impact on government, broad impact on decision making, broad impact on government programs and other governmental impacts; economic impacts such as jobs as an impact, jobs as a benefit, commercial activity as an impact, knowledge as a benefit, capital as a benefit, and other benefits; and costs such as taxes as a cost, pollution as a cost, cost of social services as a cost, cost of real estate as a cost, cost of wages as a cost, and other costs. For the costs and the benefits, these responses were coded from an open-ended response to the questions, What were the costs? What were the benefits? If the person named something as a benefit under the cost section it was recoded to be a benefit. There was also a general evaluative item regarding the coming of the plant (Has the plant meant that the community is better or worse off?), which had a five-point Likert scale response.

In addition, there were some specific institutional questions, such as the description of job; resources and program content and staff and general duties; the changes, if any, that have been made; the size of the institutional budget, and whether the priorities have shifted across categories as a result of the plant's coming; whether the clientele has changed; whether the number of pupils has changed (if it is a school);

whether the number of personnel has decreased or increased; whether the capital has increased or decreased; whether there has been an increase in programs; whether there has been an increase in training; whether there have been any increases in new facilities and, if so, which type of facility, any new program areas, any increase in staffing, either how many, what year, part-time or full time, and upgrading.

The second type of leader was called the functionary and essentially was a leader, either a political leader (such as a mayor, city manager, city council person, county commissioner) or a business leader (banker, member of the industrial bond group that brought the plant, head of a planning commission). The functionaries were asked the length of time in their position, whether they are a native or not, description of the job, the job before and the job after in terms of resources, programs, staffs, duties, and other changes.

The functionaries were also asked what were the broad impacts on the community, including the impacts on government, such as general impacts, the professionalization of public-sector jobs, the economic impacts (impacts of jobs, benefits of jobs, benefits of commerce, benefits of knowledge, influx of new capital, and other benefits), business as an impact, industry, the impacts on human services, such as the impact on education, social services, recreation, health, mental health, and fire and police protection. The leaders were asked what were the "issues" or problems—in problem-solving parlance—such as water, sewage, traffic, housing, real estate speculation, taxes, road maintenance, school bonds, annexation, wages, and pollution. The leaders were also asked if the county or city was able to negotiate the terms under which the plant would locate here. The leaders were also asked what was the current economic development strategy of the community leaders (recruitment of large industry, development of small, diversified concerns, commercial concerns, real estate development, and emphasis on service concerns). The leader was asked whether the policy preference was for growth at all costs, controlled growth, or little or no growth.

The leaders were also asked if there had been a shift in revenue toward or away from education, social services, recreation, health services, fire department revenue, police revenue, sewage, water, roads, economic development, and planning. The leaders were also asked if there had been a significant change in the character of the population, whether the following groups had been hurt or helped by the plant: young people, professionals, poor people, farmers, older adults, small business owners, workers, property owners, property developers, the well-to-do, and public servants. The leader was also asked to say whether the personnel from the plant are represented on boards of local organizations and the age and the income of the respondent. The leaders were also asked what the overall evaluation of the plant's impact is. For the precise wording of each question on both questionnaires, the reader can write the author at 347 SSB, University of Missouri Saint Louis, 8001 Natural Bridge Rd., St. Louis, MO 63121. Most of the items were close-ended. However, for the impacts items, the respondent was asked free-form to name any impacts. As the respondent listed different impacts, they were coded as a series of impacts.

The Public Opinion Data Set

The second data source for the book is the public opinion of the citizens in the four sites. A pretest was conducted on Monday, June 29, 1992, and then several items primarily were revised and put in more elementary and folksy language. The substance of all items remained the same. The telephone survey was conducted in July 1992 of 600 respondents during the hours of 5 P.M. to 9 P.M. on July 1, 2, 6, 7, 8, 9, 10, 13, 14, and 15, 1992. The interviewing and the technical aspects of the sampling were conducted under the auspices of the Centers for Public Policy Research of the University of Missouri St. Louis and were funded through a grant from the Weldon Springs Fund of the University of Missouri system. The sampling list was purchased from a commercial provider of such lists. From this every nth number was selected to yield a random sample of 150 telephone numbers by site. Since most sites included a city and a county or possibly two counties, the number selected for each site reflected the relative population numbers of the two units. For example, if the city of Georgetown is half the population of Scott County, then the sample for the Georgetown site should include one-half the phone numbers from Georgetown and one-half from Scott County.

The different jurisdictions that were sampled and their respective sites were, for the Spring Hill site: the city of Columbia, Maury County, and Williamson County; for the Smyrna site: the city of Smyrna, the city of Murfreesboro, and Rutherford County; for the Georgetown, Kentucky site: the city of Georgetown and Scott County; and for the

Marysville, Ohio, site: the city of Marysville, Union County, and Logan County.

The items on the questionnaire for the public were parallel or equivalent to those on the elite survey. There were questions concerning the impacts (jobs, government, professionalization of public-sector jobs, government decisions, government programs), including open-ended chances to respond. There were impacts on human services such as schools, recreation, fire protection, police protection, jobs as a benefit, industry as a benefit, commercial activity as a benefit, knowledge as a benefit, money as a benefit, other benefits, higher taxes as a cost, pollution as a cost, the higher cost of social services, the higher cost of real estate, increased wages as a cost, and other costs. There were questions about how the plant had set the agenda for the community: Had it caused certain issues or problems to surface in the community? The respondents were asked about each of these: water, sewage, traffic, housing, higher cost of real estate, higher taxes as a cost, the cost of roads, the cost of new school bonds, other bond issues, annexation, higher or lower wages, and pollution.

There were three evaluative questions, which tell how the public views the impact of the plant in a summary way. One was whether the citizens thought the incentive package was justified or not, measured by a five-point scale of justified, leaning toward justified, mixed, leaning toward unjustified, and unjustified. Another was a question on whether the community was better off or worse off with the plant, with the response categories being much better, a little better, about the same, a little worse, and much worse. A third question was whether the community should be the site of an additional industrial plant. Responses were yes, there should be another large industrial siting; yes; yes, but not more than one; and no. There were two questions about which economic development philosophy the public favors: large industry, small or diversified industry, commercial or real estate operations, real estate development, or service industry. The person was also asked whether he or she favored growth at all costs, controlled growth, or no growth. There were questions about how the plant has changed the makeup of the community's population.

The respondents were asked whether they viewed the plant as being redistributive across groups: Did the plant have a positive, negative, or no impact on the following groups: professionals, poor people, farmers, older people, small business owners, workers, property owners, property developers, the wealthy, and local government workers.

Finally, there were demographic questions: occupation, family member who works for Saturn, friends who are employed at auto plant, status as native, age, income, educational level attained, partisan affiliation (using a seven-point scale from strong Democrat to strong Republican), liberal-conservative in terms of government involvement, race, and gender. The actual questionnaires are available upon request from the author.

Further on in the analysis, the variables were all converted into dichotomous or trichotomous variables, and three models were constructed to predict person's positive attitude to the overall impact that the community had on the plant, the justifiability of the package, and the desire to have another large industrial siting in the community.

Documents Provided by the Elite

The citations for each document that was actually quoted are provided in the bibliography. However, to give the reader an indication of the vast range and quality of information gathered for each site, the following is the researcher's log of the documents, except budgets, from one site (Smyrna):

Category	Description/Title
1. Education/ schools	1990 Elementary school information for planning, Murfreesboro Public School District
2. Planning	Comprehensive land-use plan, city of Murfreesboro, Tennessee
3. Planning	Cycle of growth
4. Education	Rutherford County schools, 1979–90
5. Economic	Entries and exits of firms in Tennessee, 1980–85, revised edition
6. Crime	Crime data, Rutherford County
7. Employment	Employment data, Rutherford County
8. Economic	Nashville MSA, 1980–87
9. Employment	Employment data, Rutherford County
10. Sewage	Sewage and water data, Murfreesboro
11. Sewage	Consulting report, city of Murfreesboro
12. Education	City enrollment figures, Murfreesboro
13. Sewage	Historical figures for sewage and water, Murfreesboro

BUDGETARY DATA

The budgetary data came from the public budgets available for each city and county in each impact area. The units from which the budget data were gathered were: Spring Hill: Maury County and Williamson County; Smyrna site: the city of Smyrna, the city of Murfreesboro, and Rutherford County; Georgetown, Kentucky, site: the city of Georgetown and Scott County; Marysville, Ohio, site: the city of Marysville and Union County. The budgets for Logan County could not be obtained although the county fell within the impact area for the Marysville site. The Logan County courthouse documents were being moved to new offices when the field research was being conducted, and subsequent attempts to contact the county employee who kept the budgets were not successful. My most grateful and gracious thanks to those city and county employees who took the time to duplicate copies of these budgets for the book.

The coding decisions on the budgets were among the most difficult. There was no standard form for these budgets. Some of them contained minuscule itemizations such as sixty dollars for grass seed for the courthouse lawn. These had to be recoded and merged into larger categories by function—such as sewage, water, police enforcement, and so on. Some categories were transient—such as a grant from the federal EPA for water pollution control. These had to be accommodated. Capital improvements were handled in different ways in different communities.

The baseline for the budget analysis, as with the rest of the analysis, was the year before the plant was announced or the year of the announcement. The justification for this is provided in chapter 1. The impacts of the plant begin with the announcement, not with the opening. The impacts cannot be completely calibrated until years—many years—after the plant has opened, until the community is in the mature stage of development.

Methodological Challenges

The approach in this book assumes that economic development is an over-time process. The approach poses many methodological challenges. It is not as neat and tidy a technique as calculating the dollars spent per job, as had been done by other scholars. One issue is when to establish the baseline from which impacts are measured. Another issue is what constitutes the impact area of the plant. This arises from the diffuseness of the impact of the plants. In the 1950s the plant's impacts could have been measured by simply looking at the town in which it was located, not even the surrounding county. Now, with different commuting patterns and interstate highways, the plant's impact can be felt for miles around. The question becomes how far out from the bull's-eye of the plant to draw the circle called the impact area. To determine the impact area, the area was extended outward until it encompassed surrounding cities and counties accounting for 60 percent of the workforce. In the Kentucky case this was most difficult because the two counties that constituted 60 percent were not contiguous and the intervening county had few employees. Therefore, the impact area of Georgetown was determined to be Georgetown and the surrounding county, Scott. The impact of the plant was truly dispersed—even regional, crossing state lines. The process of arriving at the impact areas is also discussed in early chapters; Table 1.1 gives the political jurisdictions within each impact area.

Notes

1. Introduction

1. Funding for the interviews with the elite and the collection of the budgetary data was made possible by a grant from the Economic Development Administration (# 99-07-13727). The public opinion part of the study was made possible by a Weldon Springs grant through the University of Missouri in 1993.

2. Employment at the Honda plant—or plants—has now reached well over 10,000 employees, as a result of an addition to the plant that is in Logan rather than Union County.

3. Janet Fitchen, *Endangered Species, Enduring Places: Change, Identity, and Survival in Rural America* (Boulder, Colo.: Westview Press, 1991); see also Shirley Porterfield, "Service Sector Offers More Jobs, Less Pay," *Rural Economic Development Perspectives* 6 (June 1990): 2–7; and Shirley Porterfield and Thomas D. Rowley, "Removing Rural Development Barriers Through Telecommunications: Illusion or Reality," in *Economic Adaptation: Alternatives for Nonmetropolitan Areas*, ed. David L. Barkley (Boulder, Colo.: Westview Press, 1993), 247–64.

4. See Peter Eisenger, *The Rise of the Entrepreneurial State* (Madison: University of Wisconsin Press, 1988); H. Brinton Milward, "Estimated Impacts of the Toyota Georgetown, Kentucky, Plant" (Center for Business and Economic Research, University of Kentucky, 1988); H. Brinton Milward, "Kentucky's Automotive Supplier Industry: Trends and Implications" (report contracted by the Governor's Office of Policy and Management; Center for Business and Economic Research, University of Kentucky, 1988); H. Brinton Milward and Heidi Hosbach Newman, "State Incentive Packages and the Industrial Location Decision" (report contracted by the Governor's Office of Policy and Management; Center for Business and Economic Research, University of Kentucky, 1988).

5. See John Jackson, "Michigan," in *The New Economic Role of American States: Strategies in a Competitive World Economy*, ed. R. Scott Fosler (Oxford: Oxford University Press, 1988); Barry Bluestone and Bennett Harrison, *The Deindustrialization of America: Plant Closings, Community Abandonment, and the Dismantling of Basic Industry* (New York: Basic Books, 1982).

6. Eisenger, *Rise of the Entrepreneurial State*; Virginia Gray and David Lowery, "Holding Back the Tide of Bad Economic Times: The Compensatory Impact of State and Industrial Policy" (paper presented at the meetings of the American Political Science Association, Atlanta, August 31–September 3, 1989).

7. Bluestone and Harrison, *Deindustrialization of America.*

8. Saskia Sassen, *The Global City: New York, London and Tokyo* (Princeton, N.J.: Princeton University Press, 1991). The technical factors are deregulation, innovation, and dispersal of work and risk. Cities that are the locus of specialized service industries critical to global production are positioned to become the world's leading cities. Thus, the argument goes that the fate of these cities is linked more to the global economy than to the fate of their respective national economies. Sassen argues that many technical factors—transnational investment, the centrality of the telecommunications industry, geographic dispersion, deregulation, rapid innovation, and increased risk—all combine to concentrate power in a few financial centers as well as pose substantial barriers to the emergence of other global financial centers. In today's economy the centers of financial industry are empowered, not the regional centers of manufacturing, such as Detroit, Manchester, and Osaka.

9. Wilbur Thompson, "Urbanization," in *North American Cities and the Global Economy*, ed. Peter Karl Kresl and Gary Gappert, Urban Affairs Annual Review (Newbury Park, Calif.: Sage, 1995); Wilbur Thompson, "A Preface to Suburban Economics," in *The Urbanization of the Suburbs*, ed. Louis H. Masotti and Jeffrey K. Madden, Urban Affairs Annual Review (Newbury Park, Calif.: Sage, 1973), 409–30; Wilbur Thompson, "Alternative Paths to the Revival of Industrial Cities," in *The Future of Winter Cities*, ed. Gary Gappert, Urban Affairs Annual Review (Newbury Park, Calif.: Sage, 1987).

10. Cities that are the locus of specialized service industries critical to global production are positioned to become the world's leading cities. Thus, the argument goes that the fate of these cities is linked more to the global economy than to the fate of their respective national economies. Sassen argues that many technical factors—transnational investment, the centrality of the telecommunications industry, geographic dispersion, deregulation, rapid innovation, and increased risk—all combine to concentrate power in a few financial centers as well as pose substantial barriers to the emergence of other global financial centers. In today's economy the centers of financial industry are empowered, not the regional centers of manufacturing, such as Detroit, Manchester, and Osaka. R. Scott Bruce and George C. Lodge, *U.S. Competitiveness in the World Economy* (Cambridge, Mass.: Harvard University Business School Press, 1985); Susan E. Clarke, ed., *Urban Innovation and Autonomy: Political Implications of Policy Change* (Newbury Park, Calif.: Sage, 1989); Michael Dertouzos, Richard Lester, and Robert Solow, *Made in America* (Cambridge, Mass.: MIT Press, 1989); Peter Karl Kresl and Balwant Singh, "Competitiveness of Cities" (paper presented at OECD–Australian government conference, Melbourne, Australia, November 1994); Dennis Judd and Michael Parkinson, eds., *Leadership and Urban Regeneration: Cities in North America and Europe*. Urban Affairs Annual Review, vol. 37 (Newbury Park, Calif.: Sage, 1990).

11. Clarence N. Stone and Heywood Sanders, eds., *The Politics of Urban Development* (Lawrence: University Press of Kansas, 1987); Michael Parkinson, Dennis Judd, and B. Foley, "Urban Revitalization in America and the U.K.: Politics of Uneven Development," in *Regenerating the Cities*, ed. Michael Parkinson, Dennis Judd, and B. Foley (Manchester, United Kingdom: Manchester University Press, 1990); Timothy Bartik, *Who Benefits from State and Local Economic Development Policies?* (Kalamazoo, Mich.: Upjohn Institute for Employment Research, 1991).

12. Robert B. Reich, *The Work of Nations: Preparing Ourselves for 21st Century Capitalism* (New York: Knopf, 1991).

13. Bluestone and Harrison, *Deindustrialization of America*; Fitchen, *Endangered Species*.

14. Joseph White, "Chrysler to Shut St. Louis Plant, Third Since 1987," *Wall Street Journal*, February 2, 1990, 14.

15. Richard Hill, "Crisis in Motor City: The Politics and Economic Development in Detroit," in *Restructuring the City: The Political Economy of Urban Development*, ed. Susan Fainstein et al. (New York: Longman, 1983), 80–125. See also T. N. Clark and R. Inglehart, "The New Political Culture" (paper presented at the Biennial Meeting of the International Sociological Association, 1990); John Freeman, *Democracy and Markets: Politics and Mixed Economies* (Ithaca, N.Y.: Cornell University Press, 1989); Gray and Lowery, "Holding Back the Tide"; Virginia Gray and David Lowery, "Interest Group Politics and Economic Growth in the United States," *American Political Science Review* 82 (March 1988): 109–31; Dennis Judd, Michael Peter Smith, and Randy Ready, "Capital Flight, Tax Incentives, and Marginalization of the American States and Localities," in *Public Policy Across States and Communities*, ed. Dennis R. Judd (Greenwich, Conn.: JAI Press, 1985); Mark Schneider, *Competitive City: The Political Economy of Suburbia* (Pittsburgh: University of Pittsburgh Press, 1989).

16. George Fulton, Donald Grimes, and Alan L. Baum, "Industrial Location: Decisions and Their Impact on the Michigan Economy: Mazda Auto Assembly Case" (paper presented at the 32nd annual conference on Economic Outlook, Ann Arbor, Mich., November 15, 1984); John Friedman and Wolff Goetz, "World City Formation: An Agenda for Research and Action," *International Journal of Urban and Regional Research* 6 (1982): 309–44; Joel Garreau, *Edge City* (New York: Doubleday, 1991); John Mollenkopf and Manuel Castells, eds., *Dual City: The Restructuring of New York* (New York: Russell Sage Foundation, 1988); Thompson, "Urbanization"; Thompson, "Urbanization of Suburbs," 427–29; Clarke, *Urban Innovation and Autonomy*; Peter B. Doeringer, David G. Terkla, and Gregory Topakian, *Invisible Factors in Local Economic Development* (New York: Oxford University Press, 1988); H. Savitch, *Post-Industrial Cities: Politics and Planning in New York, Paris and London* (Princeton, N.J.: Princeton University Press, 1987); Fainstein et al., *Restructuring the City*.

17. Brian Jones and Lynn Bachelor, with Carter Wilson, *The Sustaining Hand: Community Leadership and Corporate Power* (Lawrence: University Press of Kansas, 1993), 70; Michele Hoyman, "The Impact of Economic Development on Small Communities: The Case of the Automobile Industry" (paper presented at the annual meeting of the American Political Science Association, Washington, D.C., August 29–September 1, 1991).

18. Jones and Bachelor, *The Sustaining Hand*, 70; John Blair and Robert Premus, "Major Factors in Industrial Location: A Review," *Economic Development Quarterly* 1 (1987): 72–85; H. Brinton Milward and Heidi Hosbach Newman, "Estimated Impact of Toyota on State's Economy" (Center for Business and Economic Research, University of Kentucky, 1988), 15.

19. Milward and Newman, "Estimated Impact of Toyota on State's Economy," 23.

20. Blair and Premus, "Major Factors in Industrial Location"; Milward and Newman, "State Incentive Packages and the Industrial Location Decision," 33; Milward and Newman, "Estimated Impact of Toyota on State's Economy."

21. Milward and Newman, "Estimated Impact of Toyota on State's Economy"; Kenneth Thomas, "Capital Beyond Borders: How Capital Mobility Affects Bargaining Between States and Firms" (Ph.D. diss., University of Chicago, 1992).

22. Todd Swanstrom, *The Crisis of Growth Politics: Cleveland, Kucinich, and the Challenge of Urban Populism* (Philadelphia: Temple University Press, 1985), 149. The increasing automation required to keep up with global competition is more possible in a new plant than an old. Since transportation costs have been reduced, it may be easier to bring in the parts from all over the world than to locate parts plants close to the plant.

23. Richard Feiock, "The Effects of Economic Development Policy on Local Economic Growth," *American Journal of Political Science* 35 (August 1991): 643–55.

24. Section 14.B. of the Taft Hartley Act of 1947 allowed a state to restrict the negotiation of union shops in collective bargaining agreements. Thus, the states that have opted for these restrictions, which have more open shops and a lower percentage of unionized workers, are called 14.B. states.

25. Reich, *The Work of Nations*, 214.

26. Honda has always viewed itself as a truly international company, not as a vintage Japanese company. It has been much less tied in with the tight group of insiders all of whom are Japanese. Therefore, it views itself as and in fact is a truly international company rather than a typical Japanese firm.

27. Michael A. Pagano and Ann Bowman, *Cityscapes and Capital: The Politics of Urban Development* (Baltimore: Johns Hopkins University Press, 1995); Judd and Parkinson, *Leadership and Urban Regeneration*.

28. Anthony Downs, "Up and Down with Ecology: The Issue-Attention Cycle," *Public Interest* 28 (summer 1972): 38–50. There are two key ways in which Downs's theory is distinct from the economic development issue of the plant. First, Downs

implies that the issue rises and falls and nothing is done. It is a profoundly cynical view. Baumgartner and Jones perhaps provide us with a more realistic view with their notion of punctuated equilibrium, which they explain as multiple institutional changes that result from a change in equilibrium. Second, Downs implies that there is a cycle, in other words, that the issue may indeed rise again and may be repeated. Although the author found that in this study there was a cyclical effect with regard to the possibility of facing another large economic development "event"—for instance, in Marysville, the location of a biological waste incinerator—this may not always be the case and the cycle may not repeat itself in reference to this particular automobile plant. Therefore, it may be more accurate to depict these as stages rather than as a cycle per se.

29. Jones and Bachelor, *The Sustaining Hand.*

30. Frank Baumgartner and Bryan D. Jones, *Agendas and Instability in American Politics* (Chicago: University of Chicago Press, 1993).

31. Roger Cobb and Charles D. Elder, "Issue Creation and Agenda Building," in *Cases in Public Policy Making,* ed. James Anderson (New York: Praeger, 1976), 10–21. See also Roger Cobb and Charles D. Elder, *Participation in American Politics: Dynamics of Agenda Building,* 2d ed. (Baltimore: Johns Hopkins University Press, 1983); and Matthew Crenson, *The Unpolitics of Air Pollution: A Study of Non-Decision-Making in Cities* (Baltimore: Johns Hopkins University Press, 1971).

32. Hoyman, "Impact of Economic Development on Small Communities."

33. John Kingdon, *Agendas, Alternatives, and Public Policies* (Boston: Little, Brown, 1984).

34. Fitchen, *Endangered Species.* For other treatments of rural economic development, see John T. Scott and Gene F. Summers, "Problems in Rural Communities After Industry Arrives," in *Rural Industrialization: Problems and Potentials,* ed. Larry R. Whiting (Ames: Iowa State University Press, 1974), 94–107; and, in its entirety, Larry R. Whiting, ed., *Rural Industrialization: Problems and Potentials* (Ames: Iowa State University Press, 1974); see also Gene F. Summers, Sharon D. Evans, Frank Clemente, E. M. Beck, and Jon Minkoff, eds., *Industrial Invasion of Nonmetropolitan America: A Quarter Century of Experience* (New York: Praeger, 1976). For strategies of cities see Arnold Fleischmann, G. Green, and T. M. Kwong, "What's a City to Do? Explaining Differences in Local Economic Development Policies," *Western Political Quarterly* 45 (1992): 677–700.

35. Bluestone and Harrison, *Deindustrialization of America*; John Portz, *The Politics of Plant Closings* (Lawrence: University Press of Kansas, 1990); Jeanne Gordus, Paul Jarley, and Louis Ferman, *Plant Closings and Economic Dislocation* (Kalamazoo, Mich.: Upjohn Institute for Employment Research, 1981).

36. Mary K. Marvel and William J. Shkurti, "The Economic Impact of Development: Honda in Ohio," *Economic Development Quarterly* 7 (February 1993): 50–62; Lynn Bachelor, "Michigan, Mazda, and the Factory of the Future: Evaluating Economic Development Incentives," *Economic Development Quarterly* 5 (May

1991): 126–39; Harold Wolman, Cary Lichtman, and Suzie Barnes, "Impact of Credentials, Skill Levels, Worker Training, and Motivation on Employment Outcomes: Sorting out the Implications for Economic Development Policy," *Economic Development Quarterly* 5 (May 1991): 140–51; Jackson, "Michigan," 91–112; Elaine Sharp and David Elkins, "Politics of Economic Development Policy," *Economic Development Quarterly* 5 (May 1991): 126–39; John Portz, "State Economic Development Programs: Trials and Tribulations of Implementation." *Economic Development Quarterly* 7 (May 1993): 160–77).

37. Elaine Sharp, "Institutional Manifestations of Accessibility and Urban Economic Development Policy," *World Politics Quarterly* 44 (March 1991): 121–47; Sharp and Elkins, "Politics of Economic Development Policy," 126–39.

38. See Schneider, *Competitive City*; Pagano and Bowman, *Cityscapes and Capital*; Richard DeLeon, *The Left Coast City* (Lawrence: University Press of Kansas, 1992).

39. Bachelor, "Michigan, Mazda, and the Factory of the Future."

40. Judd, Smith, and Ready, "Capital Flight."

41. Bachelor, "Michigan, Mazda, and the Factory of the Future," 119.

42. Milward and Newman, "State Incentive Packages and the Industrial Location Decision."

43. Nancy Lind and Ann H. Elder, "Who Pays? Who Benefits? The Case of the Incentive Package Offered to Diamond Starr Automotive Plant," *Government Finance Review* 2 (December 1986): 23.

44. Milward and Newman, "State Incentive Packages and the Industrial Location Decision."

45. Marvel and Shkurti, "Economic Impact of Development," 50–62.

46. Milward and Newman, "State Incentive Packages and the Industrial Location Decision"; H. Brinton Milward, "Estimated Impacts of Toyota Georgetown, Kentucky Plant" (Center for Business and Economic Research, University of Kentucky, 1988); Milward, "Kentucky's Automotive Supplier Industry."

47. Reich, *The Work of Nations*, 297–98.

48. Eisenger, *Rise of the Entrepreneurial State*; Bluestone and Harrison, *Deindustrialization of America*.

49. The author set as a goal including within each impact area 60 percent of the workers at the automobile plant. That was not always possible, however, given the great dispersion of workers and because the adjacent county in one case contained a large urban area with many employers.

50. Joe Feagin, *Free Enterprise City: Houston* (New Brunswick, N.J.: Rutgers University Press, 1988); Clarence N. Stone, *Regime Politics: Governing Atlanta, 1946–1988* (Lawrence: University Press of Kansas, 1989); Paul E. Peterson, *City Limits* (Chicago: University of Chicago Press, 1981).

51. Sassen, *Global City*.

52. Jones and Bachelor, *The Sustaining Hand*.

53. Pagano and Bowman, *Cityscapes and Capital.*

54. Thompson, "Urbanization of Suburbs," 427–29; Thompson, "Alternative Paths to the Revival of Industrial Cities."

55. Dennis Judd and Michael Parkinson, "Urban Leadership and Regeneration: Economic Restraint and Political Choice," in *Leadership and Urban Regeneration: Cities in North America and Europe,* ed. Dennis Judd and Michael Parkinson. Urban Affairs Annual Review, vol. 37 (Newbury Park, Calif.: Sage, 1990), 15.

56. Susan Fainstein, "The Changing World Economy and Urban Restructuring," in Judd and Parkinson, *Leadership and Urban Regeneration,* p. 155.

57. Included among these leaders were the mayor of the city, the county commissioner, the fire and police chiefs and/or sheriffs, planners, sewage, water, and public works department heads, employment office staff, bankers, school superintendants, city managers, and other relevant leaders involved in the plant.

58. When the other three communities tried to push for more in-lieu-of-tax payments or annexation, they were discouraged from this pursuit by the governor's office and the state economic development office. The state officials did not want the community to "push too hard" and ruin the deal between the state and the company.

59. Usually this meant one or two cities and one or two counties. The rule was that the counties had to be contiguous and that the plant could not be "drowned out" by many other plants, as in a large metropolitan area such as Nashville or Columbus. This was a problem in the case of the Georgetown site, where the plant's impact was incredibly diffuse. A full third of the workforce traveled in from Louisville each day, whereas a far lower percentage of the workers were from the county in between Louisville and Lexington. More to the point, had both Louisville and Lexington and their relevant counties been included in the impact area, this plant would have been just one of many industrial facilities in the area. The impact area was therefore defined as Georgetown and Scott County, the county in which the plant was located.

2. Four Communities in Transition

1. H. Brinton Milward and Heidi Hosbach Newman, "State Incentive Packages and the Industrial Location Decision" (Center for Business and Economic Research, University of Kentucky, 1988), pp. 28–33.

2. Bryan Jones and Lynn Bachelor, with Carter Wilson, *The Sustaining Hand: Community Leadership and Corporate Power* (Lawrence: University Press of Kansas, 1993).

3. Peter Eisenger, *The Rise of the Entrepreneurial State* (Madison: University of Wisconsin Press, 1988); Barry Bluestone and Bennett Harrison, *The Deindustrial-*

ization of America: Plant Closings, Community Abandonment, and the Dismantling of Basic Industry (New York: Basic Books, 1982).

4. Miyachi Takeo, "The Man Who Lured Toyota to Kentucky," *Economic Eye,* March 1987, 23–27.

5. Steve Mooney, former Georgetown city planner, interview with the author, May 1990.

6. Milward and Newman, "State Incentive Packages and the Industrial Location Decision," pp. 28–33.

7. Milward and Newman, "State Incentive Packages and the Industrial Location Decision," pp. 28–33; H. Brinton Milward, "Estimated Impacts of the Toyota Georgetown, Kentucky, Plant" (Center for Business and Economic Research, University of Kentucky, 1988) 28. See also "Impacts of the Toyota Plant on Scott County, Kentucky" (Report of Urban Studies Center, University of Louisville; prepared for Department of Local Government, Commonwealth of Kentucky, 1987).

8. James G. Hoaglund Jr., "Public Perceptions of Central Kentucky Communities and the Impact of Toyota Manufacturing" (Center for Development, University of Kentucky, 1990).

9. Takeo, "The Man Who Lured Toyota."

10. H. Brinton Milward, "Kentucky's Automotive Supplier Industry: Trends and Implications" (report contracted by the Governor's Office of Policy and Management; Center for Business and Economic Research, University of Kentucky, 1988), 27.

11. Milward and Newman, "State Incentive Packages and the Industrial Location Decision."

12. H. Brinton Milward and Heidi Hosbach Newman, "Estimated Impact of Toyota on State's Economy" (Center for Business and Economic Research, University of Kentucky, 1988); Milward, "Kentucky's Automotive Supplier Industry."

13. This model was developed by the Bureau of Economic Analysis at the U.S. Department of Commerce.

14. Milward and Newman, "Estimated Impact of Toyota on State's Economy"; Milward, "Kentucky's Automotive Supplier Industry."

15. In 1990, the plant manager, Mike Dodds, was from Detroit; the senior vice president came out of the automobile industry in Pennsylvania and was a graduate of the University of Kentucky. Rudy Sturma, interview with the author, May 1990.

16. Ibid.

17. "Land Use, Thoroughfare and Open Space Plan, 1977–2000, Marysville, Ohio," August 1977, B-18.

18. Leland Dorsey, president of Logan County Chamber of Commerce, interview with the author, June 26, 1990.

19. "Facts About Honda" (Honda Manufacturing Corporation of America, 1990).

20. Ibid.

21. Another way to look at these figures is to compare the absolute population of the plant with the absolute population of the town or county. Thus, in 1990 in Smyrna, the number of employees at Nissan (3,500) was roughly one-third of the town's population of 13,647. At Marysville, the number of employees was roughly one-third of the county's population. At Georgetown, there were 3,000 employees at Toyota, compared with a total population in Scott County of 22,200. And in Spring Hill there were about 3,500 plant employees, compared with a total population in Columbia of 26,372. Both Maury County and Williamson County were rather populous (54,812 and 81,021, respectively), so the proportions were much smaller there. I realize that not all employees live in the county nearest to the plant, but these rough proportions do provide a general idea of the enormous proportions of these towns' populations who worked at the plants.

22. Tennessee Advisory Commission on Intergovernmental Relations (TACIR), "Chronology of the Saturn Corporation Site Selection in Tennessee, 1985–1987," 1989, 37–39.

23. Ibid., 39.

24. William Chafin, president of Maury County Chamber of Commerce, interview with the author, May 1990.

25. Milward and Newman, "State Incentive Packages and the Industrial Location Decision," pp. 28–33.

26. TACIR, "Chrononology," 20.

27. Ibid., 9. The other variables that are included as factors to consider are covered in the report as well as in two other growth scenarios.

28. Frank Baumgartner and Bryan D. Jones, *Agendas and Instability in American Politics* (Chicago: University of Chicago Press, 1993), 100–102.

29. Ibid.

3. The View from the Top: The Plant as Agenda Setter

1. For an interesting thesis on differences between bureaucrats and elected officials in an urban setting, see Lana S. Stein, *Holding Bureaucrats Accountable* (Tuscaloosa: University of Alabama Press, 1991).

2. For Bachelor's analysis of the picture at the Mazda plant in Flat Rock, Michigan, see "Michigan, Mazda, and the Factory of the Future: Evaluating Economic Development Incentives," *Economic Development Quarterly* 5 (May 1991): 126–39. Regarding Georgetown, Kentucky, there is one estimate that only 262 out of the thousands of Toyota jobs went to workers in Georgetown; interview with Toyota official.

3. For a discussion of another measure of economic well-being, see Michele Hoyman, "The Economic Impact of Large Automobile Plant Sitings: Beyond Wages to a Notion of General Welfare" (paper presented at the meetings of the Midwest Political Science Association, Chicago, April 6–8, 1995); see also John Freeman, *Democracy and Markets* (Ithaca, N.Y.: Cornell University Press, 1989).

4. H. Brinton Milward, "Estimated Impacts of the Toyota Georgetown, Kentucky, Plant" (Center for Business and Economic Research, University of Kentucky, 1988).

5. Ibid., 5.

6. Ibid., 7.

7. Ibid., 5.

8. "Facts About Honda" (Honda Manufacturing Corporation of America, 1990). The importance of satellite industries is an economic question, but it becomes a political question if there is controversy surrounding the size of the incentive package or the limited number of direct jobs created. One of the damage control reports made some bold and far-reaching recommendations. See H. Brinton Milward and Heidi Hosbach Newman, "State Incentive Packages and the Industrial Location Decision" (Center for Business and Economic Research, University of Kentucky, 1988); and Milward, "Estimated Impacts of the Toyota Georgetown, Kentucky, Plant," 28. The latter report recommends that long-term attention be paid to the educational infrastructure of the state and that long-term planning and cooperation be developed among the "auto alley" states.

9. Bob Evans is a family-style breakfast restaurant with modest prices, not the type of world-class dining establishment to which the economic development officer was referring.

10. The citizens of Smyrna did not feel this way. Smyrna was an exception since it annexed the plant from the beginning and owned its own utility company.

11. Joe R. Feagin, *Free Enterprise City: Houston* (New Brunswick, N.J.: Rutgers University Press, 1988).

12. Don Ephelin is the official of the United Auto Workers local who negotiated the agreement with Saturn. As such, this may be the only street in the country named for a labor leader who is still alive.

13. Matthew Crenson, *The Unpolitics of Air Pollution: A Study of Non-Decision-Making in Cities* (Baltimore: Johns Hopkins University Press, 1971).

14. John Kingdon, *Agendas, Alternatives and Public Policies* (Boston: Little, Brown, 1984).

15. Janet M. Fitchen argues that the "rural crisis" looks very similar to the crisis in urban areas, characterized by NIMBYism (not in my back yard), environmental hazards, deindustrialization, low-paying service sector jobs, low-level radiation, and landfill problems. See Janet M. Fitchen, *Endangered Species, En-*

during Places: Change, Identity, and Survival in Rural America (Boulder, Colo.: Westview Press, 1991).

16. Bryan Jones and Lynn Bachelor, with Carter Wilson, *The Sustaining Hand: Community Leadership and Corporate Power* (Lawrence: University Press of Kansas, 1993).

17. Frank Baumgartner and Bryan D. Jones, *Agendas and Instability in American Politics* (Chicago: University of Chicago Press, 1993), 16.

18. Ibid.

19. Roger W. Cobb, Jeanie-Keith Ross, and Marc Howard Ross, "Agenda Building as a Comparative Political Process," *American Political Science Review* 70 (March 1976): 126–38.

20. Two issues were considered tied for a ranking if exactly the same percentage of the elite said these issues, taxes and traffic, for example, were important. Had these been the second-highest and third-highest issues, they would have both been numbered 2.5, to indicate they were tied for second place. To be listed as a problem in the center section of Table 3.3, it had to have been defined as such by 50 percent or more of the elite.

21. Real estate was ranked first by the leaders in Spring Hill and Marysville and third by the leaders in Smyrna and Georgetown. Traffic was tied for second among the leaders in Spring Hill and first at the other three sites—a remarkably consistent ranking. Housing varied among the towns in how the leaders ranked it but tended not to be ranked among the top one or two problems.

22. One reason the Georgetown elite did not identify school bonds as a problem or issue might be that Georgetown had already had a consolidated city-county school system, which may have caused it to be more wise in how it used its resources. Recall also that in Georgetown the workers lived in a much larger area than at the other sites, so there was not as large an influx of new students into the schools.

23. Perhaps some of the respondents were county, not city, officials. Annexation did not necessarily help the county; in fact, it meant that the 1 percent payroll and profit tax had to be cut in half, with the company and the county each getting half of 1 percent.

24. There were two ways to calculate this figure. The first figure, the raw mean, listed on the first row of the table, is the number of times a leader said "Yes, this is a problem" divided by the number of leaders at that site. The average was nine per site. To be considered an issue, however, the more stringent criterion of 50 percent plus one was used.

25. A note of caution is in order. This factor analysis is suggestive, not conclusive, on the question of whether the leaders considered economic development to be one-dimensional or multidimensional. This is because there are a fairly large number of variables in relation to the N.

26. Similarly, the person's role as it pertains to the economic development process—that is, whether he was a chamber of commerce or economic devel-

opment officer—influenced whether or not he viewed economic development as primary growth, secondary growth, or a sociocultural phenomenon. Whether the leader is elected or a nonelected bureaucrat should influence whether or not he conceives of economic development as a strictly economic phenomenon. The assumption is that elected officials will tend to notice the primary growth aspects associated with the plant and that nonelected bureaucrats will notice secondary and sociocultural phenomena. Finally, old-style leaders ("good old boys") will view the economic development phenomenon differently than economic boosters. The former may minimize the longer-term secondary growth and the sociocultural changes or even view the primary growth negatively.

Note that the distribution of leaders by type is uneven. Neither the size of the N nor the distribution across categories is such that we can infer anything conclusive statistically. Below is the distribution of leaders by their role:

New guard	31%	42%
Good old boy	43	58
Not elected	18	21
Elected	37	79
Not a businessperson	20	64.5
Businessperson	11	35.5

4. Impact of the Package on the Town's Budget, Revenue, and Debt

1. Dennis Judd, Michael Peter Smith, and Randy Ready, "Capital Flight, Tax Incentives and the Marginalization of American States and Localities," in *Public Policy Across States and Communities*, ed. Dennis R. Judd (Greenwich, Conn.: JAI Press, 1985); see also Dennis R. Judd, *Politics of American Cities*, 3d ed. (Glenview, Ill.: Scott, Foresman, 1988).

2. Expenditures were also evaluated. The expenditure and revenue figures differed primarily because of a miscellaneous category of government expenditures and because of capital expenditures, which are not part of the regular annual budget and may have been funded by floating a bond. For example, if the community received an Environmental Protection Agency grant or an Economic Development Administration grant, it would show up as a onetime increase in expenditures, even though it was not a consistent revenue or expenditure item. For purposes of the discussion in most of this chapter, I report revenues rather than expenditures; the same over-time information on expenditures is available upon request from the author. It should be noted that any revenue that came into the community specifically related to the plant was coded direct plant-related revenue. See also Michele Hoyman, "The Economic Impact of Large Automobile Plant Sitings: Beyond Wages to a Notion of General Welfare" (paper presented at the meetings of the Midwest Political Science Asso-

ciation, Chicago, April 6–8, 1995), in which I present per capita revenue and per capita expenditure figures for each site as rival measures to per capita income increases and other traditional measures economists use as measures of a community's well-being.

3. Peter Eisenger, *The Rise of the Entrepreneurial State* (Madison: University of Wisconsin Press, 1988; Kenneth Thomas, "Capital Beyond Borders: How Capital Mobility Affects Bargaining Between States and Firms" (Ph.D. diss., University of Chicago, 1992); John Freeman, *Democracy and Markets: Politics and Mixed Economies* (Ithaca, N.Y.: Cornell University Press, 1989).

4. See Lana Stein, *Holding Bureaucrats Accountable* (Tuscaloosa: University of Alabama Press, 1991).

5. Scholars also think that compared with corporations, large cities are vulnerable. See Paul E. Peterson, *City Limits* (Chicago: University of Chicago Press, 1981).

6. See Eisenger, *Rise of the Entrepreneurial State;* Judd, *Politics of American Cities;* and Bryan D. Jones and Lynn Bachelor, with Carter Wilson, *The Sustaining Hand: Community Leadership and Corporate Power* (Lawrence: University Press of Kansas, 1993).

7. The exception was Honda, the "quiet site."

8. See Peterson, *City Limits;* Judd, Smith, and Ready, "Capital Flight"; Judd, *Politics of American Cities;* Eisenger, *Rise of the Entrepreneurial State;* Jones and Bachelor, *Sustaining Hand;* Clarence Stone, "Preemptive Power: Floyd Hunter's Community Power Structure Reconsidered," *American Journal of Political Science* 32 (February 1988): 82–104; and Stephen L. Elkin, *City and Regime in the American Republic* (Chicago: University of Chicago Press, 1987).

9. The indicators of skillfulness were whether its chief negotiator had extensive bargaining skills, whether there was centralization of information on the community side, whether the community had access to information and time to prepare for the opening of the plant, and whether the town used negotiating strategies effectively. These strategies are covered in chapter 9. Note that no data have been available for Spring Hill since the plant opened.

10. Michele Hoyman, "The Impact of Economic Development on Small Communities: The Case of the Automobile Industry" (paper presented at the annual meeting of the American Political Science Association, Washington, D.C., August 29–September 1, 1991).

11. Mayors Ridley and Prather were similar in another way: both had been car salesmen and had owned car dealerships.

12. Jones and Bachelor, *Sustaining Hand.*

13. Tennessee Advisory Commission on Intergovernmental Relations (TACIR), Chronology of the Saturn Site Selection in Tennessee, 1985–1987," 1989.

14. The leaders interviewed in Marysville indicated that the pre-plant unemployment was 18 percent. However, the official data on the area indicated closer to 14 percent, with some surrounding counties being higher.

15. The average percentage increases in expenditure at the Spring Hill site as a whole were 1982, 8.0 percent; 1983, 5.8 percent; 1984, 15.1 percent; 1985 (announcement), 8.9 percent; 1986, 18.2 percent; 1987, 30 percent; 1988, 9.6 percent; and 1989, 13.5 percent. The average was 22.5 percent. The Williamson County percentage increases were 1984, 20.5 percent; 1985 (announcement), 1.9 percent; 1986, 16 percent; 1987, 18 percent; 1988, 10.7 percent; 1989, 13.9 percent; the average was 13.5 percent. The preannouncement average was 4.3 percent, and the postannouncement average was 16 percent for the Spring Hill site as a whole. For Williamson County, the preannouncement average was 21 percent, and the postannouncement average was 12 percent.

16. The totals in this paragraph include all revenue, not just governmental, as in Tables 4.1–4.3: Spring Hill, 1982 revenue of $7,160,044 and 1989 revenue of $112,386,793, a cumulative percentage increase of 514 percent and an average increase of 11 percent; Smyrna, 1977 revenue of $23,101,171 and 1990 revenue of $492,396,125, a cumulative increase of 2,031 percent and an average increase of 12 percent; Georgetown, 1982 revenue of $1,356,220 and 1989 revenue of $7,836,086, a cumulative percentage increase of 478 percent and an average percentage increase of 20 percent; Marysville, 1977 revenue of $4,477,470 and 1991 revenue of $10,743,904, a cumulative percentage increase of 140 percent and an average percentage increase of 11 percent. Spring Hill lacked infrastructure and had very low revenues, which may be why its revenue increased so dramatically. Georgetown had a 660 percent increase in expenditures. Smyrna had only a modest increase over time: 7 percent over the thirteen-year period. As can be seen in Table 4.2, the average annual percentage increases in revenue generally were lower for adjacent units. The exception was Williamson, where revenues increased by 22 percent.

17. The reader may wonder why there is a discrepancy in expenditures and revenues. This is because onetime items, such as large capital projects funded by the Environmental Protection Agency or through other federal funding, do not appear as revenue.

The expenditure figures by site were as follows: Spring Hill, $7,306,191 in 1981 and 134,549,661 in 1989, a cumulative percentage increase of 1,742 percent and an average percentage increase of 11.6 percent; Smyrna, $21,959,376 in 1977 and $23,455,305 in 1990, a cumulative percentage increase of 7 percent and an average percentage increase of 17.4 percent; Georgetown, $1,356,220 in 1977 and $10,384,329 in 1989, a cumulative percentage increase of 660 percent and an average percentage increase of 18.8 percent; Marysville, $8,443,032 in 1985 and $5,711,066 in 1991, a cumulative percentage decrease of 32 percent and average percentage increase of 29.5 percent. Spring Hill increased its expenditures the most. What was most striking, however, was that in Marysville expenditures decreased by 32 percent. The average percentage increases tell us a different story. Of course, these averages reflect extreme scores. Spring Hill had the lowest average annual increase in expenditures, 12 percent; Smyrna was next, Georgetown next, and Marysville last, with the highest average, although its cumulative expenditures were in the negative range.

18. The expenditure and revenue figures for the site as a whole are as follows: 1978, 10.2 percent; 1979, 15.2 percent; announcement (1980), 40.4 percent; 1981, 17.2 percent; 1982, 41.0 percent; 1983 (opening), 7.3 percent; 1984, 28.9 percent; 1985, 0.5 percent; 1986, 10.9 percent; 1987, 21.8 percent; 1988, 14.0 percent; 1989, 9.2 percent; 1990, 10.9 percent; total, 226.5 percent for the site as a whole and 17.4 percent annual average. The percentage increases by year for Murfreesboro, by comparison, were 1984, 9.3 percent; 1985, 2.9 percent; 1986, 11.0 percent; 1987, 11 percent; 1988, 12 percent; 1989, 11 percent; 1990, 1,009 percent. The preannouncement annual average for the site as a whole was 22 percent; the postannouncement annual average was 16 percent; the preopening annual average was 21.8 percent; and the postopening annual average was 13.6 percent. The comparable postannouncement figure for Murfreesboro was 9.95 percent; the postopening annual average was 152 percent; preannouncement and preopening figures were not available.

Looking at Murfreesboro's expenditures, we see that Murfreesboro expended less in the postannouncement era and much more than the average of the other government units at the Murfreesboro site during the postopening era. The percentage increase, 152 percent in the postopening era, was very heavily influenced by the surge of 1,009 percent in 1990. We can see from the preceding results that Williamson had higher average increases in its annual expenditures compared with the other units as a whole before the announcement that the auto plant was opening and Williamson had lower average annual expenditures after the announcement. Because there is only one data point for Williamson before the announcement, the results should be taken cautiously. Thus, the "one county over" hypothesis is confirmed in terms of expenditures for the Spring Hill site.

19. We can see from these figures that Williamson County had higher increases in expenditures as a whole before the announcement compared with the other units and had lower average annual expenditures after the announcement. Note that there is only one data point for Williamson before the announcement so that the results should be taken cautiously. Thus, the "one county over" hypothesis is confirmed in terms of expenditures at the Spring Hill site. The revenue percentages were as follows for the Spring Hill site as a whole: 1982, 4 percent; 1983, 2.1 percent; 1984, 15.2 percent; 1985 (announcement), 15.0 percent; 1986, 17.7 percent; 1987, 24.9 percent; 1988, 18.3 percent; 1989, .01 percent; the average percentage increase was 11.1 percent. The percentage increases for Williamson were 1984, 19.9 percent; 1985, 15 percent; 1986, 17.7 percent; 1987, 24.9 percent; 1988, 18.3 percent; and 1989, .01 percent; the average increase was 11.1 percent. Williamson County had averages as follows:

1984, 19.9 percent; 1985, 23 percent; 1986, 11.6 percent; 1987, 48.5 percent; 1988, 1.9 percent; and 1989, 24.9 percent; the average was 13.3 percent. The preannouncement average for the Spring Hill site as a whole was 7.9 percent, and the postannouncement average was 15.2 percent. For Williamson the average percentage increase in the preannouncement era was 19.9 percent, and the postannouncement increase was 12.0 percent.

20. Auto plant–related revenue data for the city of Marysville were missing for all years in the time series, 1977–90. Auto plant–related revenue for Union County was zero from 1977 to 1991.

21. Although the data were gathered from the communities in 1990, the last available year was 1991 for revenue year. Therefore, the most recent year (1991) was reported.

22. For the actual total revenue figures by site, write the author and ask for Table 4.12. Total official revenue is total revenue, both plant-related and all other. Non-plant-related revenue is revenue that is not directly attributable to the plant. For example, sales tax is non-plant-related revenue.

5. Impact of the Plants on Aspects of Public Administration of the Communities

1. ISO stands for the Insurance Services Office, an organization that rates the fire safety status of communities. There is a membership fee to belong. The insurance industry uses these ratings to determine fire risk. The higher the rating, the more fire risk. Improvements in the number of stations or number of firefighters per capita can result in an improved rating.

2. Spring Hill's absolute figures were $1,015,590 in 1982 and $5,639,437 in 1989. Smyrna's went from $0 in 1978 to $2,037,755 in 1988; Georgetown's, from $28,432 in 1983 to $2,037,755 in 1988; and Marysville's, from $189,506 in 1985 to $855,468 in 1990.

3. The biggest percentage increase in Smyrna was 132 percent, in the year the announcement of the plant was made; by contrast, there was a 26 percent increase in the year the plant opened.

4. A table showing the substantive changes in fire protection by site is available from the author. As one can see from glancing at Table 5.1, there were slight variations in the pattern—most evident in the figures for Georgetown and Marysville.

5. Obviously, insurance costs are lower in communities with better (lower) ratings.

6. The absolute numbers for each of the sites were Smyrna, 391,536 (1978) and $3,172,326 (1990); Georgetown, $131,807 (1983) and $1,585,787 (1990);

Marysville, $210,534 (1977) and $1,385,848 (1991); and Spring Hill, $1,103,581 (1982) and $2,204,567 (1989).

7. The announcement- and opening-year percentage increases, respectively, were Smyrna, 24.9 percent and –2.9 percent; Georgetown, missing data and 39 percent; Marysville, 28.2 percent and .5 percent; Spring Hill, 9 percent and missing data.

8. A table showing substantive changes in law enforcement is available on request from the author. Ask for Table 5.5.

9. The sites were in parts of the country where it was quite common for sheriffs to be elected.

10. In Murfreesboro (Smyrna), the chief reported that the cost of guns increased from $200 to $400.

11. If the reader would like a table that itemizes all the substantive changes for each site, write the author and request Table 5.5.

12. The sums of the figures for each site in the year before the plant was announced and the final year of the series were Smyrna, $281,520 (1978) and $1,314,389 (1990); Georgetown, $10,000 (1983) and $225,900 (1989); Marysville, $331,954 (1977) and $1,531,121 (1990); Spring Hill, $1,591,770 (1982) and $9,321,282 (1990).

13. The percentage increases in the years of the announcement and the opening were Smyrna, 64.5 percent and 2.4 percent; Georgetown, missing data and 42.9 percent; Marysville, 11 percent and 31 percent; Spring Hill, 6.3 percent and –4 percent.

14. Georgetown has increased its number of plants but still faces challenges in supply.

15. "Consulting Report on Water Supply," commissioned by the city of Georgetown, 1989.

16. Ibid.

17. Ibid.

18. Mark Schneider, *Competitive City: The Political Economy of Suburbia* (Pittsburgh: University of Pittsburgh Press, 1989).

19. See "Master Plan for Park Facilities for the Georgetown–Scott County Parks Department," Table B.

20. See ibid., 19.

6. Impact of the Plants on the Communities' Quality of Education

1. Williamson County schools have a ranking of thirty-fifth in the state in teachers' salaries and fortieth in per pupil expenditures.

2. Dr. Jerry Battles, superintendent of Maury County School District, inter-

view with author, May 1990; Rebecca Schwab, superintendent of Williamson County School District, interview with author, May 25, 1990; Dr. John H. Jones, superintendent of Murfreesboro School District, interview with author, May 1990.

3. Dr. Don Brown, superintendent of Franklin Special School District, interview with author, May 25, 1990.

4. Dr. Jerry Battles, superintendent of Rutherford County School District, interview with research team and supplementary information in an undated letter to author, May 1990.

5. Dr. Don Brown, interview with author, May 1990.

6. Information provided by letter dated November 17, 1990, from Dwight Spencer, superintendent of Benjamin Logan School District, contained enrollment and budget data but not staff numbers. An interview was not possible with a Benjamin Logan District representative.

7. According to Rebecca Schwab, superintendent of Williamson County School District (interview with author, May 25, 1990), there are 639 teachers in the system, 18 principals, 12 supervisors, and other employees, totaling 1,000 staff as of 1990.

8. Data provided by one of Dr. Jerry Gaither's staff, Ms. Teen, by phone to a member of the research team while the team was on site in Tennessee, May 1990.

9. "Curriculum Design: Scott County Technical School" (brochure published by Scott County Vocational Technical Education Taskforce, 1989), 1.

10. Ibid.

11. Ibid., 4.

12. Dr. Jerry Battles, superintendent of Rutherford County School District, interview with research team and supplementary information provided in an undated letter to author, May 1990.

13. Rebecca Schwab, superintendent of Williamson County School District, interview with author, May 25, 1990.

14. Dr. Gary Meier, superintendent of Marysville School District, interview with author, June 29, 1990.

15. Rebecca Schwab, superintendent of Williamson County School District, interview with author, May 25, 1990.

16. "Facts, 1989–1990" (Scott County–Georgetown Chamber of Commerce, September 22, 1989).

17. "Scott County in Transition," Local Economic Development Services, State Employment Services, and Georgetown–Scott County Consolidated Schools, 4a.

18. "Marysville Special School District Finances," a one- page document prepared by the superintendent of schools of Marysville School District and sent to the author, June 1990.

19. Dr. Gary Meier, superintendent of Marysville School District, interview with author, June 29, 1990.

20. Gerry Clark, business manager, Franklin Special School District, letter to author, June 1990.

21. Interview with professor of economics, University of Kentucky, May 1990 (a background interview).

22. "Scott County's Economy in Transition" (brochure prepared by Scott County, Scott County–Georgetown Chamber of Commerce, and city of Georgetown).

23. "Scott County in Transition," 7.

24. Ibid., 7.

25. Ibid.

26. "Scott County's Economy in Transition: Recommendations of the Economic Development Advisory Team," report prepared by the Economic Development Advisory Team, April 1990.

27. Ibid., 16.

28. Wilbur R. Thompson and P. R. Thompson, "National Industries and Occupational Strengths: The Cross-Hairs of Targeting," *Urban Studies* 24 (1987): 547–60.

7. What About the People?

1. The author wishes to acknowledge the Weldon Springs Fund, which provided a grant in 1991–92 through the University of Missouri system for the public opinion part of this study. Without this support, I would never have had the resources to conduct this part of the study. The survey was conducted under the direction of Elizabeth Sale by the Survey Center at the Centers for Public Policy Research at the University of Missouri St. Louis. The author expresses her gratitude to Ms. Sale for her extraordinary patience and competence in the execution of this project, as well as to the other center research staff person, Charles Leonard, and to the director of the center, Lance Leloup.

2. Upon request, the author can provide the reader with the three charts, asking for opinions about whether the incentive package was justifiable, whether the community is better overall since the plant, and whether the community wants an additional large industrial siting. The three questions had one version with five response categories and one with three response categories. The charts show that the number of people responding in the extremely positive category was always a minority (say, 20 percent), but these extremely positive responses, when combined with the moderately positive responses, yielded a majority of people responding favorably to these three questions.

3. Matthew Crenson, *The Unpolitics of Air Pollution: A Study of Non-Decision-Making in Cities* (Baltimore: Johns Hopkins University Press, 1971). See also Roger Cobb and Charles Elder, "Issue Creation and Agenda Building," in

Cases in Public Policy Making, ed. James Anderson (New York: Praeger, 1976), 10–21.

4. When two issues were tied for eighth place, for example, they were both given the value of 8.5 and the next item ranked 10.

5. An important question is whether there were redistributive effects associated with the plant. There is a public opinion or perceptual aspect to this, as well as an objective aspect. See the excellent treatment by Timothy Bartik in his book *Who Benefits from State and Local Economic Development Policies?* (Kalamazoo, Mich.: Upjohn Institute for Employment Research, 1991). See also Michele Hoyman, "Re-distributive Aspects of Economic Development: Who Benefits Versus Who the Public Thinks Benefits" (working paper, Political Science Department, University of Missouri St. Louis, 1995).

6. Upon request, the author can provide tables showing the exact percentages overall by site for the elite and the public.

7. The site variable in the multivariate models was actually one of several created: the Spring Hill site variable, which was Spring Hill and all others; the Georgetown variable, which was Georgetown and all others; the Smyrna variable, which was the Smyrna site and all others; and the Marysville variable, which was the Marysville site and all others. Spring Hill respondents had different attitudes than respondents at the other sites with respect to whether the community was better off overall, and so the Spring Hill site variable was included in the model predicting the community's overall reaction to having the plant. Similarly, Georgetown residents had distinctive opinions regarding whether they would want another plant and toward the incentive package, so that the Georgetown site variable was included in the two models dealing with these issues.

8. For a more detailed analysis, see Michele Hoyman, "Predictors of Attitudes to Growth and Economic Development: The People Speak" (working paper, Political Science Department, University of Missouri St. Louis, 1995). Other versions of this model, such as one in which race is omitted, do not add much to the overall explanation. When both income and education are included, neither is significant; when income is omitted, however, education is significant. When education is omitted, income is significant. If we remove both, we do not lose much explanatory power and everything remains significant.

8. Political and Cultural Transformation

1. The public opinion data were gathered from a Weldon Springs grant the author received from the University of Missouri. The survey was conducted in 1992 by the survey office (Elizabeth Sale) of the Centers for Public Policy Research under the directorship of Dr. Lance Leloup.

2. Bryan Jones and Lynn Bachelor, with Carter Wilson, *The Sustaining Hand: Community Leadership and Corporate Power* (Lawrence: University Press of Kansas, 1993).

3. Spring Hill was a slow start-up plant. The plant was announced in 1985 but not opened until 1990. Thus, it was the slowest of the four to open.

4. Floyd Hunter, *Community Power Structure* (Chapel Hill: University of North Carolina Press, 1953).

5. John Kingon, *Agendas, Alternatives, and Public Policies* (Boston: Little, Brown, 1984).

6. Ibid.

7. T. N. Clark and R. Inglehart, "The New Political Culture" (paper presented at the biennial meeting of the American Sociological Association, 1990).

8. This is not a direct quote. All of the other quotations in this chapter are direct quotes.

9. Economic Development as a Policy Choice

1. Richard Cyert and James G. March, *A Behavioral Theory of the Firm* (Englewood Cliffs, N.J.: Prentice Hall, 1963).

2. See ibid., among others.

3. Bryan Jones and Lynn Bachelor, with Carter Wilson, *The Sustaining Hand: Community Leadership and Corporate Power* (Lawrence: University Press of Kansas, 1993).

4. Michele Hoyman and Louis Ferman, "Locating New Automobile Factories in Rural Areas: Community Impacts" (report for the Economic Development Administration, U.S. Department of Commerce, Research Grant #99-07-13727, 1994), 33–35.

5. Jones and Bachelor, *The Sustaining Hand.*

6. Peter Eisenger, *The Rise of the Entrepreneurial State* (Madison: University of Wisconsin Press, 1988).

7. Lynn Bachelor, "Michigan, Mazda and the Factory of the Future: Evaluating Economic Development Incentives," *Economic Development Quarterly* 5 (May 1991): 126–39; George Fulton, Donald Grimes, and Alan L. Baum, "Industrial Location Decisions and Their Impact on the Michigan Economy: Mazda Auto Assembly Case" (paper presented at the 32nd annual conference on Economic Outlook, Ann Arbor, Mich., November 15, 1984); John Jackson, "Michigan," in *The New Economic Role of American States*, ed. R. Scott Fosler (Oxford: Oxford University Press, 1988), 91–140.

8. Michael A. Pagano and Ann Bowman, *Cityscapes and Capital: The Politics of Urban Development* (Baltimore: Johns Hopkins University Press, 1995).

9. Michele Hoyman, "The Impact of Economic Development on Small Communities: The Case of the Automobile Industry" (paper presented at the annual meeting of the American Political Science Association, Washington, D.C., August 29–September 1, 1996).

Conclusion

1. Elaine Sharp, "Institutional Manifestations of Accessibility and Urban Economic Development Polity," *World Politics Quarterly* 44 (March 1991): 121–47. See also Elaine Sharp and David Elkins, "Politics of Economic Development Policy," *Economic Development Quarterly* 5 (May 1991): 126–39.

2. Paul E. Peterson, *City Limits* (Chicago: University of Chicago Press, 1981).

3. Susan Fainstein, "The Changing World Economy and Urban Restructuring," in *Leadership and Urban Regeneration: Cities in North America and Europe*, ed. Dennis Judd and Michael Parkinson. Urban Affairs Annual Review, vol. 37 (Newbury Park, Calif.: Sage, 1990). See also the whole volume edited by Dennis Judd and Michael Parkinson, *Leadership and Urban Regeneration: Cities in North America and Europe.* Urban Affairs Annual Review, vol. 37 (Newbury Park, Calif.: Sage, 1990); and Michael A. Pagano and Ann Bowman, *Cityscapes and Capital: The Politics of Urban Development* (Baltimore: Johns Hopkins University Press, 1995).

Bibliography

Ambrosius, Margery. "Are Political Benefits the Only Benefits of State Economic Development Policies?" Paper presented at the annual meeting of the American Political Science Association, San Francisco, August 30–September 2, 1990.

Bachelor, Lynn. "Michigan, Mazda, and the Factory of the Future: Evaluating Economic Development Incentives." *Economic Development Quarterly* 5 (May 1991): 126–39.

Bartik, Timothy. *Who Benefits from State and Local Economic Development Policies?* Kalamazoo, Mich.: Upjohn Institute for Employment Research, 1991.

Battista, Philip, William Cole, and James Hoagland Jr. "Economic Self-Interest and Community Attachment: Predicting Reactions to New Industrial Development." Survey Research Center, University of Kentucky, 1989.

Baumgartner, Frank, and Bryan D. Jones. *Agendas and Instability in American Politics.* Chicago: University of Chicago Press, 1993.

Blair, John, and Robert Premus. "Major Factors in Industrial Location: A Review." *Economic Development Quarterly* 1 (1987): 72–85.

Bluestone, Barry, and Bennett Harrison. *The Deindustrialization of America: Plant Closings, Community Abandonment, and the Dismantling of Basic Industry.* New York: Basic Books, 1982.

Bruce, R. Scott, and George C. Lodge. *U.S. Competitiveness in the World Economy.* Cambridge, Mass.: Harvard University Business School Press, 1985.

"Business Education Partnership of Rutherford County Salutes Excellence in Education." *Murfreesboro (Tenn.) Daily News Journal,* June 18, 1989, 7E.

Clark, T. N., and R. Inglehart. "The New Political Culture." Paper presented at the biennial meeting of the International Sociological Association, 1990.

Clarke, Susan E., ed. *Urban Innovation and Autonomy: Political Implications of Policy Change.* Newbury Park, Calif.: Sage, 1989.

Cobb, Roger, and Charles D. Elder. "Issue Creation and Agenda Building." In *Cases in Public Policy Making,* edited by James Anderson, 10–21. New York: Praeger, 1976.

———. *Participation in American Politics: The Dynamics of Agenda Building.* 2d ed. Baltimore: Johns Hopkins University Press, 1983.

Cobb, Roger W., Jeanie-Keith Ross, and Marc Howard Ross. "Agenda Building as a Comparative Political Process." *American Political Science Review* 70 (March 1976): 126–38.

"Consulting Report on Water Supply." Commissioned by the city of Georgetown, 1989.

Cook, Kathleen. "Small Town Talk: The Undoing of Collective Action in Two Missouri Towns." Ph.D. diss., Washington University, 1993.

Crenson, Matthew. *The Unpolitics of Air Pollution: A Study of Non-Decision-Making in Cities.* Baltimore: Johns Hopkins University Press, 1971.

"Curriculum Design, Scott County Technical School." Brochure published by Scott County Vocational Technical Education Taskforce, 1989.

Cyert, Richard, and James G. March. *A Behavioral Theory of the Firm.* Englewood Cliffs, N.J.: Prentice Hall, 1963.

DeLeon, Richard. *The Left Coast City.* Lawrence: University Press of Kansas, 1992.

Dertouzos, Michael, Richard Lester, and Robert Solow. *Made in America.* Cambridge, Mass.: MIT Press, 1989.

"Development Guidelines: East Planning Area, Marysville and Paris Township, Ohio." City of Marysville.

"Development Guidelines: South Planning Area, Marysville and Paris Township, Ohio." City of Marysville.

Doeringer, Peter B., David G. Terkla, and Gregory Topakian. *Invisible Factors in Local Economic Development.* New York: Oxford University Press, 1988.

Downs, Anthony. "Up and Down with Ecology: The Issue-Attention Cycle." *Public Interest* 28 (summer 1972): 38–50.

Eisenger, Peter. *The Rise of the Entrepreneurial State.* Madison: University of Wisconsin Press, 1988.

Elkin, Stephen L. *City and Regime in the American Republic.* Chicago: University of Chicago Press, 1987.

"Facts About Honda." Honda Manufacturing Corporation of America, 1990.

"Facts, 1989–1990." Scott County–Georgetown Chamber of Commerce, September 22, 1989.

Fainstein, Susan. "The Changing World Economy and Urban Restructuring." In *Leadership and Urban Regeneration: Cities in North America and Europe,* edited by Dennis Judd and Michael Parkinson, 31–47. Urban Affairs Annual Review, vol. 37. Newbury Park, Calif.: Sage, 1990.

Fainstein, Susan, et al., eds. *Restructuring the City: The Political Economy of Urban Redevelopment.* New York: Longman, 1983.

Feagin, Joe R. *Free Enterprise City: Houston.* New Brunswick, N.J.: Rutgers University Press, 1988.

Feiock, Richard. "The Effects of Economic Development Policy on Local Economic Growth." *American Journal of Political Science* 35 (August 1991): 643–55.

Fisher, Robert, and Joseph Kling. *Mobilizing Community Leadership in the Era of the Global City.* Newbury Park, Calif.: Sage, 1993.

Fitchen, Janet M. *Endangered Species, Enduring Places: Change, Identity, and Survival in Rural America.* Boulder, Colo.: Westview Press, 1991.

Fleischmann, Arnold, G. Green, and T. M. Kwong. "What's a City to Do? Explaining Differences in Local Economic Development Policies." *Western Political Quarterly* 45 (1992): 677–700.

Freeman, John. *Democracy and Markets: Politics and Mixed Economies.* Ithaca, N.Y.: Cornell University Press, 1989.

Friedman, John. "World City Hypothesis." *Development and Change* 17 (1986): 69–83.

Friedman, John, and Wolff Goetz. "World City Formation: An Agenda for Research and Action." *International Journal of Urban and Regional Research* 6 (1982): 309–44.

Fulton, George, Donald Grimes, and Alan L. Baum. "Industrial Location Decisions and Their Impact on the Michigan Economy: Mazda Auto Assembly Case." Paper presented at the 32nd annual conference on Economic Outlook, Ann Arbor, Mich., November 15, 1984.

Garreau, Joel. *Edge City.* New York: Doubleday, 1991.

Gordus, Jeanne, Paul Jarley, and Louis Ferman. *Plant Closings and Economic Dislocation.* Kalamazoo, Mich.: Upjohn Institute for Employment Research, 1981.

Gray, Virginia, and David Lowery. "Holding Back the Tide of Bad Economic Times: The Compensatory Impact of State Industrial Policy." Paper presented at the annual meetings of the American Political Science Association, Atlanta, August 31–September 3, 1989.

———. "Interest Group Politics and Economic Growth in the United States." *American Political Science Review* 82 (March 1988): 109–31.

Hill, Richard. "Crisis in Motor City: The Politics of Economic Development in Detroit." In *Restructuring the City: The Political Economy of Urban Development,* edited by Susan Fainstein et al., 80–125. New York: Longman, 1983.

Hoaglund, James G., Jr. "Public Perceptions of Central Kentucky Communities and the Impact of Toyota Manufacturing." Center for Development, University of Kentucky, 1990.

Hoyman, Michele. "Economic Development of Rural Areas as Agenda-Setting: Of Earthquakes and Economic Development." Paper presented at the meetings of the Midwest Political Science Association, Chicago, April 1990.

———. "The Economic Impact of Large Automobile Plant Sitings: Beyond Wages to a Notion of General Welfare." Paper presented at the meetings of the Midwest Political Science Association, Chicago, April 6–8, 1995.

———. "The Impact of Economic Development on Small Communities: The Case of the Automobile Industry." Paper presented at the annual meeting of the American Political Science Association, Washington, D.C., August 29–September 1, 1996.

———. "Predictors of Attitudes to Growth and Economic Development: The People Speak," Working Paper, Political Science Department, University of Missouri St. Louis, 1995.

———. "Re-distributive Aspects of Economic Development: Who Benefits Versus Who the Public Thinks Benefits." Working paper, Political Science Department, University of Missouri St. Louis, 1995.

Hoyman, Michele, and Louis Ferman. "Locating New Automobile Factories in Rural Areas: Community Impacts." Report for the Economic Development Administration. U.S. Department of Commerce, Research Grant #99-07-13727, 1994.

Hunter, Floyd. *Community Power Structure.* Chapel Hill: University of North Carolina Press, 1953.

"Impacts of the Toyota Plant on Scott County, Kentucky." Report of Urban Studies Center, University of Louisville. Prepared for Department of Local Government, Commonwealth of Kentucky, 1987.

Jackson, John. "Michigan." In *The New Economic Role of American States,* edited by R. Scott Fosler, 91–112. Oxford: Oxford University Press, 1988.

Jones, Bryan, and Lynn Bachelor, with Carter Wilson. *The Sustaining Hand: Community Leadership and Corporate Power.* Lawrence: University Press of Kansas, 1993.

Judd, Dennis R. *Politics of American Cities.* 3d ed. Glenview, Ill.: Scott, Foresman, 1988.

Judd, Dennis, and Michael Parkinson. "Urban Leadership and Regeneration: Economic Constraint and Political Choice." In *Leadership and Urban Regeneration: Cities in North America and Europe,* edited by Dennis Judd and Michael Parkinson, 13–30. Urban Affairs Annual Review, vol. 37. Newbury Park, Calif.: Sage, 1990.

———, eds. *Leadership and Urban Regeneration: Cities in North America and Europe.* Urban Affairs Annual Review, vol. 37. Newbury Park, Calif.: Sage, 1990.

Judd, Dennis, Michael Peter Smith, and Randy Ready. "Capital Flight, Tax Incentives, and the Marginalization of American States and Localities." In *Public Policy Across States and Communities,* edited by Dennis R. Judd. Greenwich, Conn.: JAI Press, 1985.

Kingdon, John. *Agendas, Alternatives and Public Policies.* Boston: Little, Brown, 1984.

Kresl, Peter Karl, and Balwant Singh. "Competitiveness of Cities." Paper presented at OECD–Australian government conference, Melbourne, Australia, November 1994.

"Land Use, Thoroughfare and Open Space Plan, 1977–2000, Marysville, Ohio." Prepared by Hurley, Schnaufer and Associates Community Development Associates, commissioned by the Department of Housing and Urban Development and the Community Development Division of the Ohio Department of Economic and Community Development, 1977.

Lind, Nancy, and Ann H. Elder. "Who Pays? Who Benefits? The Case of the Incentive Package Offered to Diamond Starr Automotive Plant." *Government Finance Review* 2 (December 1986): 23.

Marvel, Mary K., and William J. Shkurti. "The Economic Impact of Development: Honda in Ohio." *Economic Development Quarterly* 7 (February 1993): 50–62.

Miller, Gary. *Cities by Contract.* Cambridge, Mass.: MIT Press, 1981.

Milward, H. Brinton. "Estimated Impacts of Toyota Georgetown, Kentucky, Plant." Center for Business and Economic Research, University of Kentucky, 1988.

——. "Kentucky's Automotive Supplier Industry: Trends and Implications." Report contracted by the Governor's Office of Policy and Management. Center for Business and Economic Research, University of Kentucky, 1988.

Milward, H. Brinton, and Heidi Hosbach Newman. "Estimated Impact of Toyota on State's Economy." Center for Business and Economic Research, University of Kentucky, 1988.

——. "State Incentive Packages and the Industrial Location Decision." Center for Business and Economic Research, University of Kentucky, 1988.

Mollenkopf, John, and Manuel Castalls, eds. *Dual City: The Restructuring of New York.* New York: Russell Sage Foundation, 1988.

"Ohio Water Service Company, Marysville District Long-range Plan." Prepared by Marysville Management Staff, May 1990.

Pagano, Michael A. "Urban Infrastructure and City Budgeting: Elements of a National Urban Policy." In *The Future of National Urban Policy,* edited by Marshall Kaplan and Franklin James, 131–55. Durham, N.C.: Duke University Press, 1990.

Pagano, Michael A. and Ann Bowman. *Cityscapes and Capital: The Politics of Urban Development.* Baltimore: Johns Hopkins University Press, 1995.

Parkinson, Michael, Dennis Judd, and B. Foley. "Urban Revitalization in America and the U.K.: Politics of Uneven Development." In *Regenerating the Cities,* edited by Michael Parkinson, Dennis Judd, and B. Foley, Manchester, United Kingdom: Manchester University Press, 1990.

Peterson, Paul E. *City Limits.* Chicago: University of Chicago Press, 1981.

Porterfield, Shirley. "Service Sector Offers More Jobs, Less Pay." *Rural Economic Development Perspectives* 6 (June 1990): 2–7.

Porterfield, Shirley, and Thomas D. Rowley. "Removing Rural Development Barriers Through Telecommunications: Illusion or Reality?" In *Economic Adaptation: Alternatives for Nonmetropolitan Areas,* edited by David L. Barkley, 247–64. Boulder, Colo.: Westview Press, 1993.

Portz, John. *The Politics of Plant Closings.* Lawrence: University Press of Kansas, 1990.

——. "State Economic Development Programs: The Trials and Tribulations of Implementation." *Economic Development Quarterly* 7 (May 1993): 160–77.

Premus, Robert. "Major Factors in Industrial Location: A Review." *Economic Development Quarterly* 1 (1987): 72–85.

Reich, Robert B. *The Work of Nations: Preparing Ourselves for 21st Century Capitalism.* New York: Knopf, 1991.

Sassen, Saskia. *The Global City: New York, London, and Tokyo.* Princeton, N.J.: Princeton University Press, 1991.

Savitch, H. *Post-Industrial Cities: Politics and Planning in New York, Paris and London.* Princeton, N.J.: Princeton University Press, 1987.

Schaffer, Albert. "The Houston Growth Coalition in 'Boom' and 'Bust.'" *Journal of Urban Affairs* 11 (1989): 21–38.

Schmenner, Roger. *Making Business Location Decisions.* Englewood Cliffs, N.J.: Prentice-Hall, 1982.

Schneider, Mark. *Competitive City: The Political Economy of Suburbia.* Pittsburgh: University of Pittsburgh Press, 1989.

Scott, John T. and Gene F. Summers. "Problems in Rural Communities After Industry Arrives." In *Rural Industrialization: Problems and Potentials,* edited by Larry R. Whiting, 94–107. Ames: Iowa State University Press, 1974.

"Scott County Pride." Scott County Chamber of Commerce and city of Georgetown.

"Scott County in Transition." Local Economic Development Services, State Employment Services, and Georgetown–Scott County Consolidated Schools.

"Scott County's Economy in Transition: Recommendations of the Economic Development Advisory Team." Report to the Economic Development Subcommittee of the Scott County Comprehensive Plan, Citizen Advisory Committee. Prepared by the Economic Development Advisory Team, April 1990.

Sharp, Elaine. "Institutional Manifestations of Accessibility and Urban Economic Development Policy." *World Politics Quarterly* 44 (March 1991): 121–47.

Sharp, Elaine, and David Elkins. "Politics of Economic Development Policy." *Economic Development Quarterly* 5 (May 1991): 126–39.

Smith, M. P., ed. *Cities in Transition.* Beverly Hills, Calif.: Sage, 1984.

Stein, Lana S. *Holding Bureaucrats Accountable.* Tuscaloosa: University of Alabama Press, 1991.

Stone, Clarence N. "Preemptive Power: Floyd Hunter's Community Power Structure Reconsidered." *American Journal of Political Science* 32 (February 1988): 82–104.

———. *Regime Politics.* Lawrence: University Press of Kansas, 1989.

Stone, Clarence N., and Heywood Sanders, eds. *The Politics of Urban Development.* Lawrence: University Press of Kansas, 1987.

Summers, Gene F., Sharon D. Evans, Frank Clemente, E. M. Beck, and Jon Minkoff, eds. *Industrial Invasion of Nonmetropolitan America: A Quarter Century of Experience.* New York: Praeger, 1976.

Swanstrom, Todd. *The Crisis of Growth Politics: Cleveland, Kucinich, and the Challenge of Urban Populism.* Philadelphia: Temple University Press, 1985.

Takeo, Miyachi. "The Man Who Lured Toyota to Kentucky." *Economic Eye,* March 1987, 23–27.

Tennessee Advisory Commission on Intergovernmental Relations (TACIR).

"Chronology of the Saturn Corporation Site Selection in Tennessee, 1985–1987," 1989.

Thomas, Kenneth. "Capital Beyond Borders: How Capital Mobility Affects Bargaining Between States and Firms." Ph.D. diss., University of Chicago, 1992.

———. "Trade and Investment Policy in the Automotive Industry: The Big Three and the Auto Pact." Paper presented at the meetings of the American Political Science Association, Chicago, September 5, 1992.

Thompson, Wilbur R. "Alternative Paths to the Revival of Industrial Cities." In *The Future of Winter Cities,* edited by Gary Gappert. Urban Affairs Annual Review, vol. 21. Newbury Park, Calif.: Sage, 1987.

———. "Urbanization." In *North American Cities and the Global Economy,* edited by Peter Karl Kresl and Gary Gappert. Urban Affairs Annual Review. Newbury Park, Calif.: Sage. 1995.

———. "A Preface to Suburban Economics." In *The Urbanization of the Suburbs,* edited by Louis H. Masotti and Jeffrey K. Hadden, Urban Affairs Annual Review, vol. 7. Newbury Park, Calif.: Sage, 1973.

Thompson, Wilbur R., and P. R. Thompson, "National Industries and Occupational Strengths: The Cross-Hairs of Targeting." *Urban Studies* 24 (1987): 547–60.

U.S. Chamber of Commerce. *What 100 New Jobs Mean to a Community.* 1989.

White, Joseph. "Chrysler to Shut St. Louis Plant, Third Since 1987." *Wall Street Journal,* February 2, 1990.

Whiting, Larry R., ed. *Rural Industrialization: Problems and Potentials.* Ames: Iowa State University Press, 1974.

Wolman, Hal. "Local Economic Development Policy: What Explains the Divergence Between Policy Analysis and Political Behaviors?" *Journal of Urban Affairs* 10 (1988): 27.

———. "Local Government and the Citizen: Citizen Participation and the Mental Maps of Political Elites." Paper presented at the European Consortium for Political Research, Limerick, Ireland, March 31–April 4, 1992.

Wolman, Harold, Cary Lichtman, and Suzie Barnes. "Impact of Credentials, Skill Levels, Worker Training, and Motivation on Employment Outcomes: Sorting out the Implications for Economic Development Policy." *Economic Development Quarterly* 5 (May 1991): 140–51.

Index

✓